GOD DOESN'T Try

Jim Osman & Dave Rich

Foreword by Costi W. Hinn

This book is self-published by James C. Osman II and Dave Rich in cooperation with Kootenai Community Church Publishing.

Text copyright © 2023 James Clancy Osman II and Dave Rich. All rights reserved for the intellectual content of this work. No part of this book may be reproduced in any form or by any means without the express written consent of the authors, James C. Osman II, Dave Rich, or Kootenai Community Church, P.O. Box 593, Kootenai, Idaho 83840. All rights reserved.

All Scripture quotations, unless otherwise indicated, are taken from the (NASB®) New American Standard Bible®, Copyright © 1960, 1971, 1977, 1995 by The Lockman Foundation. Used by permission. All rights reserved. lockman.org.

Scripture quotations marked ESV are taken from the ESV® Bible (The Holy Bible, English Standard Version®), copyright © 2001 by Crossway, a publishing ministry of Good News Publishers. Used by permission. All rights reserved.

Scripture quotations marked KJV are taken from the King James Version of the Bible.

Scripture quotations marked LSB are taken from the Legacy Standard Bible®. Copyright © 2021 The Lockman Foundation. Used by permission. All rights reserved. Managed in partnership with Three Sixteen Publishing Inc. 316publishing.com.

Scripture quotations marked NIV are taken from the Holy Bible, New International Version®, NIV®. Copyright © 1973, 1978, 1984, 2011 by Biblica Inc.® Used by permission of Zondervan. All rights reserved worldwide. www.zondervan.com.

Scripture quotations marked NKJV are taken from the New King James Version®. Copyright © 1982 by Thomas Nelson. Used by permission. All rights reserved.

Scripture quotations marked YLT are taken from Young's Literal Translation of the Bible.

Unless otherwise noted, all emphases in Scripture quotations have been added by the authors.

Online citations in this book were live at the time of publishing. Where possible, we have included a permalink to an archive of the website cited. That link is within parentheses next to the original link.

Editors: Jamie Rich & Diedre Osman

Cover artwork provided by Josh Comstock:
PeaceHarbor.com

Website hosting provided by Thomas Leo:
TLCWebHosting.com

For updates on the ministry of Kootenai Community Church please visit:
KootenaiChurch.org

ISBN-13: 978-0-9984550-4-4
Kootenai Community Church Publishing

First Edition: March 2024

Bulk copies of this book are available at special pricing. Please contact the authors through the contact page at KootenaiChurch.org.

Other Books by Jim Osman

Truth or Territory:
A Biblical Approach to Spiritual Warfare
Also available in audiobook.

Available in Spanish:
Verdad o territorio:
Un acercamiento bíblico a la guerra espiritual

****

Selling the Stairway to Heaven:
Critiquing the Claims of Heaven Tourists

****

The Prosperity of the Wicked:
A Study of Psalm 73

Available in Spanish:
La prosperidad de los impios:
Un estudio del Salmo 73

****

God Doesn't Whisper
Also available in audiobook.

Available in Portuguese:
Deus Não Cochicha

Dedication

To the godly men, past and present, who have taught and modeled confidence in our wise, benevolent, and sovereign King for the edification of the saints and the glory of His great name.

x

Contents

Foreword xiii
Acknowledgements xvii

PART 1: INTRODUCTION
1   Introduction: Why This Book? 2
2   "Do. Or Do Not. There Is No Try." 20

PART 2: GOD'S INFALLIBLE WORK IN BELIEVERS
3   God Doesn't Try to Save His People 40
4   God Doesn't Try to Sanctify His People 58
5   God Doesn't Try to Speak to His People 78
6   God Doesn't Try to Provide for His People 94

PART 3: GOD'S INFALLIBLE WORK IN THE CHURCH
7   God Doesn't Try to Build His Church 114
8   God Doesn't Try to Organize His Church 130
9   God Doesn't Try to Prosper His Church 154

PART 4: GOD'S INFALLIBLE WORK IN CREATION
10 God Doesn't Try to Control Creation 174
11 God Doesn't Try to Execute Justice 202
12 God Doesn't Try to Establish His Kingdom 222
13 Conclusion 240

Appendix: Discussion Questions 253
Bibliography 263
About the Authors 268

Foreword

When Jim first told me about the title for this book, we were spending time together at his and Dave's church in Idaho and I let out a laugh and a sigh of relief! Finally, someone was going to write on this subject and fix a very common misconception about our great and sovereign God. How many times have we all been under the impression that God was "trying"? With people, especially children, we coax and reason in the hopes that they will comply and achieve a desired spiritual or material outcome. Perhaps we sometimes think of God that way, as though He were trying to help us but unable to because we are getting in the way. Here are some sentiments you may have heard before or believe even this very moment:

- God is trying to save you, if only you would believe in Him.
- God is trying to bless you, if only you would claim it.
- God is trying to provide for you, if only you would receive it.
- God is trying to speak to you, if only you would listen.
- God is trying to do it, but you're getting in the way.

Even with the best of intentions, we err when we think that God is "trying" to do anything. I remember many years ago when I was immersed in prosperity (so-called) gospel theology, I would tell people, "God is trying to bless you! If only you would just give generously and believe in faith that He can do it, He would!" My conviction was genuinely rooted in a belief that God was trying so hard to do certain things, but humans (especially those who lack faith) were blocking Him from doing it. God, in my imagination, was in Heaven with His fingers crossed hoping that things would pan out. His sovereignty seemed to be handed over to us. He had set the possibilities, but it was on us to make it all happen. God, the triumphant Lord over all, was more like a try-hard deity with His hands tied by human activity. Was I ever wrong!

As I came to study Scripture, it wasn't long before the truth pressed in on my soul with the weight of a thousand tons. God wasn't trying at all. In fact, the picture I had in my mind was not only bad theology, it was blasphemous theology. God's sovereignty means that He is in complete control over every plan, purpose, and person. His authority has no limitations. He's not running a democratic process in which we vote Him into power. He's not like those old infomercials selling the Showtime Rotisserie Oven where you simply "Set it and forget it!" God didn't start the world then take a sabbatical while we work out the details. He is actively working to unfold all things after the counsel of His will (Eph. 1:11–12). We don't pick and choose what He can or cannot accomplish. He is not bound by human will, human ambition, or human opposition. God is omnipotent (all-powerful), omniscient (all-knowing), and omnipresent (all-present). He is a God who promises and delivers. He has never missed a deadline, failed a test, or lost an outcome. It is these truths—and more—that Jim and Dave have loaded into the cannons of this book. Using deep but understandable truths, and backing every claim with Scripture, they have clarified some of the most misrepresented views on God the American church has been plagued by.

Whether you have been viewing God as a distant deity who is not involved in day-to-day operations here on Earth or have simply never considered the subject of God's sovereignty, this book is a game changer that will equip, sharpen, challenge, correct, and encourage you. If you're a pastor, you'll especially be blessed by the "For the Shepherds" sections at the end of each chapter, and every Christian can build a library with the recommended reading that Jim and Dave have provided in each chapter as well.

May this book be used by the Lord to strengthen your confidence in Him. He is not trying. He is triumphant!

Costi W. Hinn
Teaching Pastor, Shepherd's House Bible Church, Chandler, AZ
Founder & President, For the Gospel Ministries

Acknowledgements—Jim Osman

With every writing project, I feel it impossible to adequately thank everyone who has had a hand in it. There are many who have offered encouragement along the way. Some have shown an undying interest in this book from the first they heard of its writing. Others have prayed diligently for it for months or even years. I know there are a number in our own congregation who have been excited for this book from the moment that Dave and I announced we were writing together. That was probably three years ago, and yet the prayers and interest from those diligent folks has not subsided. I am grateful for your kind words, encouragements, and intercession for this project. May the Lord reward it abundantly!

I must begin by thanking my coauthor, Dave Rich. Dave and I have been friends and co-laborers in gospel ministry since he and his wife, Diane, first came to Kootenai in 1999. He was quickly recognized as an elder in our fellowship and has served faithfully and diligently from the beginning. His faithful exposition of Scripture and his pursuit of the glory of God in all things is a constant encouragement to my soul. Pastoral ministry is difficult and fraught with dangers and disappointments. I can say without hesitation that without Dave's friendship, fellowship, and support, I would not be in ministry today. God providentially used Dave to thwart the enemy's many attempts to crush our small ministry. I am grateful to the Lord for His kind providence in bringing him to our fellowship and for the profound blessing that has been to my own life, family, and service. He has been a trusted friend, advisor, and co-laborer for over two decades. I pray for many more! I am thankful that he agreed to labor with me in writing this book. For both of us, this is a first. It is his first published work. It is my first coauthored work. I think I speak for both of us when I say that it has been both a challenge and a joy.

Dave and I are not alone in this work. We serve alongside two other pastors in our fellowship, Jess Whetsel and Cornel Rasor. Their faithful shepherding in church ministry allows me a bit of free time that I can give to research and writing. I am deeply thankful for their friendship and fellowship in this work. I am convinced that local church ministry is the backbone and lifeblood of the Lord's work in this world.

My administrative load has been lightened considerably over the last two decades by a fantastic secretary, Marcia Whetsel. After twenty years of meticulous service to her Lord for this local church, she has handed that position over to another fantastic secretary, Kathy Conger, who has assumed those responsibilities without the slightest glitch. Together they have kept distractions off my desk and allowed me to devote time each week to writing.

A number of great men have had editorial input into this book: Jess Whetsel, Cornel Rasor, David Forsyth, Jeff Miller, and Justin Peters. They have provided valuable encouragement and insight.

The diligent eyes of Jamie Rich (Dave's daughter) and my own wife, Diedre Osman, have made this book better than it would otherwise be. The time and effort of their editorial work could never be adequately repaid, though Dave and I would argue that a roof over their heads and a couple solid meals a day for decades has come pretty close!

Speaking of my wife, she is far more than an editor to me. She is a constant source of joy, laughter, encouragement, and strength. She has made my life great, our children blessed, and my ministry possible. "Her worth is far above jewels." Her children and "her works praise her in the gates" (Proverbs 31:10, 31).

Finally, I am thankful to the Lord, my King! He has redeemed me from the pit. He has taken a heart that was once in entrenched rebellion against Himself and caused me to love Him, praise Him, and serve Him. Except by His good grace, I wouldn't have anything good to acknowledge. To Him be glory forever and ever. Amen!

Acknowledgments—Dave Rich

This is my first writing project, and I have been amazed at the number of people who have contributed to this work in some way.

I have relied heavily on so many great expositors and biblical scholars, many of whom I will never meet before we gather together to discuss the excellencies of God in Heaven. We have listed many of these works in the Recommended Reading sections, so rather than list many of them here, I simply acknowledge the great debt owed to these faithful writers and teachers.

Closer to home, I have been blessed to sit under the teaching of a few great men in my Christian life. Tom Ruhlman, who was my shepherd for many years, contributed greatly to my understanding of the gospel, helping me to grow in my knowledge of Scripture and challenging me to lifelong service. The late Paul Heyne was my supervisor while I was a graduate student in economics, and it was him who first challenged my incomplete soteriology. I gained much from his wisdom and knowledge. He taught me economics, theology, and pedagogy.

Jim and I are two of the elders of KCC, and the work of our fellow elders Jess Whetsel and Cornel Rasor has been instrumental in allowing us both to work on this book. Their love for us and the church, expressed in wise leadership and faithful service, has been an inspiration to both of us.

I am also personally indebted to Simon Pranaitis, whose ability and enthusiastic willingness to teach my Sunday school class on occasion has enabled the work on this book to go forward.

In addition, several people have contributed to this book directly. Jeff Miller and David Forsyth provided comments on my chapters that made important improvements to the flow and content of the text. Jamie Rich and Diedre Osman were our editors, removing many of our errors and helping improve the overall readability of the book.

My coauthor, Jim Osman, has been my shepherd, friend, and co-laborer for over two decades. His faithful exposition of the Word challenges my mind and edifies my spirit, and I am forever grateful the Lord brought us to Kootenai Community Church so many years ago. While I am very proud of my contributions to this book, Jim is the creative and driving force behind it. It simply would not exist without him. *God Doesn't Try* is his idea, and I am grateful to have been a part of bringing it to life. We met regularly for "book lunches" where we updated each other and thought through next steps for the book. These lunches were bright spots in the week where I got to spend time with my good friend discussing the sovereignty of God. It was a joy to work through the implications of this important doctrine and to plan our approach to communicating these truths to His children. Our prayer is that this objective will be met for our readers.

This book also would not exist were it not for the love and patience of my wife of thirty-seven years, Diane. Much of the writing of this book took place when I took a day off from my regular work, and I spent those days in isolation in my home office, studying and writing. She has been so patient and kind to me, allowing me this time, listening to my ruminations, and encouraging me in this effort. Apart from the blessings of my salvation, she is the highest and greatest blessing the Lord has given to me, and I am eternally grateful for her.

Lastly but primarily, I recognize the centrality of Christ in this work. God has provided the ability, experience, knowledge, desire, and material for this book. He rescued an utterly helpless, totally depraved, and perfectly detestable sinner. Any good that comes from my mind and hands is entirely His work. Apart from Him, I can do nothing and have done nothing.

Part 1

Introduction

Chapter 1:

Introduction: Why This Book?

1

The god of modern Evangelicalism bears little resemblance to the God Who has revealed Himself in Scripture. For decades, pastors, serving as watchmen, have sounded the alarm as Christianity has descended into postmodern irrelevance. In 1961, A. W. Tozer observed in his day "a condition which has existed in the Church for some years and is steadily growing worse."[1] Elaborating, Tozer said,

> I refer to the loss of the concept of majesty from the popular religious mind. The Church has surrendered her once lofty concept of God and has substituted for it one so low, so ignoble, as to be utterly unworthy of thinking, worshiping men. This she has done not deliberately, but little by little and without her knowledge; and her very unawareness only makes her situation all the more tragic.
>
> The low view of God entertained almost universally among Christians is the cause of a hundred lesser evils everywhere among us. A whole new philosophy of the Christian life has resulted from this one basic error in our religious thinking.[2]

Those words are a fitting description of the modern church, the doctrine of God communicated from most pulpits, and the "Christianity" peddled in most Christian bookstores! Tozer argued that "what comes into our minds when we think about God is the most important thing about us," since "we tend by a secret law of the soul to move

---

1. Tozer, *Knowledge of the Holy*, vii.
2. Tozer, vii.

toward our mental image of God."[3] Man is made for worship. For better or worse, we become like the object of our worship. The idol worshipper becomes a moral, spiritual, and ethical reflection of the god that occupies his attention, receives his devotion, and commands his affections. The idolator is, in every way, a follower of his god. His worship forms and informs his morality, purpose, and affections. Worshipping fertility gods leads to immorality, debauchery, and impurity. The worshipper seeks to obey the moral dictates and cultic rituals demanded by his deity. He admires his god, offering his time, treasure, and talents in full devotion. What is elevated in the heart is imitated in life. Scripture condemns the folly of idolatry in Psalm 115:8: "Those who make them will become like them, everyone who trusts in them."[4]

This applies to worship of the true and living God as well. When we worship Him as He is revealed in Scripture, our hearts and minds are raised to glorious heights. Our holy God demands holiness of His people (Heb. 12:14). Those who worship a holy God love and admire holiness and will pursue those things which produce it in their lives. We mimic the God we adore. This phenomenon is supernaturally realized in the Christian as the Spirit of God uses the Word of God to conform the believer to the image of Christ (Rom. 8:29–30). We are sanctified by truth (John 17:17) and changed from one degree of glory to another. "But we all, with unveiled face, beholding as in a mirror the glory of the Lord, are being transformed into the same image from glory to glory, just as from the Lord, the Spirit" (2 Cor. 3:18).

THE MODERN DOWNGRADE

This isn't the first book lamenting the impotence and aberrations of modern Evangelicalism.[5] More than a century ago, Charles Spurgeon warned of dangerous modernistic trends that threatened the health and doctrinal purity of the church in England. He fought the doctrinal downgrade[6] tenaciously during the final years of his life

---

3. Tozer, 1.
4. See also Ps. 135:18: "Those who make them will be like them, yes, everyone who trusts in them."
5. See Johnson and White, *Whatever Happened to the Reformation?*; Gilley, *This Little Church Went to Market*; and Guinness, *Fit Bodies Fat Minds*.
6. Spurgeon was involved in the Downgrade Controversy. According to the Spurgeon Center's blog post "What Was the Downgrade Controversy Actually All About?" Charles Spurgeon had four grievances with the men of his denomination, the Baptist Union. Some in the Union were either flirting with or openly promoting the following errors: a denial of the infallibility of Scripture, a denial of the necessity and substitutionary nature of Christ's atonement, a denial of the existence and eternality of Hell, and the affirmation of universalism. Spurgeon fought

Introduction: Why This Book?

and ministry. The same cultural compromises and doctrinal dilutions that Spurgeon fought against have flourished in the church of our day, and the effects are alarming. The seeds planted in the late twentieth century have sprouted and flourished. The church in the twenty-first century is reaping the fruit, and it's rotten.

The church is suffering under a pandemic of false doctrine peddled by deceivers, false teachers, and grifters. The poison spreads like gangrene through an untaught and undiscerning Christian subculture more concerned with cultural relevance than biblical faithfulness. Christianity is suffering a famine of hearing the Word of God. Like the Jews of Amos's day, we do not lack access to the Word of God, yet the spiritual landscape is as barren, fruitless, and parched as it has ever been. "'Behold, days are coming,' declares the Lord GOD, 'when I will send a famine on the land, not a famine for bread or a thirst for water, but rather for hearing the words of the LORD'" (Amos 8:11). The increasing rarity of sound, powerful, biblical preaching in the church is an indicator of modern Evangelicalism's aversion to truth. The inevitable result of such antipathy is a dimming of the light in both the church and the world.

Church buildings, Christian programs, and sermon podcasts are ubiquitous, and Christian books are easier to access than ever. Christians have access to Scripture on smartphones and tablets. Original texts and every conceivable translation are readily available to anyone with an internet connection. Despite this embarrassment of riches, the average Christian, sitting in the average church, is as untaught, undiscerning, and ill-equipped as any illiterate peasant who lived in medieval Europe.

For the last century, ecclesiastical grifters and false teachers have exploited the weak and undiscerning. Unwittingly aided by cowardly leaders in churches and seminaries, they promote their fads, fashions, and false doctrines while the progressive spirit of the age marches through Evangelical institutions with breathtakingly destructive efficiency. Once-great bastions of orthodoxy are now hollow shells of their former selves, leaving in their wake a dystopian spiritual hellscape, theological ruin, and methodological confusion.

Clear, concise, and uncompromising expository preaching is a relic of the past. Topical, man-centered, felt-need-oriented preaching

---

against essential Christian doctrines being compromised by leaders in the church. Alex DiPrima, January 17, 2022, https://www.spurgeon.org/resource-library/blog-entries/what-was-the-downgrade-controversy-actually-all-about (https://perma.cc/4LD8-FH53).

is standard fare. Crass commercialism and cultural conformity are the clear priorities of the modern Evangelical movement. Worse yet, neither those who play the tune nor those who dance to it are the least bit ashamed of the song.

The results are nothing short of tragic. Unbelievers occupy the seats in most churches.[7] Their numbers grow, and compromises are made to keep them coming back for more. This is labeled "successful church growth" and then marketed and implemented in church after church. Consequently, ecclesiological errors reproduce faster than rabbits on spring break at Miami Beach. The small remnant of true believers in a church is surrounded by worldlings confused about the gospel and is unable to identify false doctrine when it parades across the stage on Sunday morning. They are firmly convinced that false teachers exist, but they're hard-pressed to name one. If a discerning shepherd even suggests that a favorite conference speaker might be dispensing spiritual cyanide, they'll indignantly defend the wolves.

The words of Jeremiah describe the modern church perfectly: "The prophets prophesy falsely, and the priests rule on their own authority; and My people love it so! But what will you do at the end of it?" (Jer. 5:31).

We are plagued by a low theology of God and His Word.

FILE CABINET THEOLOGY

Weak theology begets weak methodology. An ignoble view of God produces contemptible worship and hinders holiness. The doctrinal and ecclesiastical wreckage we observe on the church scene is owing to a low view of God and His Word promulgated by cowardly compromisers afraid of offending God's enemies. The carnage is the symptom of this low view of God, not the cause. Unless the church confronts head-on the low doctrine of God peddled in her midst, there

---

7. Ligonier's 2022 State of Theology survey reveals that among professing Evangelicals who claim to attend church weekly, 35 percent agree that God accepts the worship of all religions, 28 percent believe that God learns and adapts, 57 percent believe that "Jesus is the first and greatest being created by God," 23 percent agree that "Jesus was a great teacher, but he was not God," 38 percent believe the Holy Spirit is a force and not a personal being, 13 percent believe the Holy Spirit can tell them to do something the Bible forbids, 37 percent believe that "most people are good by nature," 34 percent disagree that "even the smallest sin deserves eternal damnation," 9 percent believe the Bible is not literally true, 15 percent believe science disproves the Bible, and 11 percent believe "the Bible's condemnation of homosexual behavior doesn't apply today." The State of Theology (website), Ligonier Ministries, 2022, https://thestateoftheology.com (https://perma.cc/C7VG-LSCV).

is no hope of curing any other ills that plague her, for this is the poison coursing through the bloodstream of Evangelicalism.

Our assessment is confusing to many who read the doctrinal statement of their own church and don't see much amiss.[8] In all likelihood, there is nothing amiss—on paper. The doctrinal statement may be posted prominently on the website and even nestled securely within the constitution and bylaws (if it is made public at all). The problem is not with the statement of faith as published on paper, but the statement of faith as practiced and preached. A church can have a robust, orthodox doctrinal statement on paper, but if it sits in a file cabinet never seeing the light of church life and polity, then idolatrous and blasphemous doctrinal errors breed in the pulpit. For instance, a church may profess belief in the sufficiency of Scripture while the leaders promote personal, private revelations from Heaven. They may affirm that Scripture is authoritative but applaud while the pastor exegetes the latest Hollywood blockbusters for an eight-week summer sermon series. When the music team takes the stage and when the pastor steps behind his plexiglass pulpit, the people are presented a false god, a man-centered gospel, and a serial abuse of the Word of God.

This isn't a matter of what the pastor or the church *says* they believe but what the pastor or church *shows* they believe. There is a cognitive disconnect between the doctrinal statement found in the file cabinet and the doctrinal statement flaunted on the stage. Their "file cabinet theology" may be soundly orthodox while never affecting their methodology, language, philosophy of ministry, ecclesiastical structure, or preaching. Those environments hinder holiness by withholding the very thing the Spirit of God uses to produce it: biblical preaching of the Word of God. If the congregation doesn't see a high view of God presented on Sunday, they won't have a high view of God Monday through Saturday. What is modeled in the pulpit is mimicked in the pew.

THE BIG IDEA OF THIS BOOK

Like Tozer, we are convinced that the church, more than at any time in recent years, suffers from a low view of God and His Word.

---

8. There are a number of doctrinal issues upon which orthodox, Evangelical, Bible-believing Christians can disagree while still maintaining faithfulness to the gospel and enjoying fellowship together. Positions on eschatology, church ordinances, ecclesiastical structure, liturgical expressions, and charismata will vary from church to church. While having important implications, these secondary and tertiary issues are not, in themselves, tests of orthodoxy.

God Doesn't Try

Though few Christians with any self-awareness will overtly deny the sovereign majesty of God or the sufficiency of His Word, their true convictions are laid bare by their practices and speech. An ignoble theology pervades our language, evangelism, and worship. Only a biblical view of God's absolute sovereignty, exalted majesty, and infinite glory can elevate our worship and evangelism. The Scriptures describe God in this way, making it incumbent upon us to both think and speak of Him in a manner faithful to His self-revelation. We honor our God when our thinking about Him and His works corresponds with His Word.

Thus, we should never describe God in any way that suggests the possibility that He might fail. The Bible never uses *trying* to describe the work of God. Never. The possibility of failure is precluded. Scripture simply speaks of God acting and doing. The Bible presents God in all His glory. He is truly God over all, the Master and Ruler of everything and everyone. He is always and forever the Sovereign God. He controls everything, causes everything, and does all His good pleasure.

The Psalms are full of proclamations of God's sovereignty.

> Let all the earth fear the LORD;
> Let all the inhabitants of the world stand in awe of Him.
> For He spoke, and it was done;
> He commanded, and it stood fast.
> The LORD nullifies the counsel of the nations;
> He frustrates the plans of the peoples.
> The counsel of the LORD stands forever,
> The plans of His heart from generation to generation. (Ps. 33:8–11)

David described God's complete sovereignty, saying, "The LORD has established His throne in the heavens, and His sovereignty rules over all" (Ps. 103:19). God's absolute sovereignty sets Him apart from all the gods of the nations. Look at the contrast in Psalm 135:5–6: "For I know that the LORD is great and that our Lord is above all gods. Whatever the LORD pleases, He does, in heaven and in earth, in the seas and in all deeps." Similarly, Psalm 115 contrasts Yahweh with impotent idols saying,

> But our God is in the heavens;
> He does whatever He pleases.
> Their idols are silver and gold,
> The work of man's hands.

Introduction: Why This Book?

> They have mouths, but they cannot speak;
> They have eyes, but they cannot see;
> They have ears, but they cannot hear;
> They have noses, but they cannot smell;
> They have hands, but they cannot feel;
> They have feet, but they cannot walk;
> They cannot make a sound with their throat. (Ps. 115:3–7)

Nebuchadnezzar affirmed that the kings of the Earth are powerless against Him.

> But at the end of that period, I, Nebuchadnezzar, raised my eyes toward heaven and my reason returned to me, and I blessed the Most High and praised and honored Him who lives forever;
>
> > For His dominion is an everlasting dominion,
> > And His kingdom endures from generation to generation.
> > All the inhabitants of the earth are accounted as nothing,
> > But He does according to His will in the host of heaven
> > And among the inhabitants of earth;
> > And no one can ward off His hand
> > Or say to Him, "What have You done?" (Dan. 4:34–35)

None can question God, stay His hand, or call Him to account. He is totally sovereign over all things. David humbly acknowledged,

> Yours, O LORD, is the greatness and the power and the glory and the victory and the majesty, indeed everything that is in the heavens and the earth; Yours is the dominion, O LORD, and You exalt Yourself as head over all. Both riches and honor come from You, and You rule over all, and in Your hand is power and might; and it lies in Your hand to make great and to strengthen everyone. (1 Chron. 29:11–12)

Consequently, none can stay His hand or thwart His work, "for the LORD of hosts has planned, and who can frustrate it? And as for His stretched-out hand, who can turn it back?" (Isa. 14:27).

When God exerts His power over His creation, it is an expression of His sovereignty. Wayne Grudem says, "God's exercise of power over his creation is also called God's *sovereignty*. God's sovereignty is his exercise of rule (as 'sovereign' or 'king') over his creation."[9] God has a divine right to do as He pleases. Given that all He pleases

---

9. Grudem, *Systematic Theology*, 217 (emphasis in original).

is good, righteous, and wise, His use of His authority is always good, righteous, and wise. His sovereignty is never isolated from His character.

A. W. Pink similarly described sovereignty this way:

> The sovereignty of God may be defined as the exercise of His supremacy.... Being infinitely elevated above the highest creature, He is the Most High, Lord of heaven and earth. Subject to none, influenced by none, absolutely independent; God does as He pleases, only as He pleases always as He pleases. None can thwart Him, none can hinder Him. So His own Word expressly declares: "My counsel shall stand, and I will do all My pleasure" (Isa. 46:10); "He doeth according to His will in the army of heaven, and the inhabitants of the earth: and none can stay His hand" (Dan. 4:35). Divine sovereignty means that God is God in fact, as well as in name, that He is on the Throne of the universe, directing all things, working all things "after the counsel of His own will" (Eph. 1:11).[10]

Pink quotes part of Ephesians 1:11: "We have obtained an inheritance, having been predestined according to His purpose who works all things after the counsel of His will." "All things" includes our election (v. 4); predestination to adoption (vv. 5, 11); redemption by blood and forgiveness (v. 7); the revelation of His will (v. 9); the consummation of all things in Christ (v. 10); our eternal, imperishable inheritance (v. 11); our belief in the gospel (v. 13); and our sealing in the Spirit (vv. 13–14). God doesn't *try* to work these things after the counsel of His immutable will. He does it.

OUR APPROACH

We'll demonstrate from Scripture that God doesn't try. We will study the doctrine of sovereignty as exercised in His soteriological (salvation), ecclesiastical (church), and eschatological (world) works. We'll consider God's infallible work in individuals, His church, and creation. Our examination of God's sovereignty in salvation focuses on His work in the individual. Our study in ecclesiology gives consideration to His sovereignty in the church. Our survey of God's sovereignty in eschatology encompasses all of His creation and Kingdom. We have structured the book to increase in scope from the individual (believers) to the group (the church) to all things (creation).

---

10. Pink, *The Attributes of God*, 32.

Introduction: Why This Book?

We'll see that God's infallible work in individuals necessarily means that He doesn't try to save (chapter 3), sanctify (chapter 4), direct (chapter 5), or provide for His people (chapter 6). What is true of God's work for the individual must be true for the corporate body of His people as well. He doesn't try to build (chapter 7), organize (chapter 8), or prosper His church (chapter 9). God's sovereign rule within His church is a microcosm of His rule over all creation. Therefore, God doesn't try to control creation (chapter 10), execute ultimate justice (chapter 11), or establish His Kingdom (chapter 12). God's perfect power and infinite wisdom ensure the success of His designs for all creation. God doesn't try to do any of these things. He can't try because He can't fail.

We won't spend an undue amount of time explaining and defending foundational doctrinal truths, though each chapter could warrant its own book. Instead, we will state our theology clearly, provide necessary exegetical treatments of key passages, and answer some common objections. We don't intend the theological teaching in each chapter to be exhaustive. We will point the reader to reliable resources and authors who offer more thorough work on the subject for further reading. The explanations of biblical doctrine will guide our thinking through certain practical and devotional implications.

The polemical sections will apply theology in critique of unbiblical traditions, practices, and verbiage woven into the warp and woof of modern church life. Though painful, it is necessary to assess our thinking so that we may conform our lives, speech, prayer, and worship to the truth. We will take aim at the manifestations of bad theology on the flashy megachurch stage, the quiet prayer closet, and everything in between.

The devotional reflections should conform our affections to the truth, applying sound doctrine to how we feel about God. Truth should set the heart aflame that we may strive to love the Lord our God with all our heart, soul, and might (Deut. 6:5). Affection for God grows out of a proper understanding of His truth, nature, and works. Only truth lifts our hearts Heavenward, that we might love God as He is, not as we wish or vainly imagine Him to be.

The idol of American Evangelicalism can't fall soon enough. This book aims to accelerate its demise. We hope to challenge Christians, especially our fellow undershepherds, to thoughtfully examine their methods and ministries in light of biblical truth. We want Christians to think of God biblically, speak of God accurately, and relate to God properly. Every believer is called to think biblically and live accordingly.[11] We aspire to live, minister, speak, and serve in a way that honors God as He is revealed in Scripture.

FOUR KINDS OF READERS

You, dear reader, are likely to find yourself in one of four groups. Imagine them on a spectrum.

Group 1: The unaware, undiscerning, and satisfied believer.

This describes most who sit in churches across the country. In most churches, Christians experience a shallow, superficial Christianity. The sermons are weak, doctrinally benign pablum baptized in Christian lingo. They are never given God's Word on the controversial issues of the day, hearing only the most superficial handling of any theological subject. The "shepherds" are either too cowardly or ill-equipped to address pressing issues. Spiritually speaking, congregants are starving to death and don't know it. The weekly spiritual teaching provided by the unqualified leaders of their church during the sermon, Sunday school lesson, or midweek Bible study is no more spiritually nutritious to the soul than Styrofoam is to the body.

Believers in this environment never grow. Occasionally, they inadvertently stumble onto solid biblical teaching, but the tapeworms growing in their soul ensure that no spiritual nutrients survive long enough to produce fruit. They are susceptible to false teaching, tossed about by every fad and fashion that blows across the church landscape (Eph. 4:14). Some linger in these environments for decades, never moving beyond the elemental teachings of the Christian faith (Heb. 6:1–3). After decades of Bible studies, sermons, service projects, church activities, worship services, small groups, book clubs, men's fellowships, women's ministries, accountability groups, conferences, and retreats, they have all the doctrinal depth of a puddle of spilled milk, without its clarity.

Worse yet, they are unaware of their plight. They don't know anything different is available. Their only exposure to "Christianity" consists of this weak imitation. They've never been exposed to doctrinally robust, exegetical, expository preaching. They are accustomed to shallow, inane, and puerile preaching. They have never heard preaching that exalts God and humbles man. They have no taste for it. They have never heard a gospel presentation that mentions God's

---

11. I have borrowed this phrase from David Wheaton of The Christian Worldview radio program.

wrath, Hell, and eternal damnation. They have never read the Puritans, been warned of false teachers, or had their worldliness confronted. A theological ocean is available to them, but all they have known is the shallow, stinking, debris-strewn tide pools on the shore.

These poor believers are oblivious to their spiritual malnourishment, undiscerning of their peril, and comfortable in their weakened state.

Group 2: The aware, undiscerning, and uncomfortable believer.

These believers are in the same kind of environment as the first group but sense that something is wrong. Something feels off, but they can't put their finger on it. Aware that the preaching they hear hasn't equipped them for life, trained them for evangelism, or grown them in faith, they leave each service feeling empty and spiritually unsatisfied, longing for something more.

Though not sure what's wrong with the preaching they hear, they know it's not right. They can't explain the difference between a sermon by John MacArthur and one by Joel Osteen, but they can tell there is one. They don't have an insatiable hunger for expository preaching, but they aren't satisfied with the banal, clichéd pablum they have imbibed for so many years. They know the church they attend on Sunday isn't healthy, but they don't have a clue how to identify one that is. They aren't sure what they're looking for, but they know they haven't found it.

They are spiritually unsettled. Every worship service reminds them of their spiritual weakness and malnourishment, despite the incessant, vapid, flatteringly inoffensive "talks" they repeatedly endure. Their frustration is intensified with the realization that they've invested so much time, treasure, and work with so little real growth to show for it. Intellectually, they know they should walk away and find a better church. Emotionally, they are attached to the people and place they have invested in for so many years. They love the people in their church, and they wonder why others don't see the same things and feel the same frustrations.

They are aware that something is wrong, they cannot discern what to do about it, and the whole situation makes them uncomfortable.

Group 3: The aware, discerning, and uncomfortable believer.

A third group, further along the spectrum, are aware of their unhealthy church environment. Though able to discern why it's unhealthy, they have no good options for remedying their situation.[12] They are more uncomfortable than those in the previous groups because they *know* something more exists. They've tasted it.

They know the difference between a doctrinally rich expository sermon and the weak-kneed topical tripe they tolerate every Sunday. Their pastor is either unable or unwilling to preach truth clearly, accurately, and unapologetically. Nearly nothing offered up by their church leadership nourishes their soul, challenges their intellect, or advances their holiness. If not for a steady diet of podcasts and sermons by doctrinally sound expositors, and reading books by the same, they would spiritually starve.

Though they would gladly move to another church fellowship for the good of their family and their soul, they have no better options. A survey of the church landscape nearby turns up only far less desirable alternatives. As weak and unhealthy as their current church home might be, it's all they have. Their town offers nothing more. They live in a spiritual wasteland, a desert, where like-minded believers are few, and strong, vibrant, healthy churches are nonexistent.

They know something is wrong. They know what it is. They are miserable because they feel they can't do anything about it.

Group 4: The aware, discerning, and comfortable believer.

This is a small group. Many of these believers have come out of, or even through, the previous stages. They were made aware of their spiritually malnourished state, discerned the cause of it, and found a healthy church environment near them. Now they're in a church with a biblical leadership structure, sound doctrine, and exegetical, expository preaching. Consequently, they are spiritually thriving and fruitful. They know that being in a church family united by the truth is a priceless blessing. They enjoy doctrinally rich Christian fellowship with like-minded believers, and they don't take it for granted.

Group 1 is unaware that group 4 exists. When someone speaks of the blessing of a healthy church, those in group 1 think that they are in such a place. They are blissfully and dangerously ignorant, describing themselves as doctrinally sound, spiritually nourished, and fruitful.

---

12. I (Jim) regularly get email correspondence from people in this group.

Introduction: Why This Book?

Group 2 suspects that group 4 exists. But they aren't sure where to find such a church or even how to know if they did. They are hesitant to go searching for it because they don't want to make the same mistake twice.

Group 3 knows that group 4 exists. They know what they're looking for and would give nearly anything to have it.

FOR THE SHEPHERDS (AND REALLY FOR EVERYONE!)

We will end each chapter with a "For the Shepherds" section. Though specifically addressed to men serving as undershepherds in their church (i.e., pastors/elders), we encourage every reader to give thoughtful, prayerful consideration to those closing encouragements.

I (Jim) have served as a preaching/teaching elder at Kootenai Community Church since 1996. Dave Rich has faithfully and diligently served alongside me since 2001. We love the work of shepherding God's people and desire to help others joyfully and lovingly do the same (1 Pet. 5:1–4).

Some pastors reading this will observe the conditions we have mentioned and feel the same frustrations described above, but from the other side. Perhaps you serve a church largely composed of people with no love for sound doctrine or hunger for expository preaching. Many sit before you on Sunday with itching ears (2 Tim. 4:3), comfortable in their worldliness, expecting you to affirm their self-centered ways. You wish they were interested in doctrinal precision, theological perspicuity, or Bible exposition. The sheep you are called to shepherd might come from various backgrounds, having imbibed nearly every false teaching or aberrant theology circulating in the church. They don't have a high view of God or His Word nor see the need for one. Without any previous exposure to biblical preaching, they have no discernment.

Pastor, your task is a difficult one! You must fulfill your calling in a challenging environment. Take comfort in the fact that young Timothy faced a similar situation.[13] We know it's not easy; the right and

---

13. Timothy faced down the false teachers who had infiltrated the church in Ephesus. Paul encouraged him to confront doctrinal error for the good of the entire church body:

> As I urged you upon my departure for Macedonia, remain on at Ephesus so that you may instruct certain men not to teach strange doctrines, nor to pay attention to myths and endless genealogies, which give rise to mere speculation rather than furthering the administration of God which is by faith. (1 Tim. 1:3–4)

> This command I entrust to you, Timothy, my son, in accordance with the prophecies previously made concerning you, that by them you fight the good fight, keeping faith and a good conscience, which some have rejected and suffered shipwreck in regard

necessary thing seldom is. The current Christian culture pressures you constantly from every direction to be content with mediocrity and avoid conflict at all costs. You live with the constant threat that those under your care can easily move on to the nearest "goat farm" where their immaturity will be coddled, false doctrines tolerated, and favorite false teachers promoted.

Righting that ship won't be easy. In fact, being faithful to the truth may be costly. We would offer the following encouragements.

First, make changes slowly and deliberately. Not everything needs to be changed at once. Some things are immediate threats to the spiritual health and vitality of a church. Those are your priorities. The long-standing tradition that visitors stand and introduce themselves during announcements may irritate you, but the ladies' Bible study going through a Beth Moore book takes precedence. Adopt a long-term perspective. Run the marathon, not the sprint. Take the time to teach your people through the issues. Let the Word of God do the work. Show the truth. Model the truth. Preach the truth. With love and grace, showing concern for the sheep, bring people along toward the goal. Lead, teach, and love them out of error. Be patient. The Spirit of God frequently sanctifies His people slowly. Be loving, gentle, and firm as you seek to instill in them, through biblical preaching, a love for the truth. Labor to give God's people a high view of their God.

Second, read at least one book a year on preaching. Evaluate your own preaching. Pursue excellence and growth in your study,

---

to their faith. Among these are Hymenaeus and Alexander, whom I have handed over to Satan, so that they will be taught not to blaspheme. (1 Tim. 1:18–20)

But the Spirit explicitly says that in later times some will fall away from the faith, paying attention to deceitful spirits and doctrines of demons, by means of the hypocrisy of liars seared in their own conscience as with a branding iron, men who forbid marriage and advocate abstaining from foods which God has created to be gratefully shared in by those who believe and know the truth. For everything created by God is good, and nothing is to be rejected if it is received with gratitude; for it is sanctified by means of the word of God and prayer.

In pointing out these things to the brethren, you will be a good servant of Christ Jesus, constantly nourished on the words of the faith and of the sound doctrine which you have been following. But have nothing to do with worldly fables fit only for old women. On the other hand, discipline yourself for the purpose of godliness; for bodily discipline is only of little profit, but godliness is profitable for all things, since it holds promise for the present life and also for the life to come. It is a trustworthy statement deserving full acceptance. For it is for this we labor and strive, because we have fixed our hope on the living God, who is the Savior of all men, especially of believers. (1 Tim. 4:1–10) preparation, and delivery. Labor in the Word. Dig deep to feed your own soul, and feed your people out of the overflow.

These encouragements are nothing more than what Paul said to Timothy.

> Prescribe and teach these things. Let no one look down on your youthfulness, but rather in speech, conduct, love, faith and purity, show yourself an example of those who believe. Until I come, give attention to the public reading of Scripture, to exhortation and teaching. Do not neglect the spiritual gift within you, which was bestowed on you through prophetic utterance with the laying on of hands by the presbytery. Take pains with these things; be absorbed in them, so that your progress will be evident to all. Pay close attention to yourself and to your teaching; persevere in these things, for as you do this you will ensure salvation both for yourself and for those who hear you. (1 Tim. 4:11–16)

DISCUSSION QUESTIONS

1. What role does your church's doctrinal statement play in directing and evaluating its ministries? When was the last time you carefully and thoughtfully read through it?

2. Have you gone through the stages of discernment described in this chapter? Which group most closely describes you? If you identify with groups 1–3, what efforts are you willing to make to remedy your situation?

3. If you're in group 4, what responsibility do you have to your church body? What can you do to further the influence and gospel impact of your healthy church?

4. Who in your life knows and loves you enough to prayerfully speak God's Word to you for encouragement and correction? Are you providing that kind of encouragement to anyone yourself? What changes do you need to make in your weekly schedule to make such mutual edification more than wishful thinking?

5. How does your view of God affect your worship, either positively or negatively? What does the modern worship methodology communicate about God and His Word?

6. How can we encourage faithful, diligent shepherds in their work?

7. Can you name three modern false teachers and describe their main heresies? Name three biblical doctrines that must be included in an orthodox doctrinal statement.

RECOMMENDED READING

This Little Church Went to Market: The Church in the Age of Entertainment by Gary E. Gilley

Fit Bodies Fat Minds: Why Evangelicals Don't Think and What to Do About It by Os Guinness

Whatever Happened to the Reformation? edited by Gary L. W. Johnson and R. Fowler White

Chapter 2:

*"Do. Or Do Not.
There Is No Try."*

2

What does it mean to try?

The word *try* can have different meanings in different contexts. The most common meaning is "to make an attempt at."[1] The word can also mean "to test." We try something to see what the result will be, as in trying a new recipe, hairstyle, or restaurant. This meaning is related to trying a person in court or trying someone for information, as in "I don't know where the keys are, you might try Diane." We use it to refer to testing our mettle or courage ("This hardship is trying my patience").

Whether we use the word to describe an attempt or a test, the meaning necessarily includes the idea of discovering if something is or isn't so. There is, in both uses, the possibility of more than one outcome. Trying always assumes the possibility, though not the certainty, of failure. We may succeed or fail in the attempt. We may try a new recipe and love it, or it may be awful. The criminal may be guilty or innocent. Diane may or may not know where the keys are. The hardship may prove my patience to be strong or weak.

For the purposes of this book, we'll focus on the primary meaning, "to make an attempt." *Try*, in that sense, always implies the possibility of failure. It's an attempt only, with no guarantee of success. It reminds me of the saying I have used after an unsuccessful day of fishing: "That's why they call it fishing and not catching." Fishing is an attempt (trying) to catch fish. Catching isn't guaranteed. Similarly, trying isn't always succeeding, and, in fact, failure is always possible.

---

1. Merriam-Webster, s.v. "try (v.)," accessed December 7, 2023, https://www.merriam-webster.com/dictionary/try (https://perma.cc/KP5A-6SVS).

God Doesn't Try

For example, you might tell your boss you'll try to get all the work done today, but you wouldn't say you'll try to work. What's the difference? Getting all the work done may or may not be possible, but doing some work is certain (unless you're extremely lazy, in which case "trying to work" would make sense—but would also get you fired). We might try to lift something heavy, but we don't try to lift something light. We try to read through our Bibles in a year or try to read a passage every day, but we don't try to read (unless we're learning to read, in which case the attempt can potentially result in failure, making the word *trying* appropriate). We use *try* to describe attempting things difficult or uncertain. We don't use it to describe attempting things simple or certain. Those we just *do*.

FAILURE IS ALWAYS AN OPTION

The famous quote "Failure is not an option"[2] is attributed to Gene Kranz, the NASA Flight Director for many of the Gemini and Apollo missions, but Kranz never actually said it himself. It was written for the Kranz character in the movie *Apollo 13*. The statement means that failure is so horrible to contemplate that we'll never willingly consider it. Instead, we will exhaust all other options, putting the prospect of failure out of our minds, as if denying its possibility guarantees success.

The title of this chapter—"Do. Or Do Not. There Is No Try."—comes from a famous scene in *The Empire Strikes Back* in which Yoda trains Luke Skywalker in the swamps of Dagobah. Young Skywalker arrives on Dagobah at the direction of a disembodied Obi-Wan Kenobi. There, he meets the strange creature Yoda. Luke begins his Jedi training, and it doesn't go well. When Yoda instructs Luke to raise his X-wing fighter from the swamp, Luke responds with a lackadaisical "All right, I'll give it a try." Yoda quickly rejoins, "No! Try not. Do. Or do not. There is no try."[3] Even with that great wisdom received, Luke . . . fails to raise the fighter.

These are useful illustrations of the point of this chapter. Quotes like "failure is not an option" and "there is no try" are used in motivational speeches, corporate sales meetings, and locker rooms at halftime. They encourage the power of positive thinking, as if resolve and determination are all that are necessary to overcome reluctant buyers, rival high school volleyball squads, or any other obstacle.

---

2. *Apollo 13*, directed by Ron Howard.
3. *Star Wars Episode V: The Empire Strikes Back*, written and produced by George Lucas.

"Do. Or Do Not. There Is No Try."

Yoda and Kranz share a similar erroneous view—namely, that failure is due only to a lack of human will. According to them, allowing for the possibility of failure leads to failure. Therefore, to deny the possibility of failure will lead inevitably to success. By easily raising Luke's fighter, Yoda demonstrated that his power with the Force was great. He denied the possibility of failure and was successful. By denying that failure was an option, Kranz and his team avoided catastrophe in *Apollo 13*.

But is recognizing the realistic probability of failure the chief reason people fail? If we all decided that failure wasn't an option and willed to do (or do not) but never to try, would we never fail? Of course not! Denying that a thing can happen doesn't prevent it from happening, even if you're an aerospace engineer or a Jedi Grand Master.[4] The real Gene Kranz was involved in many space missions, one of which ended in tragic failure. Even Yoda failed to defeat Count Dooku and Emperor Palpatine, though he certainly tried.

Failure was an option on the Apollo 13 mission (and in fact the mission did not achieve its ultimate objective of a lunar landing) but happily, tragic failure was not the outcome in that case. There apparently was *try* for our fictional hero Yoda in that his efforts did sometimes end in failure. For humans, failure is always an option. The only people who never fail are those who never try. To attempt anything difficult will result in failure at least occasionally. Players on opposing teams might tell reporters that "failure is not an option" prior to a game, but failure certainly is possible for both teams, and one of them will certainly fail. That's why we play the game!

A RECIPE FOR FAILURE

Failure remains possible in spite of our resolve, positive thinking, and denials, but why is that? What is it about human nature that prohibits us from *doing* with 100 percent success? What shortcomings make failure possible, and in some cases inevitable?

All failures in human endeavors arise from two basic limitations of our nature: inability and ignorance. Think carefully about your own

---

4. I'm not saying that denying the possibility of failure or putting it out of your mind has no value in promoting success or encouraging resolve. I'm not suggesting it's immoral. I am pointing out that it's preposterous to believe that doing so *guarantees* success. Clearly, it doesn't, so failure must result from something other than just allowing for its possibility.

failure. What was the cause? It had to be either inability or ignorance.[5] Either you lacked the ability or the knowledge required for the task.

If I try to dunk a basketball, I'll fail. Why? Because I'm unable to jump that high. I can't overcome the pull of gravity. It's a physical inability. I may make an honest, vigorous attempt, but I'll still fail. If I try to run a two-minute mile, lift an elephant, reach from my desk to my refrigerator in the next room, go without sleep for a year, hold my breath for an hour, swim the English Channel, or see through a wall, I'll fail. In all these cases, my failure would result from inability. We often attribute our failures to inability, saying things like, "I tried, but I just couldn't do it."

Many failures are due to inability, but perhaps more are due to ignorance. I can't solve the Riemann hypothesis or even describe it intelligently. That mathematical hypothesis has never been solved, and if I tried, I would certainly fail due to a lack of knowledge. As an economics student, I (Dave) failed to answer some exam questions correctly because I didn't know the answers. One may fail to dunk a basketball not because of physical inability (it's not that they can't jump high enough) but because they don't know when or how hard to jump. Practice may remedy that ignorance. A person may try to get a job but fail the interview because they didn't know the answer to a question. Many have had failed investments because they didn't know the price of an asset would go down instead of up. Imagine how financially successful you could be if you had perfect knowledge of tomorrow's prices today. That fundamental lack of knowledge often results in failure. How often have you said, "If I had only known then what I know now"? That's an admission that knowledge would have prevented failure.

TRYING IN THE BIBLE

In the Old Testament, there is one main Hebrew word that means "to attempt," and it has a much broader semantic range than our English word *try*. That word is *bāqaš*. In the NASB, it's most often translated "sought" or "seeking" and only translated "tried" twice in the Old Testament:

---

[5]. I am dividing inability and ignorance into two distinct limitations for clarity, but ignorance is really a subset of inability. Ignorance is a lack of knowledge, an inability to know everything.

> When Pharaoh heard of this matter, he *tried* to kill Moses. But Moses fled from the presence of Pharaoh and settled in the land of Midian, and he sat down by a well. (Exod. 2:15)

> Saul *tried* to pin David to the wall with the spear, but he slipped away out of Saul's presence, so that he stuck the spear into the wall. And David fled and escaped that night. (1 Sam. 19:10)

The English word *sought* is another way to express the idea of "trying." When *bāqaš* is used with an infinitive form of a verb (i.e., the word *to* followed by the verb) it could be properly translated as either "try," "desire," or "intend," as in Deuteronomy 13:10: "So you shall stone him to death because he has *sought* to seduce you from the LORD your God who brought you out from the land of Egypt, out of the house of slavery." "To seduce" is an infinitive, so *bāqaš* is translated "sought." It would have no loss of meaning if it were translated "tried,"[6] as in "tried to seduce." The word often describes both wanting to do something and attempting to follow through on the desire. For example, Esther 2:21: "In those days, while Mordecai was sitting at the king's gate, Bigthan and Teresh, two of the king's officials from those who guarded the door, became angry and *sought* to lay hands on King Ahasuerus." The traitors desired to attack the king, and actually attempted to do so. *Bāqaš* is the Hebrew word that most closely corresponds to our English word *try*, though it has a range of meaning broader than "to attempt."

In the New Testament, there is one main Greek word, *zēteō*,[7] that most closely expresses the meaning of our English word *try*. It has a range of meaning similar to *bāqaš* and is the primary translation of *bāqaš* in the Greek Septuagint. Like *bāqaš*, *zēteō* is most often translated "seek." It's translated "tried" or "trying" eight times in the NASB.[8] Here are three examples:

---

6. Many English translations do translate *bāqaš* as "tried" in this verse. For example, the NIV translates it, "Stone them to death, because they *tried* to turn you away from the LORD your God, who brought you out of Egypt, out of the land of slavery."

7. There are cases where *try* in the New Testament isn't a translation of *zēteō*. *Peirazó* is normally used more narrowly as "testing" or "tempting" but is translated "trying" in Acts 16:7, where it definitely has the meaning "to attempt": "And after they came to Mysia, they were trying to go into Bithynia, and the Spirit of Jesus did not permit them." *Dokimazō* is translated "try" in Luke 14:19 and Eph. 5:10 but doesn't mean "attempt" in either case. Rather, it means "to prove or discern." The English word *try* is sometimes added in translation in cases where the original is an infinitive verb, as in Acts 18:4: "trying to persuade" rather than "persuading."

8. John 19:12 says, "As a result of this Pilate *made efforts* to release Him, but the Jews cried out saying, 'If you release this Man, you are no friend of Caesar; everyone who makes

Now the chief priests and the whole Council *kept trying* to obtain false testimony against Jesus, so that they might put Him to death. (Mat. 26:59)

But as the sailors *were trying* to escape from the ship and had let down the ship's boat into the sea, on the pretense of intending to lay out anchors from the bow . . . (Acts 27:30)

Zaccheus *was trying* to see who Jesus was, and was unable because of the crowd, for he was small in stature. (Luke 19:3)

These uses of *zētéō* closely correspond to the primary meaning of our English word *try* (i.e., "to attempt"). They nicely demonstrate that the possibility of failure is implied in the meaning of the word. The chief priests and the Council at first failed to find someone to provide false testimony that would stand up in a Roman court. They kept trying until they eventually succeeded: "They did not find any, even though many false witnesses came forward. But later on two came forward . . ." (Matt. 26:60). The sailors' attempt to escape the ship was thwarted when the centurion and the soldiers cut away the lifeboat (Acts 27:32). Zaccheus's initial attempt to see Jesus failed because of his stature, but the "wee little man" ultimately found a way (Luke 19:4). In all these instances, trying was accompanied by initial failure.

To summarize, there is a main Hebrew word and a main Greek word used to express (among other ideas), the notion of trying—attempting to do something with a real possibility of failure. Here is the point of this brief word study—*these words are never used of God in this sense.*[9] While the words are used over three hundred times in Scripture, they are never used in this way to describe an act of God. God is never said to try in the sense of "attempting something" He may fail to accomplish. Why? Because God doesn't try!

---

himself out to be a king opposes Caesar.'" "Made efforts" has the same meaning as "tried," so this may be counted as a ninth usage of *zētéō* in this way.

9. The verb *bāqaš* is applied to God, but never in the sense of "to make an attempt at." God is said to examine, intend, require, set about, or find (*bāqaš*). It's very interestingly used by Job in Job 10:6 to describe God seeking for Job's guilt. In that verse, Job was asking if God is like a man, trying to find out if he is guilty of sin. Clearly, this isn't true of God, just as it isn't true that God has "eyes of flesh" or sees "as a man sees" or has "days as the days of a mortal" or "years as man's years" (Job 10:4–5). Job would later repent of suggesting this, saying, "I have declared that which I did not understand" (Job 42:3). The verb *zētéō* is used to describe Christ seeking to save the lost (Luke 19:10), seeking to do the will of the Father (John 5:30), and seeking the glory of the Father (John 7:18). It is also used of the Father seeking worshippers (John 4:23). In none of those instances is the possibility of failure in any way implied.

God can't try because God can't fail. God can't fail because He has neither inability nor ignorance. God's omnipotence (absolute ability) and omniscience (complete knowledge) preclude the possibility of failure. Since He can't fail, He can't be said to try.

THE POWER OF GOD

God is absolutely, completely, infinitely able. God can do anything He wills, decrees, or intends that is consistent with His holy and perfect nature.[10] Wayne Grudem's definition of omnipotence is helpful: "God's omnipotence means that God is able to do all his holy will."[11] Richard Mayhue and John MacArthur define it thus: "God's omnipotence describes his ability to do anything consistent with his nature."[12] Charles Hodge brilliantly contrasts the power of man (who tries) with the power of God (Who doesn't):

> We get the idea of power from our own consciousness. That is, we are conscious of the ability of producing effects. Power in man is confined within very narrow limits. We can change the current of our thoughts, or fix our attention on a particular object, and we can move the voluntary muscles of our body. Beyond this our direct power does not extend. It is from this small measure of efficiency that all the stores of human knowledge and all the wonders of human art are derived. It is only our thoughts, volitions, and purposes, together with certain acts of the body, that are immediately subject to the will. For all other effects we must avail ourselves of the use of means. We cannot will a book, a picture, or a house into existence. The production of such effects requires protracted labor and the use of diverse appliances. . . . It is by removing all the limitations of power, as it exists in us, that we rise to the idea of the omnipotence of God. We do not thus, however, lose the idea itself. Almighty power does not cease to be power. We can do very little. God can do whatever He wills. We, beyond very narrow limits, must use means to accomplish our ends. With God

---

10. God can't do anything inconsistent with His nature and character. He can't lie, sin, change, or deny Himself. He can't do something logically impossible like create a square circle or make one plus one equal three. Logic is part of God's nature, and consequently, violations of logic are rational impossibilities. Rational impossibilities, such as the famous immovable rock dilemma (whether God can create a rock so heavy He can't lift it), can't be postulated of a rational, logical God.

11. Grudem, *Systematic Theology*, 216.

12. MacArthur and Mayhue, *Biblical Doctrine*, 177.

means are unnecessary. He wills, and it is done. He said, Let there be light; and there was light. He, by a volition created the heavens and the earth. At the volition of Christ, the winds ceased, and there was a great calm. By an act of the will He healed the sick, opened the eyes of the blind, and raised the dead. This simple idea of the omnipotence of God, that He can do without effort, and by a volition, whatever He wills, is the highest conceivable idea of power, and is that which is clearly presented in the Scriptures.[13]

The biblical testimony to the omnipotence of God is so extensive as to be utterly undeniable. Here are just a few clear descriptions of God's absolute power.

Now when Abram was ninety-nine years old, the LORD appeared to Abram and said to him, "I am God Almighty; walk before Me, and be blameless." (Gen. 17:1)

Whatever the LORD pleases, He does, in heaven and in earth, in the seas and in all deeps. (Ps. 135:6)

Ah Lord GOD! Behold, You have made the heavens and the earth by Your great power and by Your outstretched arm! Nothing is too difficult for You. (Jer. 32:17)

And looking at them Jesus said to them, "With people this is impossible, but with God all things are possible." (Matt. 19:26)

In his book, *Reprobation and God's Sovereignty*, Peter Sammons writes,

That God is all-powerful means that God is never hindered by any external force in the exercise of his power. There is no personal being (such as Satan), impersonal law (such as the principle of "free will"), or force (such as evil) that is able to challenge or frustrate God's efforts. What God wills, he does. And because his power is infinite, he never gets tired or exhausts his power when he uses it.[14]

The implications of God's omnipotence are manifold, being of great comfort to the Christian and causing terror to the honest, self-aware unbeliever. God's omnipotence ensures success in all His intentions and acts. There is no possibility of failure due to inability.

---

13. Hodge, *Systematic Theology*, 1:406–7.
14. Sammons, *Reprobation and God's Sovereignty*, 24.

"Do. Or Do Not. There Is No Try."

THE KNOWLEDGE OF GOD

Is it possible for God to act as He intends, but for His actions to have unintended consequences? As we saw earlier, this is a common cause of human failure. We lack the information, knowledge, or intellectual capacity to succeed. I was physically capable of filling in the correct bubble on a multiple-choice question on an economics exam. I had the physical ability to move a pencil appropriately on the paper to form the correct words on an essay or problem. I didn't lack ability but knowledge. I didn't know the right answers. Could this be true of God? Could He fail because of a lack of knowledge?

If you think this is a stupid question, your instinct is correct. But in some Evangelical circles, this very idea has gained some traction in recent years. Those who defend the supremacy and sovereignty of the human will must, at some point, jettison the biblical teaching of God's omniscience.[15] Those who deny God's omniscience deny a basic truth regarding Yahweh's nature. Denying omniscience places one outside the bounds of orthodoxy. They are idolators worshipping another god.

God's omniscience precludes the possibility of failure due to a lack of knowledge. There are no gaps in God's knowledge related to time (He knows the past and future perfectly) or space (there are no hidden corners of the universe or additional universes where God's knowledge doesn't extend).

God's omniscience may be defined in this way: "God fully knows himself and all things actual and possible in one simple and eternal act."[16] There are three components to that definition that deserve our consideration. First, God fully knows Himself. This captures the concept of God's knowledge entirely. To know God fully is to know all that can be known. Since God is sovereign, His full knowledge of Himself is a full knowledge of everything, as everything is in the mind of God and occurs only by the will of God. To know God fully is to know everything. In order to fully understand God, a being would have to know all that has ever happened, ever will happen, and ever could've happened, as well as all the implications of all those potential events. That being would have to know everything about everything in the past, present, and future, as well as everything about all

---

15. We'll deal with objections to God's omniscience and examine the relationship between God's omniscience and the will of man in chapter 10.
16. Grudem, *Systematic Theology*, 190. This is a common definition, and variations on it are found in multiple sources. See Berkhof, *Systematic Theology*, 54; Hodge, *Systematic Theology*, 1:397–98; and MacArthur and Mayhue, *Biblical Doctrine*, 174–75.

things that didn't happen and don't exist but could have within the will of God.

Second, God fully knows all things actual and possible. Though nothing exists outside the will of God or the mind of God, complete knowledge includes information not directly pertaining to the nature of God. This includes all scientific knowledge, history, current events, future events, and the thoughts of every person or creature that has ever existed, could have existed, will exist, or could exist. God knows not only what is, but what will be and what could possibly be, so long as those possible things are consistent with His character.

> Woe to you, Chorazin! Woe to you, Bethsaida! For if the miracles had occurred in Tyre and Sidon which occurred in you, they would have repented long ago in sackcloth and ashes. Nevertheless I say to you, it will be more tolerable for Tyre and Sidon in the day of judgment than for you. And you, Capernaum, will not be exalted to heaven, will you? You will descend to Hades; for if the miracles had occurred in Sodom which occurred in you, it would have remained to this day. Nevertheless I say to you that it will be more tolerable for the land of Sodom in the day of judgment, than for you. (Matt. 11:21–24)

Third, God's knowledge is one simple[17] and eternal act. God's knowledge isn't incremental. Grudem uses the example of counting grains of sand to ascertain how many exist.[18] God needn't do that. All knowledge has always resided in God. He doesn't need to make logical connections, count, add, subtract, reason, or research in order to answer a question. He doesn't discover truth or learn. This always has been and always will be so.

As with omnipotence, the biblical testimony to omniscience is ubiquitous and overwhelming. Here are a few relevant passages.

> For to us God revealed them through the Spirit; for the Spirit searches all things, even the depths of God. For who among men knows the thoughts of a man except the spirit of the man which is in him? Even so the thoughts of God no one knows except the Spirit of God. (1 Cor. 2:10–11)

---

17 By "simple" we mean not divided into parts.
18 Grudem, *Systematic Theology*, 192.

> And there is no creature hidden from His sight, but all things are open and laid bare to the eyes of Him with whom we have to do. (Heb. 4:13)

> We will know by this that we are of the truth, and will assure our heart before Him in whatever our heart condemns us; for God is greater than our heart and knows all things. (1 John 3:19–20)

Back to our question: is it possible that God may fail from lack of knowledge? Obviously not. The omniscience of God precludes failure. With perfect knowledge of all facts, actual and potential, God cannot err or fail for want of knowledge because He has no such deficiency.

WHY GOD'S SOVEREIGNTY MATTERS

This is the theological underpinning of this book: God doesn't try. To speak of trying is to admit the possibility of failure. Failure is always due either to a lack of power or a lack of knowledge. These are the ontological limitations that cause humans to fail, making almost all human actions mere attempts. Humans try because humans can fail. Humans fail because we lack absolute ability and perfect knowledge. God can never try (and in Scripture is never said to try) because His nature precludes the possibility of failure inherent in the meaning of *try*. For God, failure truly isn't an option. God does or does not. For Him, and Him alone, there is no try.

A Christian would willingly give hearty assent to the basic theological truths covered in this chapter. The omnipotence and omniscience of God are among the most well-known of His attributes. If you were to ask the average Christian to name the attributes of God, the "omnis" would be among the first ones mentioned. I have demonstrated in this chapter that the perfections of God preclude the prospect of failure. Why go through this exercise? What are we seeking to address?

A quick internet search for "God has been trying" turns up multiple results that suggest God is "trying to get your attention," "trying to tell you something," or "trying to call you to something," such as a ministry or vocation. These all offer the same thing: tips and tricks from biblically illiterate advisors on how to hear the voice of God clearly. These tricks are needed to help a poor, weak, incoherent

God Doesn't Try

god[19] speak to his people.[20] They suggest we look for signs like repeated messages and advice from friends. We're to read our unsettled feelings or unhappiness as signs that God is trying to tell us something that He's unfortunately incapable of communicating infallibly. Jim has written extensively on the unbiblical practice of "hearing the voice of God" in his book *God Doesn't Whisper*, showing that God speaks clearly and sufficiently in His Word. He doesn't need signals, signs, and inaudible whispers. He isn't impotently trying to give His sheep the guidance necessary for their sanctification. God has written a book which is sufficient for every decision, belief, and work in the life of the believer. 2 Timothy 3:16–17 promises that "all Scripture is inspired by God and profitable for teaching, for reproof, for correction, for training in righteousness; so that the man of God may be adequate, equipped for every good work."

The central premise of *God Doesn't Whisper* is that God doesn't *try* to communicate to His people. God has spoken! His Word is sufficient to equip the man or woman of God for the work to which He has called them. God doesn't whisper. He doesn't *try* to speak to us. He has inspired and preserved His Word. He didn't try. He didn't fail. This book applies the truth behind *God Doesn't Whisper* to all aspects of the Christian life.[21]

We pray that reading this book will convince you that God hasn't failed, can't fail, and doesn't try. He doesn't try to speak. He doesn't try to heal. He doesn't try to provide. He doesn't try to execute justice. He doesn't try to save. He doesn't try to get your attention. He doesn't try to guide you. He doesn't try to change culture. He doesn't try to accomplish His will. God either does or He doesn't.

This is vital to Christian living in a multitude of ways. In his sermon "Divine Sovereignty," Charles Spurgeon said,

> There is no attribute of God more comforting to his children than the doctrine of Divine Sovereignty. Under the most adverse circumstances, in the most severe troubles, they believe that Sovereignty hath ordained their afflictions, that

---

19. We use lowercase *g* when describing this false god, a figment of the imagination, and not the God of the Bible. In this book, that is how we will refer to a god who tries.

20. On the first results page, there were lists of three, seven, nine, ten, and twenty signs that God is trying to get your attention or tell you something. Page two fills in some of those gaps with lists of four, five, and eight signs. Apparently, we need to add "inarticulate" to the list of this god's attributes.

21. See chapter 5 for more on this point.

"Do. Or Do Not. There Is No Try."

Sovereignty overrules them, and that Sovereignty will sanctify them all.[22]

It's only in the sovereignty of God that the Christian can find peace and comfort. If God only tries, if God may fail, then life is beyond terrifying and the future is paralyzingly uncertain. If God merely tries, we can't have assurance of salvation, future hope, or ultimate victory over the grave. We are consigned only to a life of fear and anxiety.

But God doesn't try. God does or doesn't. If you're a child of God, this is your comfort and peace. We can find joy in the words of Paul in Romans 8:28–30:

> And we know that God causes all things to work together for good to those who love God, to those who are called according to His purpose. For those whom He foreknew, He also predestined to become conformed to the image of His Son, so that He would be the firstborn among many brethren; and these whom He predestined, He also called; and these whom He called, He also justified; and these whom He justified, He also glorified.

Believing this promise is only reasonable if God is sovereign. Rejoicing in this promise is only possible if we have certainty that His decretive will[23] can't be thwarted. He has purposed to redeem for Himself a people, a Kingdom, a family. He sent His Son, our God and Savior, the Lord Jesus Christ, to be born on this Earth. This sinless Man, this Divine Son, lived a perfect life and died on a cross to bear the wrath of God for the sins of all who would ever repent of their sins and put their faith in Him. Having suffered the wrath of God, paying the penalty for the sins of all the redeemed from all time, He rose from the dead victorious over sin and death. Those who come to Him in humble, repentant, God-given faith receive forgiveness and righteousness. He atoned for our sins through His death and provided

---

22. Spurgeon, "Divine Sovereignty."
23. Reformed theology distinguishes between God's decretive will (will of decree), referring to those things God has ordained to occur, and God's preceptive will (will of precept), referring to those things God has commanded of moral agents. God's decretive will was established in eternity past and can't be altered or thwarted. God's preceptive will is revealed in the commands and principles of Scripture. Sin is that lawlessness that transgresses the preceptive will of God. God's decretive will is secret, while His preceptive will is revealed. This terminology is important. God's decree is unknown to us but revealed as events occur. A small part of God's decree is revealed in prophecy, which tells us of some future elements of His decretive will which are yet to happen. Thus, a small fraction of God's secret will is revealed.

perfect righteousness for us through His sinless life. He didn't *try* to save His people. He did it. He did it all. And we can have assurance of our future inheritance because, and only because, God doesn't try. If we question His ability or knowledge, if we believe that He tries and doesn't always succeed, then our faith is in someone no greater than ourselves, someone who may fail to save.

Further, we strongly believe that saying God is trying (and so implying that He could fail) is sinful blasphemy that should be rooted out of our language, conversation, writing, thinking, preaching, and teaching. It leads to the ungodly and heretical doctrines of demons we describe later on, but more subtly, it misrepresents God by portraying Him as a fallible salesman working on His pitch to persuade men of the value of His product. That god is like a suitor wringing his hands outside our door, desperately hoping to win our hearts. That god has a you-shaped hole in his heart and hopes his efforts are sufficient to earn your love. He is subject to the true sovereign—human will—for the decisive move.

We pray that this work can be a part of a "back to the Bible" approach to living the Christian life. Let's believe God's Word. Let's think of Him, speak of Him, and worship Him as He has revealed Himself in Scripture. Sovereign. Powerful. Able. Independent. Absolute. God.

FOR THE SHEPHERDS

Does your preaching and teaching undermine the sovereignty of God? Do you speak of God as if He were trying? You may be tempted to get God off the hook by claiming He doesn't have anything to do with evil, whether natural or moral. For example, after a natural disaster impacts your congregation, you might be tempted to say, "A disaster like this doesn't come from God. This is a result of sin and comes from the evil one, Satan." Aside from being entirely unbiblical, how does this answer comfort the believer? Is God trying (but failing) to prevent these sorts of things from happening? Is He too weak? Doesn't He know about them? Doesn't He care?

How does denying God's sovereign control in the wake of a traumatic event bring comfort to God's people? If God had no part in the terrible thing that happened to you, how can you have confidence in any of His promises? How can you trust Him if He has no control over a virus, a cancer, a fire, an earthquake, a tornado, or a person who would do you harm? Where is our comfort if God is impotent or ignorant?

"Do. Or Do Not. There Is No Try."

God is sovereign over everything that happens. He can prevent (or cause) natural disasters as He pleases. To suggest otherwise is to deny the clear teaching of Scripture and make Him out to be something less than He is. It makes something or someone superior to Him in power and/or knowledge.

It is a careless use of language to say things like "God is trying to tell us something in this verse," or "God is trying to get our attention with what's happening," or "God was trying to save this person for years before they finally bowed the knee and turned to Christ." These are unbiblical and blasphemous descriptions of God. For all the reasons outlined here, to say that God *tries* is to bear His name in vain. As teachers and preachers, we must be clear about the power, knowledge, and sovereignty of God. We must describe Him truthfully and accurately. God doesn't try!

DISCUSSION QUESTIONS

1. Do you find the teaching of God's sovereignty to be a source of comfort? Why or why not?

2. Do you know anyone who struggles to understand or embrace this truth? How can you help them see God's sovereignty as a glorious reality?

3. Can you name causes of human failure other than lack of knowledge and lack of power? Do those other causes fit under the two categories listed?

4. In what ways do you think your language fails to honor God? How do you misrepresent Him and His works through sloppy language?

5. Is there anything God is unable to do? Why?

6. What does *omniscience* mean? How is omniscience related to God's power?

7. What is the difference between simple, eternal knowledge and incremental knowledge?

RECOMMENDED READING

The Mystery of Providence by John Flavel

Biblical Doctrine: A Systematic Summary of Bible Truth by John F. MacArthur Jr. and Richard Mayhue

God Doesn't Whisper by Jim Osman

Evangelism and the Sovereignty of God by J. I. Packer

Almighty Over All: Understanding the Sovereignty of God by R. C. Sproul Jr.

Part 2

God's Infallible Work in Believers

Chapter 3:

God Doesn't Try to Save His People

3

Some years ago, we attended a funeral service for a man in our community who died unexpectedly. We will call him John.

John grew up in a well-known family with a long history in our area. Some of John's family attended the church Dave and I pastor, and he had worked for the same company as Dave. We both attended the funeral. John had a reputation for rowdy living, sinful indulgences, and reckless adventures. However, a couple years prior to his passing, he started attending a local church and reportedly turned from sin and came to faith in Christ. After years of rambunctious carousing, he had an impressive number of friends and acquaintances, many of whom were present for the funeral. It was held in a local church, a venue large enough to accommodate the expected attendance. The place was packed. It was a perfect opportunity to preach the gospel to hundreds of unbelievers, most of whom knew of John's riotous life and recent conversion to faith in Christ.

What I am about to describe, the reader has undoubtedly witnessed a time or two. After some introductory statements and a couple of songs, the pastor proceeded to the "message." With *brief* references and, in some cases, mere allusions to Scripture, he spoke of the tragedy of dying young and the grief it causes for those left behind. He mentioned, in the most cursory fashion possible, John's faith and church attendance. Then, without any explanation of sin, the wrath of God, or the death and resurrection of Christ, the pastor said in a weak and wimpish tone, "Since we'll all die, we all need to make a decision for God just like John did. I hope you'll make that decision yourself someday."

That was it. That was his "gospel message," and it was no gospel at all. This travesty is repeated every day in every city in this country.

WEAK GOSPEL APPEALS

We have suffered through more weak-kneed, flaccid, and vague "gospel presentations" than we care to count. Funerals, weddings, Awana events, conferences, concerts, camp meetings, outreaches, church services, baptisms, and conventions provide opportunities to present the gospel to large gatherings. Some are intentionally designed to gather unbelievers so they can be "evangelized." With all the effort and money poured into these events, we might expect a bold, hard-hitting, straightforward presentation of the truth. A large gathering is the perfect opportunity to swing for the fences and hold nothing back. The encouragement to be "straightforward about the truth of the gospel" (Gal. 2:14) is for just such occasions. The funeral service was a slow pitch directly over the plate with the bases loaded. The batter chose to leave the bat on his shoulder.

Why do men do this? Why, when those gathered in a church expect the preacher to give a religious message, quote Scripture, and talk about Heaven and Hell, God and judgment, sin and righteousness, do men intentionally obfuscate the truth? The preacher has home field advantage. The people are in a church building. They've come to a service officiated by a pastor. They expect to hear a pastor, in a church, at a religious event, talk about life, death, and eternity.

When I (Jim) do wedding ceremonies for couples in our congregation, I unapologetically teach what Scripture says concerning the marriage covenant.[1] I teach that there are only two genders created by God, that God created marriage, and that God assigned the gender roles in the marriage covenant. Men are to lovingly lead their wives, and women are to respectfully submit to the loving leadership of their husbands. I say that marriage isn't a contract to be legally dissolved when one or more parties no longer accept the terms. Marriage isn't a convenience to make our lives easier. Marriage isn't a convention invented, defined, or described by the state. Rather, marriage is a covenant. God's design for marriage is one man and one woman becoming one flesh for one lifetime. This, by definition, rules

---

1. We (the elders of Kootenai Community Church) will not perform wedding ceremonies in our church for any couple unless at least one of them is a member in good standing. Our church building isn't available for use for weddings to anyone who isn't a member. We don't perform civil ceremonies nor recognize the authority of the state to define or govern the institution of marriage. Biblical marriage is a covenant made before the Lord's people.

out any perversion of marriage sanctioned by human governments, customs, cultures, or the courts.

Not surprisingly, I'll hear complaints from non-Christians in attendance. I've offended more than one person with so "dogmatic," "narrow-minded," and "judgmental" a perspective. My response is always the same: "You came to a Christian marriage ceremony in a Christian church to wed two Christian people in a Christian institution officiated by a Christian pastor and you're surprised I spoke about the Christian view of marriage? What did you expect?" Sometimes I have to lovingly point out that the ceremony was not about them and their enjoyment.

Why do men entrusted with proclaiming the gospel and unflinchingly preaching the whole truth (Acts 20:27; Eph. 6:20) avoid the hard edges of the gospel and dance around the truth like a tribal shaman conjuring a rainstorm? This gross dereliction of duty is due to a low view of God, His Word, and His ability to save. Men lack confidence in God, Who, for His own eternal glory, has foreordained the salvation, sanctification, and security of all His elect. They don't preach as men convinced that God infallibly accomplishes the salvation of all those the Father has given to the Son in eternity past.

They preach as if God were only *trying* to save people. They won't risk offending a potential convert with the hard truths of Scripture lest they walk away, never to give the gospel another hearing. The person God was trying to save would be forever lost because the preacher didn't craft the message to avoid offense. They avoid anything that might hinder God's efforts to save and, ironically, end up withholding from the sinner the very thing that God uses to do so—namely, the fullness of gospel truth (Rom. 1:16).

They approach evangelism as if God were trying to save sinners and dangerously close to failing. Since many enter the gate that leads to destruction (Matt. 7:13), they conclude that God is unable to save the bulk of humanity, though He's desperately trying. He needs our clever, subtle methods of covert evangelism. Like trapping wild prey, they try to lure the unsuspecting sinner into making a "decision for Jesus" before they're scared off by truth. Some lack the courage to unapologetically present the truth because they lack the conviction that God will infallibly use it to accomplish His ordained purposes.[2] He needs us to do better PR work.

---

2. This isn't the only cause of modern cowardice, but it's the cause we are addressing in this book. Some don't accurately or boldly present the gospel because they don't know how.

God isn't *trying* to save sinners! He isn't making every attempt or even doing His best. God isn't *trying* at all. In fact, such descriptions of God's redeeming work aren't worthy of Him. Describing God's saving work in this way is blasphemous. He *is* saving sinners. In fact, God is infallibly saving every person whom He has chosen in Christ (Eph. 1:4), appointed to eternal life (Acts 13:48), and given to His Son (John 6:37–39). God can't fail to accomplish this since God can't fail. He lacks neither the knowledge nor the power to do what He intends. God suffers from neither ignorance nor inability; therefore, God doesn't *try* to save sinners.

FROM WHENCE COMES MY HELP?

If we were to summarize the Scripture's teaching on salvation, we couldn't do better than the statement made by Jonah in the belly of the great fish: "Salvation is from the LORD" (Jon. 2:9).

This is a most God-glorifying, man-humbling truth. It's impossible for salvation to be a synergistic work whereby God cooperates with men in their redemption. If it were, salvation would be "from the Lord *and men*." However, salvation is from the Lord. It originates with God. It's granted and accomplished by God and God alone. Man can't take credit for even the least part of his salvation. We can boast of nothing—not even our faith (Eph. 2:8–9). God doesn't share His glory with another (Isa. 42:8; 48:11).

We affirm that salvation is of the Lord both in part and in whole. If any individual part of salvation comes from man—his ability, willingness, or cooperation—then we can't say salvation as a whole is of the Lord. We can't say of the whole what we can't affirm of the individual parts. All of salvation is from the Lord.

Salvation began in eternity past. The Father chose a people in Christ before the foundation of the world (Eph. 1:4). By that sovereign and unconditional act of divine grace, the Father gave His chosen people to His Son (John 6:37–39). That grace was granted to them from all eternity (2 Tim. 1:9).[3] Salvation wasn't planned by sinful men.

They've never been trained or discipled to do so. Others don't understand the gospel. Some fear men, afraid they'll lose their job, reputation, or church members. This is the implicit assumption that lies behind the seeker-centered church growth movement. Some fear the physical or financial harm that may come. Others fear the world's scorn or being branded a pariah in their communities. These concerns rise from a low view of God and His word. Fear of man is a lack of faith in and proper fear of God.

3. Some teach that God looked forward in time to observe what men would do when offered the gospel, then "chose" all those whom He foresaw would freely choose Him. We categorically and vehemently reject this view of divine election for a number of reasons. First, it makes God's

Those God would save were predestined to salvation before anything was created (Rom. 8:29–30; Eph. 1:5, 11).

Salvation wasn't procured by sinful men. Men are fallen in Adam (Rom. 5), dead in their sins (Col. 2:13), and alienated from the life of God (Eph. 4:18; Col. 1:21). Our hearts are hardened, desperately wicked, and in love with the darkness that enslaves us (John 3:19). Born spiritually dead and under the wrath of God (Eph. 2:1–3), men have no ability to keep God's law or please Him (Rom. 8:6–8). All our good deeds are offensive in the sight of a holy God (Isa. 64:6) since the thoughts of men's hearts are only evil continually (Gen. 6:5; Jer. 17:9–10). Man is hopeless, helpless, and unable to change his condition. God must do the work.

Our sin debt is so enormous, and our inability so complete, that another had to accomplish salvation on our behalf. We were unable to fulfill the righteous demands of the law and merit God's blessing. What God required, we failed to do. What He forbade, we transgressed. Guilty of breaking the law, we were unable to pay the penalty our sin warranted.

Jesus Christ bore the full wrath of God that our sin deserved. He took the punishment for all the sin of all the sinners who would ever believe. Christ did what we could never do. He lived the perfect life the law demanded to provide us righteousness (2 Cor. 5:21). His righteous life is credited to our account, so we can stand in the presence of the Father not just forgiven, but righteous. Then He died the death that divine justice demanded of us, paying the price for our sin (Heb. 9:11–14, 27–28; 10:11–18; 1 Pet. 2:24).

Salvation isn't planned by man, procured by man, or applied by man. Man has no ability to deliver himself from sin, the kingdom of darkness, or Satan. Though commanded to do so, fallen man is unable to turn from sin and savingly believe.[4] God's grace must attend

---

"choice" a reaction to man's choice. Rather than being the cause of our salvation, God's election turns out to be nothing more than observing what we would do on our own. Second, God can't learn anything. At no point did God peruse history and discover what I would do when offered salvation. God always knew my response from eternity past, not because He's a good prognosticator but because He's sovereignly and perfectly omniscient. Third, apart from divine grace, nobody would respond to the gospel. Scripture teaches that men are dead in sin and unable to come to Christ. Fourth, this view denies that salvation is God's work, since God's choice actually accomplishes nothing. Man's choice is determinative. By this view, if God hadn't chosen anyone, all the same people would be saved and all the same people would be lost.

4. We must distinguish between ability and responsibility. Though man is responsible to turn from sin and believe the gospel, apart from divine grace he is unable to do so since he is spiritually dead, blinded, and captive to Satan. Man is commanded to be perfect (Matt. 5:48) despite being utterly unable to obey that command (Rom. 3:9–20; 8:7–8). It isn't unjust for God

the gospel proclamation by the power of the Holy Spirit (1 Thess. 1:5) to secure the obedient response of God's elect. Both repentance and faith are said to be gifts of God granted to those who believe (Acts 16:14; 2 Tim. 2:25; Phil. 1:29; Eph. 2:8–9).

The Father chose a people as a love gift for His Son in eternity past. The Son died for those given to Him by the Father. The Father draws them to the Son (John 6:44), and the Holy Spirit regenerates their hearts (Titus 3:4–7) and causes them to be born again to a living hope (John 3:4–8; 1 Pet. 1:3). The Holy Spirit gives new life to those chosen by the Father and purchased by the Son. He infallibly applies the work of Christ to those whom the Father chose, accomplishing in time the salvation planned in eternity past.

Man can't apply the benefits of salvation to himself. It must be granted by God and accomplished by a work of divine grace. From first to last, "salvation is from the LORD" (Jon. 2:9).[5]

JOHN 6: JESUS EXPLAINS UNBELIEF[6]

Jesus didn't shy away from presenting hard truths. Those who avoid uncomfortable topics to mollify audiences are nothing like the Lord Jesus Christ. Jesus declared His unity and oneness with the Father (John 5:16–23), confronted sin (Matt. 5:17–48), opposed self-righteousness (Matt. 23:1–39), incited the hatred of the Pharisees (Matt. 12:1–14), described man's slavery to sin (John 8:31–47), spoke of the torments of Hell (Mark 9:44, 46, 48), and warned of judgment to come (Matt. 25:31–46). He never avoided controversy, offense, or truth. The malleable milksops claiming to represent Him demonstrate with every concession how un-Christlike they actually are. This is glaringly obvious to any observer with a cursory knowledge of the Gospels.

John 6 is an occasion when Jesus spoke hard and offensive truth to a large crowd. In the Bread of Life Discourse (John 6:26–65), Jesus taught the sovereignty of God in election, the inability of man to turn from sin, and the necessity of believing upon Him for eternal life. With that sobering sermon, Jesus offended the "large crowd" that followed Him (v. 2), winnowing it down from more than five thousand to only a few, including the twelve (vv. 66–71).

---

to demand of sinful man something that, due to the fall, he has no ability to perform. That God requires something of His creatures doesn't imply they have an ability to do it.

5. See also Ps. 3:8, Isa. 45:17, and Rev. 19:1.

6. Jim preached a seven-year-long series on the Gospel of John, including twenty-six sermons on John 6. Those sermons are archived on our website at https://kccjohn.transistor.fm.

To appreciate the significance of the Bread of Life Discourse, we must remember the context in which Jesus spoke the offensive words. John 6 begins with a miracle: the feeding of the five thousand. The crowd gathered near the Sea of Galilee "because they saw the signs which He was performing on those who were sick" (v. 2). John mentions later that "Jesus knew from the beginning who they were who did not believe, and who it was that would betray Him" (v. 64). He knew the crowd was following Him for all the wrong reasons. They were interested in signs, physical healing, and material provision.

Though their motives were corrupt, Jesus graciously multiplied bread and fish to feed the hungry multitude (vv. 5–13). The miracle proved that "this [was] truly the Prophet who [was] to come into the world" (v. 14).[7] The crowd was ready to "make Him king" (v. 15). They had a correct understanding of Who Jesus was. His withdrawal from the crowd only tempered their enthusiasm momentarily.

The following day, the crowd crossed the Sea of Galilee in small boats to find Jesus at Capernaum (vv. 22–25).[8] Knowing their hearts, He reproved them for their base motives and unbelief.

> Jesus answered them and said, "Truly, truly, I say to you, you seek Me, not because you saw signs, but because you ate of the loaves and were filled. Do not work for the food which perishes, but for the food which endures to eternal life, which the Son of Man will give to you, for on Him the Father, God, has set His seal." (John 6:26–27)

Jesus used the physical bread provided the previous day as an object lesson to show their need for spiritual life. Just as physical bread provides physical life, spiritual bread (Jesus) provides eternal life. After calling the crowd to "believe in Him whom He [the Father] has sent" (v. 29), He spoke of "the bread of God . . . which comes down out of heaven, and gives life to the world" (v. 33). The crowd thought He was describing another kind of physical bread and didn't perceive that He was speaking of Himself. "Then they said to Him, 'Lord, always give us this bread'" (v. 34).

---

7. "The Prophet" is a reference to Moses's prophecy of a Messiah, promised in Deut. 18:15–22. By describing Jesus as "the Prophet," they were correctly identifying Him as the Messiah.

8. At night, the disciples got into a boat to cross the sea to Capernaum. During a storm, Jesus came to them walking on the water and brought them safely to shore (vv. 16–21). When the crowd woke up the next morning, they saw that Jesus and His disciples were gone and pursued Him to Capernaum.

We can't ignore the spiritual condition of the crowd. Every indication shows they were following Jesus for all the wrong reasons. They had seen Him heal the sick. They had eaten the physical bread of His miraculous provision and wanted more. The previous day, they were willing to take Him by force and make Him king. They saw in Jesus Someone Who could provide military leadership to overthrow Roman oppression, physical healing from all their diseases and discomforts, and an endless free lunch. This wasn't a crowd poor in spirit, feeling the gravity of their sin, the wrath of God, and their need of salvation. Everything they sought was temporal, earthly, and physical. They weren't true believers in any sense of the word. Jesus indicated that they didn't have eternal life (v. 27). They hadn't come to Him for salvation and hadn't received it. They remained dead in their sins, desiring only physical satisfaction. They had no thirst for righteousness or desire for forgiveness and eternal life. But Jesus wasn't surprised by the crowd's unbelief.

> Jesus said to them, "I am the bread of life; he who comes to Me will not hunger, and he who believes in Me will never thirst. But I said to you that you have seen Me, and yet do not believe. All that the Father gives Me will come to Me, and the one who comes to Me I will certainly not cast out. For I have come down from heaven, not to do My own will, but the will of Him who sent Me. This is the will of Him who sent Me, that of all that He has given Me I lose nothing, but raise it up on the last day. For this is the will of My Father, that everyone who beholds the Son and believes in Him will have eternal life, and I Myself will raise him up on the last day." (John 6:35–40)

Jesus unashamedly pointed to Himself as the source of eternal life and the object of saving faith. The spiritual need for eternal life is described as "hunger" and "thirst" (v. 35). "Coming to Him" and "believing in Him" are parallel ideas. Though they had seen Him and witnessed the demonstration of His power, they didn't truly believe (v. 36). Intellectually, they affirmed He was the Prophet promised by Moses. They acknowledged His miracle-working abilities. Still, they remained dead in their sins.

What explains their unbelief? How could they see Him heal the sick and multiply food yet remain spiritually dead in unbelief? How could they believe He was the Messiah (vv. 14–15) without believing *in Him* as Messiah? Though they had come to Him for physical bread,

God Doesn't Try to Save His People

they wouldn't "come to Him" (believe upon Him) as the Bread of Life. They wanted a Messiah Who would provide physical food. They didn't see their need for spiritual life.

In John 6:37, Jesus explained their unbelief: "All that the Father gives Me will come to Me, and the one who comes to Me I will certainly not cast out." That verse describes two glorious complementary truths: divine sovereignty and human responsibility. Faithfulness to Scripture requires that we affirm both, preach both, and never view them as opposed to one another. They are not contradictory, but complementary.

There are four notable features of this verse. First, the One Who gives: the Father. Second, the One Who receives the gift: Jesus, the eternally Divine Son. Third, those who are given: all who will believe in Jesus for salvation. Fourth, an infallible result: the salvation of those given.

Using the terms *all* (vv. 37, 39) and *everyone* (v. 40), Jesus described something true of the elect as a whole (the entire company given to Him by the Father). But the reference to the group doesn't mean election is not personal and individual. Individuals are in view even as Jesus described the group: "the *one* who comes to Me" (v. 37), and "I will raise *him* up on the last day" (vv. 40, 44). References to individual elect within the group appear throughout the passage. Individuals are chosen, and together they comprise the group known as "the elect." They are given to the Son.[9]

Those given to the Son are individuals chosen before time. This group doesn't include all men, but only some. If all had been given to Him, then all would come to Him: "*All* that the Father gives Me will come to Me" (John 6:37). Those in the crowd hadn't come to Him; they hadn't believed (v. 36). If they had been given to Him, they would have come to Him for eternal life. This is the explanation for their unbelief: they hadn't been given by the Father to the Son.

The giving of the Father precedes the believing by the elect. The giving of the Father secures their belief, salvation, and resurrection on the last day. Our belief doesn't cause us to belong to the Son. Our belonging to the Son guarantees our believing. Those given by the

---

9. Contrary to a view known as "class election," Scripture doesn't teach that the Father chose to save a nameless, faceless, nondescript group of people for salvation—whoever by their own volition comes to Christ. Rather, specific individuals are chosen to salvation. Election doesn't refer to a vague intention by the Father to save a group of yet-to-be-determined people. References to those chosen by God for salvation are abundant in Scripture. See Acts 13:48; Rom. 9; Eph. 1:3–5; 2 Thess. 2:13; 2 Tim. 1:9–10; and 1 Pet. 1:1–2.

Father come to Christ, believe upon Him, receive eternal life, and are raised up. This is true of *all* those the Father gives to the Son. Jesus promised that every last one (all) would come to Him and none would be cast out. He will not reject a single one chosen by the Father for salvation.

The Father has a saving intention in His election. He wills the salvation of those He chose. Christ, the Divine Son, came into the world to do the will of the Father: "For I have come down from heaven, not to do My own will, but the will of Him who sent Me. This is the will of Him who sent Me, that of all that He has given Me I lose nothing, but raise it up on the last day" (John 6:38–39). The Father wills the salvation and preservation of every last one He chose for His Son. Jesus came to accomplish that will.

The Father didn't send the Son to try to save a group He hasn't chosen. The Son's mission was to save those the Father gave Him. God the Father chose an innumerable multitude to receive the blessings of the Son's saving work. He chose a bride for His Son, a people for His own possession. Those that belong to the Father belong to the Son (John 17:6, 9–10). He committed His elect to the saving work of His Son and wills the salvation, sanctification, and resurrection of *every last one*.

What explains the unbelief of the crowd that witnessed His miraculous works? They didn't belong to Him. If they had been chosen, they would have believed. That is the explanation Jesus provided.

Apart from the sovereign, unmerited, and unconditional grace of the Father in choosing a people for the Son, none would be saved. If the Father had not secured our salvation by His choice, we wouldn't come to Christ. "No one can come to Me unless the Father who sent Me draws him; and I will raise him up on the last day" (John 6:44). As in the previous verses, the language is comprehensively inclusive. "No one" describes not just a few in the crowd, and not just that particular crowd, but all of fallen humanity.

The Greek word translated "can" (vv. 44, 65) is *dynamai* and describes an ability or capability. No one has the power to come to Christ. All lack the ability. The meaning of the word is clear in other places where John uses the same language (John 3:2–3; 8:21–22; 10:29). Those passages describe a lack of ability, power, or capacity. Jesus wasn't describing a lack of permission, but a lack of power. It is essential we understand the difference.

God Doesn't Try to Save His People

When my child asks, "Daddy, can I watch TV?" and I respond, "No, you can't," I am not describing a lack of ability, but a lack of permission. My child doesn't lack the physical ability or strength to sit and watch TV. They lack my permission. If my child asks, "Daddy, can I lift your truck?" and I respond, "No, you can't," I am describing a lack of power, not of permission. I'm not saying they don't have permission to lift my truck. I'm saying they are physically unable to do so.

In John 6:44 (repeated in 6:65), Jesus said that no man has the power to come to Him unless the Father draws him. Fallen man doesn't lack permission, he lacks power. Sinners are commanded to repent and believe (6:29, 35, 47) and graciously offered eternal life (6:46–58) but have no ability to turn from sin and come to Christ.

It's vain imagination to suppose that men desire Heaven and long to be liberated from sin but are kept from salvation by a lack of permission to enter Heaven's gates. Some teach that turning to Christ is easy and within the capacity of every sinner. According to Jesus, it's not. We're fallen in Adam, dead in our trespasses and sins, and enslaved to our lusts. We have a moral inability to turn from sin and come to Christ.[10] Our impotence lies in our will. Sinners *cannot* come because they *will not* come. J. C. Ryle wrote,

> The nature of man since the fall is so corrupt and depraved, that even when Christ is made known and preached to him, he will not come to Him and believe in Him, without the special grace of God inclining his will and giving him a disposition to come. Moral suasion and advice alone will not bring him. He must be "drawn."[11]

Graciously, the Father, through the Holy Spirit, draws to the Son those whom He chose and gave to Him. According to James White, the word *draw* (*helkýō*) is used twice in John 21 to speak of "hauling a net, either into a boat, or up onto land. *It speaks of a force being applied to move something from one place to another.*"[12]

The Father draws to the Son all those whom He has chosen. All those drawn will come to the Son. The Son will reject none but give them all eternal life. He will raise them all up on the last day, losing

---

10. Just as a physically dead person lacks the physical ability to get up and walk, so the spiritually dead sinner lacks the spiritual ability to leave his sin and come to the light.
11. Ryle, *Ryle's Expository Thoughts*, 3:388.
12. White, *Drawn by the Father*, 74 (emphasis added).

none. This is the glorious promise of the Son regarding the salvation and glorification of those the Father has chosen and given to Him.

JOHN 10 AND 17

The same group is described in John 10 and 17 where Jesus returned to this familiar theme.

> Jesus answered them, "I told you, and you do not believe; the works that I do in My Father's name, these testify of Me. But you do not believe because you are not of My sheep. My sheep hear My voice, and I know them, and they follow Me; and I give eternal life to them, and they will never perish; and no one will snatch them out of My hand. My Father, who has given them to Me, is greater than all; and no one is able to snatch them out of the Father's hand. I and the Father are one." (John 10:25–30)

Though the setting is different, the themes are the same. In this passage, Jesus described those given to Him by the Father as "My sheep."[13] The results of the Father's giving are the same as in chapter 6. Those who are given by the Father come to Christ, and He gives them eternal life and security out of love and obedience to the Father. Similarly, the unbelief of some (vv. 19–20) is explained in verse 26: "But you do not believe because you are not of My sheep." The unbelieving Jews weren't of His sheep. They didn't belong to Him. They hadn't been given to Him by the Father. This is Jesus's explanation for their unbelief. They didn't have eternal life and weren't secured everlastingly because the Son didn't come to try to save those whom the Father hadn't given to Him. He came to lay down His life for His sheep (vv. 11, 15, 17), give them eternal life (vv. 10, 28), and secure them everlastingly for the Father's glory (vv. 28–30).

A TRINITARIAN SALVATION

The Father, the Son, and the Holy Spirit are one in substance, will, and purpose. The three Persons of the Trinity are not in conflict with One Another. The Son didn't come to atone for and try to save a multitude the Father hasn't chosen and the Spirit won't regenerate. The Spirit isn't attempting to regenerate men and women not chosen by the Father or secured by the Son. The Father didn't choose for salvation a vast number whom the Son will fail to save or the Spirit

---

13. We recommend reading both chapters alongside John 6 and observing the consistent way that Jesus described those who are His. He described them as "My own," "My sheep," and "those whom You [the Father] have given Me" (John 10:11–18, 25–30; 17:2, 6, 9, 24).

will fail to regenerate. No individual Person of the Trinity is working in conflict with, or contrary to, the purposes and intents of either of the other two Persons. There is no disharmony among the Persons of the Godhead.

All the elect will be saved. None of the elect will be lost. This is the promise of our triune God. All whom the Father has chosen, the Son will save. He'll lose none. If even one of the elect should be lost, the Son will have failed to do the will of the Father. The Son came to do all the Father's will and only the Father's will.[14]

Can Jesus fail to do what the Father sent Him into the world to accomplish? Are the Father and Son at odds in Their redeeming intentions? Does the Father intend the salvation of a multitude the Son will fail to save, secure, and bring to eternal glory? Is Jesus trying to save a multitude not given to Him by the Father?

Jesus described the salvation, preservation, and eventual resurrection of all His people as an absolute certainty because He doesn't *try* to save anyone. He saves. He saves perfectly, completely, and infallibly. He saves to the uttermost and forever (Heb. 7:25). He doesn't try to do this. He does it!

WORDS OF COMFORT

Jesus's words in John 6 bring tremendous comfort, encouragement, and confidence to the believer.

We are comforted by the truth that salvation doesn't rest in our ability, performance, or choice, but in God's gracious work. We've been loved by the Father, drawn to the Son, and regenerated by the Spirit. Jesus has promised that we'll never be lost. God isn't *trying* to save us. He has saved us from our sin and will deliver us safely to His eternal Kingdom on the final day.

Persecution threatens us, suffering awaits us, and death stalks us. Though trials and tribulations come, we have nothing to fear. The Captain of our Salvation can't fail. He doesn't lack the power to see us safely through. He doesn't lack the wisdom or knowledge to preserve us from every threat and fully accomplish the Father's gracious redeeming purposes. He can't be thwarted. He can't fail.

Our assurance of salvation doesn't rest on our ability but His. He's able to complete what He has started (Phil. 1:6). He'll keep what you've entrusted to Him, your soul and salvation, until the day of His Kingdom (2 Tim. 1:12). He "is able to keep you from stumbling, and

---

14. See John 5:19–23, 30, 36; 6:38; 17:4; 18:11.

to make you stand in the presence of His glory blameless with great joy" (Jude 24).

We're encouraged in our evangelistic efforts by the truth that the effectiveness of gospel preaching doesn't rest on our abilities, cleverness, or creativity. We don't have to be well-polished orators, slick-styled, smooth-tongued salesmen, or pithy pitchmen to be effective witnesses for Christ. God calls us to faithfulness, not success. He grants salvation. He does the work of drawing the sinner to His Son. He grants the gifts of faith and repentance. He changes the heart, inclines the will, opens the eyes, and regenerates the soul. None of that is our work.

Our task is to speak the truth boldly, clearly, and faithfully. The conversion of the sinner isn't within our power, but faithfulness to share the gospel is. We speak the truth and leave the results to God. When we stand before a crowd to preach the Word and present the gospel, it is comforting to remember that we're not responsible for their salvation. We're responsible for our faithfulness. Only God can save the sinner.

Finally, Jesus's words give us great confidence in the truth. He wasn't concerned that it might offend people. He didn't shy away from it, soften its rough edges, or seek to make it palatable to rebels that love darkness. He didn't avoid the truth in order to mollify the hardhearted and unbelieving, and neither should we. Speak the truth with confidence and boldness!

FOR THE SHEPHERDS

We live in an age of confusion, compromise, and cowardice. The church needs bold and courageous preaching. The people of God need to hear the truth preached with clarity and conviction. They need deep, doctrinal preaching—precise preaching with precise language. The true sheep long for this. They hunger for it. It feeds their souls, informs their minds, and lifts their hearts in praise to our great God. To that end, we encourage you to do the following:

First, when you have opportunity to present the gospel, swing for the fences. At funerals, weddings, concerts, outreach events, and special services, go for broke! Be clear. Don't avoid speaking of sin, wrath, Hell, and eternal damnation. Don't dabble in man-centered, inoffensive, milquetoast drivel that leaves your hearers thinking that Jesus is just another of their many options for satisfaction and fulfillment. Don't be afraid to bring the law of God to the conscience and His justice before their mind's eye. The sinner won't understand their need for a Savior unless they first tremble before the just demands of God's holiness. Don't fear that you might alienate them; they're already alienated (Eph. 2:2)! Don't worry that they might hate God; they already do (John 3:19–21)! Don't let them leave with any confusion about what Scripture says concerning the state of their eternal soul.

Second, be courageous. 2 Timothy 1:7 says, "For God has not given us a spirit of timidity, but of power and love and discipline." Don't worry about what the crowd will think or say. Ultimately, you preach for an audience of One. You must please Him. If unbelievers hate you, take comfort in the fact that they hated Him first (John 15:18–25). If you're scorned and rejected by the world, you'll be among a large company of faithful men and women who've been despised by the devil's brood. Rejoice that you've been considered worthy to suffer shame for His name (Acts 5:41) and take your place among the many who've born the reproach of faith (Heb. 11). You will receive faith's reward!

Mortify the sin of fearing men instead of God. Do it aggressively and perpetually. Stand before those you shepherd and be clear. Stand before them and be courageous. Remember the words of Psalm 27:1: "The LORD is my light and my salvation; whom shall I fear? The LORD is the defense of my life; whom shall I dread?"

DISCUSSION QUESTIONS

1. Do you have a clear understanding of Who does what among the Members of the Godhead regarding the salvation of sinners? Can one Member of the triune Godhead do a work without the Others being involved?

2. In what ways is a clear understanding of the sovereignty of God in salvation a source of comfort to our souls and boldness in our witness?

3. How can you encourage your pastors/elders to either become or remain faithful to this truth?

4. Do you think the fear of man causes weak gospel preaching? How else does this fear manifest itself in our lives?

5. In what ways does Jesus's clarity on doctrinal truths serve as an example to us? How can we follow that example?

6. How does the doctrine of predestination show the power, love, grace, omnipotence, wisdom, and omniscience of God?

RECOMMENDED READING:

Evangelism and the Sovereignty of God by J. I. Packer

Almighty Over All: Understanding the Sovereignty of God by R. C. Sproul Jr.

Drawn by the Father by James R. White

The Sovereign Grace of God by James R. White

Chapter 4:

God Doesn't Try to Sanctify His People

4

The previous chapter argued that God infallibly saves all He intends to save. Jesus Christ purchased our salvation through His life, death, and resurrection. The Holy Spirit applies the accomplished redemption to the individual elect sinner in time. By means of an outward gospel proclamation and an inner, irresistible call, the elect sinner is confronted, sometimes repeatedly, with the convicting and liberating message of the gospel.

God accomplishes the salvation of His individual elect. While salvation would ultimately include all aspects of the *ordo salutis*,[1] in the prior chapter the emphasis was on election, effectual calling, regeneration, conversion, and justification. Confidence in those verities gives us courage and boldness to preach the gospel and God's Word faithfully without addition or dilution. We are confident that God saves sinners.[2] This chapter will argue that God is just as sure and certain to sanctify His elect as He is to save them.

---

1. *Ordo salutis* is a Latin phrase meaning "order of salvation" and refers to the logical order of the various components in God's saving work. While there are reasonable intrafamily debates over the order of some elements, most Reformed theologians would list them as (1) election, (2) calling, (3) regeneration, (4) conversion (repentance and faith), (5) justification, (6) adoption, (7) sanctification, (8) perseverance, and (9) glorification.

2. J. I. Packer summarizes Reformed soteriology in his introductory essay to John Owen's *The Death of Death in the Death of Christ*: "For to Calvinism there is really only *one* point to be made in the field of soteriology: the point that *God saves sinners*" (p. 6). Reformed theology claims that God does all the saving work. God's salvation is an actual salvation and not just a potential salvation leaving the decisive act to "sovereign" human will. God infallibly saves sinful people incapable of saving themselves by any means. He doesn't *try* to save sinners.

SANCTIFICATION DEFINED

Here we shall address the element of the *ordo salutis* referred to as "sanctification."[3] The group of words that speak of sanctification describe the state of being "set apart." They're related to the words translated as "holy," "holiness," and "saint." Here are three good definitions of sanctification from well-known Reformed systematic theologies. According to Louis Berkhof, "Sanctification may be defined as that gracious and continuous operation of the Holy Spirit, by which He delivers the justified sinner from the pollution of sin, renews his whole nature in the image of God, and enables him to perform good works."[4] John Frame's definition is more concise: "God's work to make us holy is called sanctification."[5] Finally, Wayne Grudem says, "Sanctification is a progressive work of God and man that makes us more and more free from sin and like Christ in our actual lives."[6]

While not strictly a definition, John Murray's characterization of the human side of sanctification is both clarifying and edifying:

> Sanctification involves the concentration of thought, of interest, of heart, mind, will, and purpose upon the prize of the high calling of God in Christ Jesus and the engagement of our whole being with those means which God has instituted for the attainment of that destination. . . . The prospect it offers is to know even as we are known and to be holy as God is holy.[7]

In sanctification, God sets us apart, makes us holy, delivers us from sin, renews our nature, and makes us more like Him in our practice and conduct. We're declared holy positionally or forensically when justified by grace alone through faith alone. We're sanctified in practice at the moment of regeneration/conversion when we're made spiritually alive and capable of responding positively to God's commands, including His command to repent and believe. We've only

---

3. All the elements of the *ordo salutis* are parts of God's saving work in the sinner. Sanctification is involved in all the elements of salvation in one form or another. Sanctification is part of election if one defines it broadly as "being set apart." Sanctification happens in time when one is called and regenerated. Repentant faith is the evidence of sanctification. Progressive sanctification only happens to the justified, adopted child of God; it continues throughout their lifetime by the faith that perseveres in the power of God. Final and complete sanctification occurs when our redeemed soul/spirit is joined to our resurrected and glorified body.

4. Berkhof, *Systematic Theology*, 513.
5. Frame, *Systematic Theology*, 983.
6. Grudem, *Systematic Theology*, 746.
7. Murray, *Redemption Accomplished and Applied*, 158–59.

begun the sanctification process at that point.[8] Conversion begins a lifelong progressive growth in Christlikeness and experiential holiness. That work of God is sanctification.[9]

THE INEVITABILITY OF SANCTIFICATION

The definitions above indicate that sanctification is the work of God the Holy Spirit in the believer to make him or her more like Christ. While there is clearly a human component, we contend strongly that God sanctifies all His elect in precisely the manner He desires and exactly to the degree He desires. In other words, God's efforts in sanctification always achieve His desired end. God doesn't *try* to sanctify. The surest way to show this is by the exposition of several Scripture passages.

SANCTIFICATION IN 1 PETER 1

Peter wrote his first Epistle to suffering and persecuted Christians to provide comfort, encouragement, and instruction for enduring difficult times. It has stood for two millennia as a primary text for believers suffering persecution and dealing with trials inherent to life on this sin-cursed asylum of a planet. From a shepherd's heart, Peter gives instruction to his brothers and sisters in Christ. We learn how to view "the time of your stay on earth" (1 Pet. 1:17). We learn the purpose for life and how focusing on that purpose makes life tolerable and brings "joy inexpressible and full of glory" (1 Pet. 1:8).

What is that purpose? What is the meaning of life? A careful, considered reading of this letter demonstrates that, for the Christian, the purpose of this life is our increasing holiness and conformity to the character of God. In a word, the purpose of your life on Earth is sanctification.

> Peter, an apostle of Jesus Christ,
>
> To those who reside as aliens, scattered throughout Pontus, Galatia, Cappadocia, Asia, and Bithynia, who are chosen according to the foreknowledge of God the Father, by the sanctifying work of the Spirit, to obey Jesus Christ and be sprinkled with His blood: May grace and peace be yours in the fullest measure. (1 Pet. 1:1–2)

---

8. Our life before conversion is undoubtedly used by God to prepare us for salvation, but in no way are we in the process of sanctification prior to conversion. Prior to the extension of God's grace in the gospel, we're Hell-bound, totally depraved sinners without a hint of authentic holiness in our lives (Eph. 2:1–3).

9. We must distinguish between initial or definitive sanctification, which occurs at conversion, and progressive sanctification, which is the focus of this chapter.

Peter identified his audience using two adjectives and a noun: *eklektois parepidēmois diasporas*. That is translated in various ways:

LSB: "To those who reside as exiles, scattered . . . , who are chosen . . ."

NASB: "To those who reside as aliens, scattered . . . , who are chosen . . ."

ESV: "To those who are elect exiles of the Dispersion . . ."

NKJV: "To the pilgrims of the Dispersion . . . , elect . . ."

YLT: "To the choice sojourners of the dispersion . . ."

NIV: "To God's elect, exiles scattered . . ."

The most literal translations, such as the YLT, reflect the word order of the original Greek, though not the parts of speech. The first word, *eklektois*, is a Greek adjective translated "chosen" or "elect." It's worth noting that, in a letter written to ease the suffering and promote the happiness of believers, the first blessing Peter points to is their (and our) election to salvation by God in eternity past. Why does Peter describe his readers this way? There is tremendous comfort in the doctrine of election, as it so clearly points to the sovereignty of God in salvation, and by extension, the sovereignty of God over everything. The two twin truths of theology proper, that God is sovereign and good, mean that the trials of life have a good purpose, even if that good purpose isn't apparent to us in the moment.

The second adjective is translated in the LSB as the noun phrase "those who reside as exiles." Other translation choices include "strangers," "sojourners," "temporary residents," "those temporarily residing abroad," or "pilgrims." It's the Greek adjective *parepidēmois*, meaning "residing" or "sojourning in a strange place." It contains the notion of "passing through" and describes one who, while living actively among a people, has some degree of detachment from both the place and the people.

The third word in Peter's description of his audience is the noun *diasporas*. We get our English terms *diaspora*, *disperse*, and *dispersion* from this word. It means "scattered" or "dispersed." It could describe seed scattered in a field, for example. Here, Peter uses it to describe those scattered amongst the locations listed in verse 1. Later readers of this text can legitimately understand it to include all the "elect exiles scattered" across a sin-cursed world, living among the worldly reprobate.

What does his description of us as "those who reside as aliens, scattered" tell us about our identity? These words telegraph the point of the entire Epistle. Knowing we are strangers in a strange land enables us to understand and embrace our differences. We see this repeatedly in 1 Peter. We're God's people, called out, chosen to be different, holy, and formed into the image of Christ. "But you are a chosen race, a royal priesthood, a holy nation, a people for God's own possession, so that you may proclaim the excellencies of Him who has called you out of darkness into His marvelous light" (1 Pet. 2:9). We can embrace that identity and live lives of happiness and joy in this foreign land while looking forward to our home in the presence of our Master (Phil. 3:20), forever free from sin's presence and curse. We're here to be sanctified; that is the purpose of suffering. The trials of life produce holiness in believers.

We see God's sanctifying purpose in 1 Peter 1:2, where Peter describes our election as being "by the sanctifying work of the Spirit, to obey Jesus Christ." We live as exiles, scattered throughout a world that hates Christ and His bride, for this purpose: to be sanctified by the work of the Spirit and live in obedience to Jesus Christ. We may reasonably wonder, Why am I here? Having turned from sin toward Christ in repentant faith, why can't I be free from the presence of sin and enjoy the presence of the Lord? Why doesn't He take us home at the point of our conversion? Why must we live out this sojourn on Earth? This Epistle is Peter's answer.

> Blessed be the God and Father of our Lord Jesus Christ, who according to His great mercy has caused us to be born again to a living hope through the resurrection of Jesus Christ from the dead, to obtain an inheritance which is imperishable and undefiled and will not fade away, reserved in heaven for you, who are protected by the power of God through faith for a salvation ready to be revealed in the last time. In this you greatly rejoice, *even though now for a little while, if necessary, you have been distressed by various trials, so that the proof of your faith, being more precious than gold which is perishable, even though tested by fire, may be found to result in praise and glory and honor at the revelation of Jesus Christ*; and though you have not seen Him, you love Him, and though you do not see Him now, but believe in Him, you greatly rejoice with joy inexpressible and full of glory, obtaining as the outcome of your faith the salvation of your souls. (1 Pet. 1:3–9)

The trials of life, though distressing, are temporary. They are "for a little while" and "necessary." They serve a purpose. They demonstrate to us and all who observe that our faith is a great and powerful gift of God, absolutely invincible, even in the face of the most horrendous trials and persecution. Trials are intended to make us holy, sanctifying us by God's gracious work. God is glorified as we, the angels, and the watching world observe the supernatural nature of a faith that brings "joy inexpressible and full of glory" (1 Pet. 1:8) in the midst of grievous trials.

SANCTIFICATION IN 1 JOHN

John's Gospel is an evangelistic masterpiece. He states the purpose in John 20:31: "These have been written so that you may believe that Jesus is the Christ, the Son of God; and that believing you may have life in His name." The Gospel of John is a true "evangel" intended to persuade the unbeliever of the truth of the gospel and their need to trust in the Person and work of Christ for salvation. His intended audience is unbelievers.

John's first Epistle is about sanctification and the assurance that accompanies it. A key purpose statement is found in 1 John 5:13: "These things I have written to you who believe in the name of the Son of God, so that you may know that you have eternal life."[10]

1 John is written to believers. While it provides evidence for the truth claims of the gospel (1:1–4, 5:6–10), the body of the letter isn't intended to elicit belief but to provide assurance of genuine faith. John does this by giving multiple tests of the genuineness of faith. He contrasts the fruit of the changed life of a believer with the fruit of the natural unregenerate life of an unbeliever or false convert. John points to the progressively sanctified life of the Christian as evidence of eternal life.

ETERNAL LIFE IN 1 JOHN

It's important we understand what John means by "eternal life." This is vital for understanding Scripture as a whole, particularly as it pertains to teaching on sanctification and its practical implications for the mundane issues of Christian living.

---

10. John gives five purpose statements (1:4, 2:1, 2:12–14, 2:26, 5:13). All are related to assurance of faith. John wishes for his readers to have the same certainty regarding the gospel as he does, resulting in joy (1:4), avoidance of sin (2:1), a close relationship to Christ (2:12–14), theological discernment (2:26), and assurance of salvation (5:13), particularly in light of the incipient proto-Gnostic ideas John contradicted in this Epistle.

John starts with this preface:

> What was from the beginning, what we have heard, what we have seen with our eyes, what we have looked at and touched with our hands, concerning the Word of Life—and the life was manifested, and we have seen and testify and proclaim to you the eternal life, which was with the Father and was manifested to us—what we have seen and heard we proclaim to you also, so that you too may have fellowship with us; and indeed our fellowship is with the Father, and with His Son Jesus Christ. These things we write, so that our joy may be made complete. (1 John 1:1–4)

John introduces the Epistle by describing "the Word of Life," a shorthand way of referring to the Person and work of Christ. The message of Jesus Christ was "from the beginning."[11] He has been "heard," "seen," "looked at," and "touched." He was and is fully human with a real physical body, something denied by the proto-Gnostic heresy John corrected throughout the Epistle. Jesus Christ is called "the Word" in John 1:1. He is Himself a proclamation of life from God to man. He is the source of life and thus gives eternal life. He was "manifested" in His incarnation and made visible, audible, and fully perceptible to us in His humanity. John, with the other apostles, had "proclaimed" the person and work of Christ.

The life of Christ is eternal in the truest sense. It is without beginning or end. He provides that same life to His people, a life that produces obedience, brotherly love, and holy living. Jesus Christ possessed eternal life with the Father from eternity past. Every believer shares the same eternal life of the resurrected Christ. The life possessed by the Father, the Son, and the Holy Spirit vivifies every regenerated Christian. This is the life John describes throughout the letter. Possession of this life makes our joy complete. Proclamation of Christ and His work results in fellowship among believers (i.e., "with us") because our fellowship is "with the Father, and with His Son Jesus Christ."

---

11. Whether "from the beginning" refers to Jesus's eternality or the beginning of His earthly ministry is up for debate. John uses similar language ("in the beginning") in his Gospel to describe the eternal preexistence of the Divine Son, the Word Who became flesh (John 1:1, 14). The reference to "from the beginning" here probably refers to the beginning of gospel preaching when the readers would have first heard the message of Christ. As John MacArthur notes, "The phrase also emphasizes the stability of the gospel message; its contents do not change but remain stable from the very beginning; it is not subject to change due to current worldly fads or philosophical thinking" (note on 1 John 1:1 in *The MacArthur Study Bible*, p. 1934).

This is the vital truth, the linchpin, and the center of the Epistle. Eternal life isn't merely having pre-conversion physical life extended for eternity. What a curse that would be! No, Christians have much more than this. "Eternal life" refers to more than just duration of living. It refers to the *nature* of the life we possess. Eternal life is the very life of God! It is the spiritual life of the life-giving Spirit! We have the Spirit of God within us. We're changed, made different, in a tangible, testable way. This increasing difference will be seen and appreciated as the evidence of regeneration. In other words, sanctification gives us assurance of salvation, producing the confidence, peace, and joy that John mentions.[12]

THE TESTS OF FAITH IN 1 JOHN

John provides three different tests by which Christians can examine their lives and grow in assurance of salvation. Taken together, they offer a comprehensive evaluation of the fruits of eternal life.

First, the moral test. John unapologetically and repeatedly asserts that a believer "keeps" God's commandments (2:1–6; 3:24; 5:2–4). While acknowledging that Christians sin (1:8–10), he instructs Christians to "walk in the Light" (1:7) and not darkness (1:6). Why? Because we share in the life of God, and "in Him there is no darkness at all" (1:5). Remarkably, John rarely expresses the necessity of obedience, rejecting sin, and pursuing righteousness as commands. He describes a concern for the ethical requirements of the new covenant[13] as something Christians possess rather than something they must do. He assumes that Christians have a desire for righteousness and a hatred for sin as a result of their salvation and union with Christ. Since you are partakers in the eternal life of Christ, says John, that has been in and with the Father and proceeds from God to us through Christ, you will do, think, and act like Him, at least to some degree. While we admit we sin, it is also true that we hate it and desire to live in obedience to Christ. This is the moral test.[14]

---

12. This doesn't preclude gaining assurance from fixing our hope on Christ, looking away from the world toward Him, or considering the apologetic evidence for Christianity (prophetic accuracy, historical evidence of the resurrection, etc.). The point is that every Christian can look to their own imperfect but progressively sanctified life as evidence of their participation in the eternal life of the triune God.

13. While the antinomian view (that the Christian is subject to no moral law) is popular in some circles, there are, in fact, moral commands in Scripture addressed to the Christian under the new covenant.

14. The verbs John uses for keeping the commandments don't imply perfect obedience to them. He could've used verbs to express obedience, but he didn't. He used verbs for "do" or

Second, the social test. Love for Christians is an inevitable fruit of fellowship with God. If you have eternal life, you'll love your brothers and sisters in Christ (2:9–11, 3:10–20, 4:7–21, 5:1). John put it bluntly: "The one who loves his brother abides in the Light and there is no cause for stumbling in him. But the one who hates his brother is in the darkness and walks in the darkness, and does not know where he is going because the darkness has blinded his eyes" (1 John 2:10–11). It's either love or hate, living in light or living in darkness. For John, the vast gray middle, in which many Evangelicals find comfort, simply doesn't exist. A Christian is one who possesses the life of God. He loves those whom God loves. "Whoever believes that Jesus is the Christ is born of God, and whoever loves the Father loves the child born of Him" (1 John 5:1). No one who has experienced the saving love of Christ and His work for them on the cross could fail to cherish fellow partakers of the divine nature (2 Peter 1:4). Christians have, at the core of their being, an eternal life, a new type of life that hates sin and loves Christ. They want to please Him. They are necessarily and inevitably attracted to those who share the same life. As John says, "We love, because He first loved us" (1 John 4:19). That is a great summary of this truth. John was describing a love for both Christians and God. Christians love. It's the new nature of the believer and therefore an inevitable reality and implication of the fact that "He first loved us." His love for us is the efficient cause of our love for others.

Third, the doctrinal test. John wasn't a Pelagian who believed that men have no need for saving faith. Before setting out these tests of the genuineness of faith, John describes the content of saving faith. We must believe the gospel. Regardless of our claim, if we deny those propositional truths that define the faith (Jude 3), we aren't Christians. We see this test in the preface (1 John 1:1–4) and again in 4:1–6:

"keep," which together imply cherishing, esteeming, and paying attention to the ethical requirements of the new covenant. They don't imply perfection. There is much written about the tense of the verbs claiming they indicate a sinless perfection in the life of the believer. That discussion is beyond the scope of this book, but it's an important matter in the exposition of 1 John and the Christian's understanding of various theological controversies. It seems very clear to the authors that John is speaking not of perfection but of an absence of habitual, regular sin, or what Peter refers to as a "futile way of life" (1 Pet. 1:18). Such conduct is inconsistent with a claim to the fellowship with God that defines our union with Christ.

Beloved, do not believe every spirit, but test the spirits to see whether they are from God, because many false prophets have gone out into the world. By this you know the Spirit of God: every spirit that confesses that Jesus Christ has come in the flesh is from God; and every spirit that does not confess Jesus is not from God; this is the spirit of the antichrist, of which you have heard that it is coming, and now it is already in the world. You are from God, little children, and have overcome them; because greater is He who is in you than he who is in the world. They are from the world; therefore they speak as from the world, and the world listens to them. We are from God; he who knows God listens to us; he who is not from God does not listen to us. By this we know the spirit of truth and the spirit of error.[15]

John describes genuine faith as a confession that "Jesus Christ has come in the flesh" (4:2). Those who "confess Jesus" (4:3), bearing witness that "the Father has sent the Son to be the Savior of the world" (4:14), confessing that "Jesus is the Son of God" (4:15), and believing that "Jesus is the Christ" (5:1) have eternal life. John didn't tolerate the proto-Gnostic heretics of his day who denied the essential truths of the gospel. He repeatedly appealed to his readers' knowledge of these truths and gave them assurance contrary to the false teachers' claim that saving knowledge was available only to the elites within their heretical sect. According to John, believing the gospel is being a Christian, and being a Christian is doing what Christians do.

There is no middle ground when it comes to these tests. We can't help but be struck by John's certainty, something missing in modern-day preaching on these topics. Christians walk in light rather than darkness. They have a desire to obey God's commands. They don't persist in unrepentant sin. They love other believers. These Christian traits are always present in the life of a believer, at least to some degree.

SANCTIFICATION IN HEBREWS 12

Hebrews 12:4–17 describes the Lord's discipline of His children. It's a remarkably comforting passage. Verses 7–8 tell us that God lovingly disciplines all His children.

---

15. See also 1 John 4:14–16; 5:1–12.

> It is for discipline that you endure; God deals with you as with sons; for what son is there whom his father does not discipline? But if you are without discipline, of which all have become partakers, then you are illegitimate children and not sons.

Verses 9–11 tell us why all Christians receive God's discipline:

> Furthermore, we had earthly fathers to discipline us, and we respected them; shall we not much rather be subject to the Father of spirits, and live? For they disciplined us for a short time as seemed best to them, but He disciplines us *for our good, so that we may share His holiness.* All discipline for the moment seems not to be joyful, but sorrowful; yet to those who have been trained by it, afterwards *it yields the peaceful fruit of righteousness.* (Heb. 12:9–11)

What is God's purpose for discipline in the lives of His children? God's discipline makes us more holy. It sanctifies us (v. 10), strengthens us for our race (v. 1), and fixes our eyes on Jesus (vv. 2–3). While discipline isn't a punishment for our sin, it does purge sin from our lives. This is necessary if we are to share God's holiness (Heb. 12:10). Matthew Henry said, "The best of God's children need chastisement. They have their faults and follies, which need to be corrected."[16] Discipline produces holiness. Holiness yields the peaceful fruits of righteousness (Heb. 12:11).

Without the holiness produced by discipline, no one will see God. "Pursue peace with all men, and the sanctification without which no one will see the Lord" (Heb. 12:14). Does this mean sanctification is necessary for salvation? No, it doesn't.

I love the account of the penitent thief:

> One of the criminals who were hanged there was hurling abuse at Him, saying, "Are You not the Christ? Save Yourself and us!" But the other answered, and rebuking him said, "Do you not even fear God, since you are under the same sentence of condemnation? And we indeed are suffering justly, for we are receiving what we deserve for our deeds; but this man has done nothing wrong." And he was saying, "Jesus, remember me when You come in Your kingdom!"

---

16. Henry, *Matthew Henry's Commentary*, "The Benefit of Afflictions" (commentary on Heb. 12:4–17).

And He said to him, "Truly I say to you, today you shall be with Me in Paradise." (Luke 23:39–43)

That beautiful encounter gives the lie to so many false doctrines pertaining to the necessity of works for salvation. Beyond his expression of repentant faith, the thief had no opportunity to engage in anything we would consider evidence of salvation, but he was undoubtedly saved. He was unbaptized, unchurched, and had never taken the Lord's Supper. A horribly blasphemous sinner only moments prior, the only evidence of his conversion was the cessation of his cursing and mockery and his confession of Christ's innocence: "This man has done nothing wrong" (Luke 23:41). Expecting Christ's coming Kingdom, he acknowledged his own guilt. His repentant faith was sufficient for salvation. His sanctification was limited to positional and initial sanctification. He had no opportunity to pursue a life of righteousness, grow in holiness, or persevere under trial. In other words, as a believer, he experienced very little of God's discipline. This exceptional case demonstrates clearly that works are not required for salvation. While progressive sanctification is the inevitable result and, indeed, the purpose of post-conversion life on Earth, that sanctification is not necessary for our justification.

Hebrews 12 shows that, normally speaking, a saved person will enter into the Lord's presence with at least some degree of sanctification. It's ludicrous, immature, and ill-conceived to suggest a Christian, after living years as a new creation, could enter into the presence of Christ still characterized by sin, depravity, and a futile way of life (1 Pet. 1:18). Without the sanctification that comes to every believer through the Lord's discipline, no one will see the Lord.

The writer of Hebrews develops this further in the context of verse 14:

Pursue peace with all men, and the sanctification without which no one will see the Lord. See to it that no one comes short of the grace of God; that no root of bitterness springing up causes trouble, and by it many be defiled; that there be no immoral or godless person like Esau, who sold his own birthright for a single meal. For you know that even afterwards, when he desired to inherit the blessing, he was rejected, for he found no place for repentance, though he sought for it with tears. (Heb. 12:14–17)

This is a stern warning to any who profess faith while living lives that bear no evidence of eternal life and union with Christ. If you aren't changed, well, you aren't changed. If there is no demonstrable, outward transformation, what would make you think you're inwardly a new creation? Why should you think your spirit is alive, you're new in Christ, and your heart of stone has been changed to a heart of flesh, if your affections and behaviors remain unchanged?

SANCTIFICATION IN PAUL'S LETTERS

Paul expected that sanctification would be an obvious reality in the life of every believer.

> Therefore be imitators of God, as beloved children; and walk in love, just as Christ also loved you and gave Himself up for us, an offering and a sacrifice to God as a fragrant aroma.
>
> But immorality or any impurity or greed must not even be named among you, as is proper among saints; and there must be no filthiness and silly talk, or coarse jesting, which are not fitting, but rather giving of thanks. *For this you know with certainty, that no immoral or impure person or covetous man, who is an idolater, has an inheritance in the kingdom of Christ and God.*
>
> Let no one deceive you with empty words, for because of these things the wrath of God comes upon the sons of disobedience. Therefore do not be partakers with them; for you were formerly darkness, but now you are Light in the Lord; walk as children of Light (for the fruit of the Light consists in all goodness and righteousness and truth), trying to learn what is pleasing to the Lord. (Eph. 5:1–10)

How can anyone read verses 5–8 (in italics) and deny that every Christian is sanctified? There are many commands for new covenant believers in the Bible, and you see some of them in this passage. We're progressively sanctified. While we aren't made immediately perfect in practice, we are in the process of being made more holy. The fruit of the light possessed by believers "consists in all goodness and righteousness and truth" (v. 9). Those who are "Light in the Lord" walk as "children of Light" (v. 8).

Romans 6 also demonstrates the inevitability of sanctification in the life of the believer. Paul describes our freedom from sin and union with Christ. His question in verse 2 shows the vital connection between our union with Christ and the new life that inevitably flows from it: "How shall we who died to sin still live in it?" The answer is obvious to Paul. We won't! We can't! Paul says in verse 4, ". . . as Christ was raised from the dead through the glory of the Father, so we too might walk in newness of life." The believer lives a new life. We don't live as we did before conversion. We're no longer slaves to sin but to Christ! Once we obeyed the dictates of sin. Now we obey our good Master. "But thanks be to God that though you were slaves of sin, you became obedient from the heart to that form of teaching to which you were committed, and having been freed from sin, you became slaves of righteousness" (Rom. 6:17–18).

Paul concludes his argument, saying,

> Therefore what benefit were you then deriving from the things of which you are now ashamed? For the outcome of those things is death. But now having been freed from sin and enslaved to God, you derive your benefit, resulting in sanctification, and the outcome, eternal life. For the wages of sin is death, but the free gift of God is eternal life in Christ Jesus our Lord. (Rom. 6:21–23)

Astonishingly, he describes the benefits of our redemption as "resulting in sanctification, and the outcome, eternal life." *Outcome* here doesn't mean "the final thing" but the "ultimate purpose" or "reason for" a thing. In other words, the benefit of this earthly life for Christians, in contrast to the fruit of their prior sinful lives as unbelievers, is sanctification! Peter referred to the outcome of this sanctifying life as "the salvation of your souls" (1 Pet. 1:9). Paul and John both describe the result of sanctification as "eternal life."

God's work in sanctifying all who are His is so certain Paul could say, "For I am confident of this very thing, that He who began a good work in you will perfect it until the day of Christ Jesus" (Phil. 1:6).

THE HEART OF THE MATTER

"For just as the body without the spirit is dead, so also faith without works is dead" (James 2:26).

The Bible is clear, and we should understand the implications of its teaching regarding sanctification: a Christian will always be sanctified. Holiness is the point of this life according to Peter, the evidence of salvation according to John, and the outcome of God's discipline according to Hebrews. An unsanctified life is indistinguishable from an unregenerate life and strong evidence of a lack of regeneration, as Ephesians teaches. A new and sanctified life, progressing in holiness, results from redemption, as seen in Romans.

This is the consistent and unmistakable testimony of Scripture. The God Who saves doesn't *try* to save. The God Who sanctifies doesn't *try* to sanctify. His sanctifying work is as certain as His saving work. God doesn't try.

FOR THE SHEPHERDS

For the shepherds in God's flock, we would offer the following encouragements.

First, be aware of the controversy around this topic and make a determined effort to study the Scriptures and the books, both good and bad, written about it. We would strongly recommend reading all of John MacArthur's books on this topic. His extensive writings on the lordship salvation controversy are the definitive resources for biblical teaching on the role of repentance in salvation. Begin with MacArthur's groundbreaking work *The Gospel according to Jesus*.[17] We highly recommend a short, powerful book by Wayne Grudem, *"Free Grace" Theology: 5 Ways It Diminishes the Gospel*. For a thorough presentation of Free Grace Theology, we would recommend *A Defense of Free Grace Theology: With Respect to Saving Faith, Perseverance, and Assurance,* edited by Dr. Fred Chay. Though other books explain and defend Free Grace Theology, this seems to be the most thorough and one that most honestly engages with its critics.

Second, stand and deliver on the ethical requirements of the new covenant and the power of the Holy Spirit to grow the believer in holiness. The seeker-friendly philosophy of ministry that dominates the church scene is characterized by an unwillingness to call out sin. This is, in part, because these pitchmen-preachers don't believe there is sufficient power in the gospel to overcome sin in the hearts, minds, and bodies of believers. Be unashamed of the gospel! Why? Because "it is the power of God for salvation to everyone who believes" (Rom. 1:16). It is the power of God for every aspect of salvation, including sanctification. We're no longer slaves to sin. We must tell our people to obey Christ and that they're made capable of doing it. Like John, be unafraid to admit we sin but just as unapologetic in teaching that a sinful life is inconsistent with a claim to union with Christ. The notion that your congregation of God's children is unable to obey the commands of Christ is a satanic lie. We'll never be perfect in this life,

---

17. See also these other books by MacArthur: *Ashamed of the Gospel, The Gospel according to the Apostles, The Gospel according to God, The Gospel according to Paul*, and *Hard to Believe*.

but we ought to strive toward it. We should pursue the holiness of Christ like Paul in Philippians 3:12–14:

> Not that I have already obtained it or have already become perfect, but I press on so that I may lay hold of that for which also I was laid hold of by Christ Jesus. Brethren, I do not regard myself as having laid hold of it yet; but one thing I do: forgetting what lies behind and reaching forward to what lies ahead, I press on toward the goal for the prize of the upward call of God in Christ Jesus.

Preach to image-bearers that they should bear His image. The unbeliever's first duty is to believe. The believer's duty is to reflect the image of God and progress in Christlikeness. "For those whom He foreknew, He also predestined to become conformed to the image of His Son" (Rom. 8:29).

Third, remind your people of God's purpose for their sufferings. If they don't see sanctification as a goal to pursue, they won't live an overcoming life. Why should they try? It's hard. If trials aren't working for our sanctification to prepare us for an ultimately satisfying eternal life in the new creation, then why persevere through them? Life might as well end now if it has no purpose. We can certainly do better than the nihilistic worldview offered by atheism:

> As far as we can tell, from a purely scientific viewpoint, human life has absolutely no meaning. Humans are the outcome of blind evolutionary processes that operate without goal or purpose. Our actions are not part of some divine cosmic plan, and if planet Earth were to blow up tomorrow morning, the universe would probably keep going about its business as usual. As far as we can tell at this point, human subjectivity would not be missed. Hence *any* meaning that people ascribe to their lives is just a delusion.[18]

Your people have struggles. Show them why those struggles are necessary and beneficial! Show them how to endure them and find joy in them. Move them from despair to a confident expectation of their eternal future. Lift their eyes to Heaven!

Fourth, much of the sanctification of God's people occurs through the activities of the local church. Solid biblical teaching,

---

18. Harari, *Sapiens*, 391 (emphasis in original). Harari is a popular atheist in the political and pop-cultural circles that influence your people.

preaching, and counseling, observation of the ordinances, the exercise of spiritual gifts, the blessings of giving, participation in Christian fellowship, corporate prayer and worship, and church discipline are all essential means of grace, and all are essential activities of the local church. It's vital that the shepherds of the church work to develop a fellowship of believers that performs its purpose, part of which is the sanctification of the church body. The activity of "going to church" to "hear a talk" and "do some singing" is not participation in the life of the body of Christ. Part of your accountability as a shepherd of your church is to see that the gifts of the believers in your church are used for the benefit of the church, including her sanctification. Work to develop a fellowship committed to living in obedience to the commands to love and serve one another in the local church context.

Fifth, while Christians in the United States haven't faced persecution yet, it isn't likely to remain that way forever. The history of the church is the history of the martyr. Persecution is the norm. That is the case in many parts of the world today, and hostility to biblical truth is increasing in the Americas. We have seen imprisonments of pastors in Canada and legal persecution of the church in the United States over COVID-19 mandates. Christians who refuse to affirm gay marriage or use "correct pronouns" are being targeted by both the private and public sectors. As Romans 1 is increasingly lived out before our eyes, we can expect a continued assault on biblical morality and any who fail to affirm the most disgusting, damaging, and demonic conduct this lost world can conjure.

1 Peter was written to Christians in such circumstances. It is a manual for dealing with persecution. That manual tells us that suffering is for our ultimate good and God's glory. Suffering is for our sanctification. How will your people, their children, or their grandchildren endure increasing persecution bravely, joyfully, confidently, if you don't teach them that God sanctifies His people through their afflictions? How will you, as a shepherd and primary target of persecution, endure harsh treatment and glorify God if you don't understand the purpose of those trials? If the lesser trials of the Christian life and profession cause you despair, what will you do in a reeducation camp, a prison, or under threat of torture or execution? This is no idle consideration. Prepare yourself, your family, and your flock for persecution by teaching that though our faith may be "tested by fire," it will ultimately "result in praise and glory and honor at the revelation of Jesus Christ" (1 Pet. 1:7).

DISCUSSION QUESTIONS

1. Have you ever engaged in an extended study of the doctrines of sanctification? In what ways did that study change your view of the subject? In what ways has this chapter changed your view on sanctification? How has it clarified your understanding?

2. How would you utilize your biblical knowledge of the doctrine of sanctification to help a fellow believer who is struggling with sin? To what Bible passages would you turn to help them?

3. Do you struggle to embrace life's difficulties and afflictions as a gift from the hand of a loving heavenly Father? Why or why not? Why does God discipline believers?

4. What are you doing to prepare your loved ones to face the possibility of suffering for the faith? In what ways are you preparing your own heart for this? How does God use persecution to accomplish His designs for the church? What are the negative results of persecution?

5. Discuss how suffering makes us holy. Can suffering have the opposite effect? Why or why not?

6. Describe how sanctification differs from justification.

7. How is sanctification inevitable for the believer?

8. Describe the moral test in one sentence.

9. How do we demonstrate our love for the children of God?

10. What does an unchanged life communicate to the world about the gospel? What does it communicate to other believers?

RECOMMENDED READING

A Defense of Free Grace Theology: With Respect to Saving Faith, Perseverance, and Assurance edited by Dr. Fred Chay[19]

---

[19] We do not agree with the conclusions of this book or the distinctive tenets of Free Grace Theology. This book is recommended to help the reader understand this false doctrine, not to commend it.

"Free Grace" Theology: 5 Ways It Diminishes the Gospel by Wayne Grudem

Ashamed of the Gospel: When the Church Becomes Like the World by John F. MacArthur Jr.

The Gospel according to God: Rediscovering the Most Remarkable Chapter in the Old Testament by John F. MacArthur Jr.

The Gospel according to Jesus: What Does Jesus Mean When He Says, "Follow Me"? by John F. MacArthur Jr.

The Gospel according to Paul: Embracing the Good News at the Heart of Paul's Teachings by John F. MacArthur Jr.

The Gospel according to the Apostles: The Role of Works in the Life of Faith by John F. MacArthur Jr.

Hard to Believe: The High Cost and Infinite Value of Following Jesus by John F. MacArthur Jr.

Chapter 5:

**God Doesn't Try
to Speak to His People**

5

One of the most exciting moments for a parent is hearing their child's first word. It might be "mama," "dada," or some garbled form of a sibling's name. Sometimes it's simply the word *no*. Children hear it and are able to articulate it sooner than other words. It's an easy word to learn, and children use it frequently.

Long before they can articulate words and complex sentences, they're able to understand them. A young child will know what a parent means by "Would you like some ice cream?" or "It's time for bed" long before they're able to express those sentiments themselves. As children grow, they learn more words and start forming complex sentences. Some of the funniest moments come from listening to children talk as they learn language by trial and error.

The stuttering, bumbling, and undecipherable mutterings of a two-year-old are cute. The same behavior from an adult suggests some form of mental incapacitation, like drunkenness, dementia, or a stroke. But when that kind of communication is attributed to God, it is blasphemous.

MODERN EVANGELICAL BELIEF

Christians affirm that God is a communicating God, but few have thought through the implications of their beliefs about how God speaks and the form of His revelation. In most Evangelical circles, it's assumed that God continues to speak apart from and outside Scripture. This belief isn't relegated to the fringes of the Charismatic movement. Many Christians who would call themselves "cessationist" and decry the abuses of the Charismatic movement are continuationists[1] in practice, believing that God speaks through still small voices, whispers, impressions, inner promptings, random thoughts, signs, fleeces, dreams, visions, or a peace in the heart. Almost any sign, confluence of circumstances, or coincidence is regarded as the "voice of God" by those who hold this view.

Advocates of "hearing the voice of God" (HVG) theology[2] believe God *needs* to speak to us today because Scripture doesn't give sufficient information for day-to-day decision-making. The Bible doesn't specifically reveal which house to buy, person to marry, or school to attend. This is regarded as a deficiency in Scripture. While the Bible contains plenty of general guiding principles and generic counsel, it lacks necessary specifics. That specific guidance is presumed necessary for the believer to live a God-honoring and obedient life.

For instance, Robert Morris claims that Scripture contains "God's general will for our lives"[3] but also promises us specific guidance for major decisions. Morris cites examples of God giving personal direction to Abram and Saul of Tarsus, then says, "If God guided His servants in specific manners in times past, then why would God not guide His servants specifically in present times—particularly in light of John 10?"[4] He explains,

> Every one of us has major decisions to make in our lives, when we need to hear God. God gives His general counsel, and He also graciously gives us specific counsel. It comes back to the foundational truth set forth in John 10. We are

---

[1]. A continuationist, broadly speaking, believes that sign and revelatory gifts continue to operate today just as they did in the early church during the lives of the apostles. While some continuationists wouldn't believe this revelation is on par with Scripture in authority, inerrancy, and inspiration, others have no problem equating their revelations with the Word of God. A cessationist believes that the supernatural sign and revelatory gifts (tongues, interpretation of tongues, miracles, prophecy, healing) have ceased. Cessationists believe that God still does miraculous works but that He doesn't give those spiritual gifts today. For more on this, see MacArthur, *Charismatic Chaos*; and Waldron, *To Be Continued?*

[2]. In my (Jim's) book *God Doesn't Whisper*, I have dubbed this "HVG theology" (Hearing the Voice of God) and deal with this subject *thoroughly*. I answer the three wrong assumptions of this theological position: I *need* to hear from God outside Scripture, I should *expect* to hear from God outside Scripture, and I can *learn* to hear from God outside Scripture. I provide a comprehensive study of the passages often cited by proponents of HVG theology and answer common questions and objections. This chapter isn't going to deal with all the issues connected to this theology. For a detailed and comprehensive treatment of HVG theology, I would recommend *God Doesn't Whisper*.

[3]. Morris, *Frequency*, chap. 1.

[4]. Morris, chap. 1.

sheep. Jesus is the Good Shepherd. We were designed to hear the voice of God.[5]

The implication is clear: Scripture isn't sufficient for major decisions. It's great as far as it goes, but what is a child of God to do when he really needs to decide something important? According to Morris, he needs to hear from God directly. Scripture isn't enough. Since apparently God can't communicate to you without your help, He needs you to take some time, even extended time, away to get quiet and listen. Morris explains,

> When you need to hear God about a specific decision or direction you need to take, set aside even more time, at least an extra hour or two. And if it's a very important decision, then you might even go away and spend half a day or even a weekend with the Lord to really be able to hear Him and spend time with Him.[6]

If only the Bible contained all we need for life and godliness (2 Pet. 1:3)! But lo, we are left without any sure word (2 Pet. 1:19). We need some specific revelation that fills in where the Bible falls short. Morris says,

> But as we've discussed throughout this book, sometimes we want a specific word from God too. We have the Bible, and we're already reading the Bible, but God is being silent on an issue about which the Bible doesn't speak directly. We wonder then how to act. What do we do? Which direction do we turn? What decision do we make? It's at such a time that we're invited to ask God to speak to us specifically. We long to hear God's voice. Sometimes God will speak to us by using a specific portion of Scripture, pointing our attention to it. Sometimes God will speak to our hearts by a nudging, an inclination. This is harder to quantify, yet it is God speaking nevertheless.[7]

---

5. Morris, chap. 1.
6. Morris, chap. 3.
7. Morris, chap. 10. In that same context, Morris encourages us to read Scripture in order to hear from God. My point is not that Morris doesn't believe Scripture is God's Word, but rather he doesn't believe it *alone* is God's Word. The approach Morris takes to interpreting Scripture and hearing God speak through the Bible is seriously problematic. It is an approach I (Jim) have thoroughly addressed in chapter 8 of *God Doesn't Whisper*. Notice that Morris claims, "We're invited to ask God to speak to us specifically" (chap. 10). He doesn't bother citing a passage in Scripture where we are invited to do so. There is no such invitation in Scripture. We

This methodology is thoroughly unbiblical and disparages the treasure that is the Word of God. It is a doctrine of divine revelation that isn't taught or modeled in Scripture. Morris, like all HVG teachers, cites John 10 as proof that believers can expect to hear personal messages from Jesus.[8] John 10:27 is serially abused by advocates of this theology. In the verse, Jesus says, "My sheep hear My voice, and I know them, and they follow Me." Charles Stanley writes,

> Jesus made it clear in John 10:27 that the believer's normal experience is to hear God accurately. "My sheep hear My voice, and I know them, and they follow Me." . . . The natural walk of Spirit-filled, committed believers is such that when God speaks, we can identify His Voice.[9]

Contrary to these confident claims, John 10 teaches nothing of the sort. The Good Shepherd Discourse has nothing to do with hearing private and personal revelations. In fact, John identifies Jesus's words as a "figure of speech" (John 10:6). Jesus was not speaking of literal hearing. He was describing salvation. Those who hear His voice come to Him (vv. 4, 16, 27) and receive eternal life (v. 28). Jesus was not promising that believers will hear His whispers in their daily lives through impressions and nudges. He was describing His work of bringing His sheep to salvation. The Good Shepherd calls, gathers, saves, and secures His sheep everlastingly.

> John 10 has NOTHING to do with receiving personalized private revelations. It has nothing to do with hearing Jesus whisper a message to you. It isn't describing an innate or cultivated ability to pick up a frequency of divine whispers, nudgings, and promptings. It isn't describing a conversational walk with Jesus as He whispers directives into our spiritual ears through feelings and impressions. Jesus was talking about salvation, the work of gathering His sheep to Himself (10:16), saving and securing them in spite of the spiritual threat of false shepherds, robbers, and hirelings.[10]

---

are never invited to ask for revelation outside Scripture. We are never encouraged to go beyond it or long for something more than God has provided in His Word.

8. Morris identifies John 10 as "one of the foundational Bible passages that describe this type of close relationship with God" (*Frequency*, chap. 1). Morris writes, "Who is Jesus? Jesus is our Good Shepherd. And what are we? We're sheep. And how does the Good Shepherd guide His sheep? By His voice. That's how we're to live: by listening to Jesus' voice. We're to depend on hearing His voice regularly and clearly" (chap. 1).

9. Stanley, *How to Listen*, 50.

10. Osman, *God Doesn't Whisper*, 67.

God Doesn't Try to Speak to His People

One of the many bad fruits of HVG teaching and methodology is the way in which it disparages God's ability to communicate. HVG proponents envision a god *trying* to speak to his people. According to them, God's success hinges on our ability to listen, quiet our hearts, and tune into His frequency. We have to cultivate an ability and practice the discipline of hearing His voice to ensure His missives are not missed. As Morris claims, "We need to tune in to the frequency of heaven and hear the voice of God" because "God is speaking all the time, but the only ones who hear are those who tune in to the right frequency through humility and obedience."[11] According to Morris, God is always speaking, hoping to be heard, *trying* to be heard, but He needs our cooperation for His communication to be successful.

According to HVG teaching, the consequences of not hearing from God can be tragic. So much is at stake. According to Blackaby and King, we may miss God's work in this world if we fail to hear from Him.

> You need to know what God has on His agenda for your church, community, and nation at this time in history. Then you and your church can adjust your lives to God, so that He can move you into the mainstream of His activity *before it is too late*. Though God likely will not give you a detailed schedule, He will let you know one step at a time how you and your church need to respond to what He is doing.[12]

Blackaby and King presuppose that we *need* information not contained in Scripture. They aren't suggesting we thoroughly search the Scriptures for truth "once for all handed down to the saints" (Jude 3). They're not saying Scripture is the sufficient repository of divine truth whereby God has granted us everything we need for the work of the church in our community and nation "at this time in history." Rather, they are promoting a method of divining the will of God through sources outside Scripture.

Likewise, Robert Morris claims the only way we can "walk in certainty" is if we "hear God's voice in so many areas of our lives—our jobs, our families, our friendships, our health, our areas of service, our futures."[13] According to Charles Stanley, we can't make the right

---

11. Morris, *Frequency*, chap. 7.
12. Blackaby and King, *Experiencing God*, 68 (emphasis added).
13. Morris, *Frequency*, chap. 1.

decisions apart from God giving us "definite and deliberate direction" outside Scripture through personal and private revelations.[14]

The consequences of failing to help God be heard could be catastrophic. If we fail to receive God's situation-specific directions, we won't be able to fully obey His will. We'll miss out. Our obedience will be incomplete, our service hampered, and our walk with God severely truncated. Imagine a god who leaves the fulfillment of his purposes up to us and our ability to decipher his quiet, mysterious, and opaque promptings—this is the god of HVG theology.

This is an implicit denial of the sufficiency of Scripture. To teach that believers *need* further revelation beyond what is provided in Scripture is, by definition, a denial of sufficiency. Further, the methodology employed by HVG teachers to "hear from God" is a tacit denial of God's ability to successfully speak clearly, coherently, and intelligibly. I have documented copious examples of this elsewhere,[15] but here I shall offer two examples I haven't previously critiqued.

JOHN ELDREDGE AND HIS STUTTERING GOD

John Eldredge became wildly popular in the early 2000s with the publication of *Wild at Heart*. By the time *Walking with God* (2008) was published, Eldredge's writings and ministry had secured a large audience among Evangelicals, ensuring that the dangerous doctrines promoted in that book would be widely embraced.[16]

Eldredge offers a method for hearing from God. He cites examples from Scripture of God speaking to people and assumes such revelation is the portion of every child of God in every age. His method of hearing God's voice bears no resemblance to anything in Scripture. Neither the mode nor the content of the revelation that Eldredge claims to receive is akin to the examples in Scripture of God speaking to people. The messages Eldredge claims to receive are nothing more than hints, figures, and vague, confusing clues. For instance, when he asked the Lord, *"What are you saying, Lord?"* Jesus

---

14. Stanley, *How to Listen*, 9. Stanley claims that God gave him special necessary revelation for purchasing a Thanksgiving turkey. His retelling of this story in answer to a viewer's question regarding hearing from God can be found in a video entitled "'How Can I Hear God's Voice?' (Ask Dr. Stanley)," posted on the In Touch Ministries YouTube channel (https://www.youtube.com/watch?v=V4ocm31RJ7g).

15. See my (Jim's) book *God Doesn't Whisper*.

16. I have published an extensive review of *Walking with God* on our website: https://kootenaichurch.org/articles-pdf/book_reviews/CR/cr-walking-with-god.pdf (https://perma.cc/UFZ5-MS5C). I commend that review to the reader for a thorough presentation of the grave theological issues present in the book.

allegedly responded with *"My love."*[17] Eldredge admits that the response is anything but clear. He says, "Every time I've stopped to listen, I've heard, *My love*. Over and over again, *My love*. And I've wondered why. When there are so many things going on in the world and in my life, so many things I know I need to hear from him, still he says to me, *My love*."[18] Then Eldredge frankly admits, "I haven't really known what to do with this."[19]

Later in the book, Eldredge claims, "God has been speaking to me through hawks."[20] After seeing a hawk while out looking for shed antlers, Eldredge claims that God said to him, *"A symbol of My heart."*[21] We're left to wonder what a hawk has to do with God's heart or even why such a statement would be beneficial. On a separate occasion, when Eldredge asked the Lord what the appearance of a hawk meant, he heard, *"My love."*[22]

When deciding whether or not to put down a pet, Eldredge claims he heard God say, *"Two days,"* and then later, God sputtered, *"Your hearts."*[23]

Apparently, God is unable to communicate in clear, complex, and carefully constructed sentences. Is God able only to speak a couple of words at a time? Why are these missives from God so vague, banal, and perplexing? They aren't even complete sentences. I would expect a two-year-old to speak like this, not the God of Scripture. This revelation bears no resemblance to the examples we have in Scripture where God speaks with clarity, complete sentences, and remarkable precision. God's conversation with Moses from the burning bush consisted of arguments, questions, and answers. God gave precise instructions. He didn't just mumble "My love" and "Egypt" and

---

17. Eldredge, *Walking with God*, 75–76.
18. Eldredge, 76. Eldredge doesn't put the words that God speaks in quotation marks. Instead, he sets them apart by putting them in italics. I have accurately represented his style in these quotations, though that style does not fit standard conventions. I have also accurately reflected the capitalizing convention used by Eldredge for pronouns referring to God when I quote him.
19. Eldredge, 76.
20. Eldredge, 117.
21. Eldredge, 117.
22. Eldredge, 118. Notice that Eldredge is allegedly giving information not contained in Scripture. Scripture doesn't use a hawk as a symbol of God's love or God's heart. This is, in every way, new revelation. It is something about God that was not previously revealed. I would challenge the continuationist with two questions. First, if God has said this, should it not be added to Scripture? This is divine revelation concerning the nature of God and His love. Second, why are such revelations even needed? We have entire chapters of Scripture that speak of God's love. Isn't that enough?
23. Eldredge, 126.

leave it to Moses to piece together the meaning of His stammering incomplete sentences and dependent clauses. Listening to Eldredge, you would think that God has no idea how to use a subject and predicate together.

Like others who promote such a weak and feeble deity, Eldredge offers pointers on how to hear God speak: "I find that to hear the voice of God, we must be in a posture of quiet surrender."[24] However, in Scripture, no recipient of divine revelation had to be in "a posture of quiet surrender" to hear the voice of God.

MATT CHANDLER AND PIRATE SHIPS

Matt Chandler also believes that God's voice today is unclear. Chandler teaches that while the canon of Scripture is closed, God still speaks, but in a more opaque and ambiguous manner. He claims that prophecy given through Old Testament prophets like Jeremiah and Isaiah is markedly different than modern prophetic revelations. Whereas prophets of old spoke with clarity, precision, and certainty, modern prophets should only *suggest* that they *might* be getting a *sense* of what the Lord *might* have them share with someone. In a 2018 sermon at The Village Church, Chandler said,

> So you will never prophesy in a way that's on par, equal to, anywhere near the inerrant, infallible Word of God. That's closed, shut. And so the best you've got—the best you've got—is the humility to say, "I think the Lord would have me lay this before you."[25]

In the same sermon, he offered a hypothetical example of how God might speak if he asked how to encourage his friend Danny: "And then I'm quiet again, trying to listen. And then automatically in

---

24. Eldredge, 30. Eldredge admits that he is not always certain he has heard from God and offers numerous ways of confirming what he feels God might be saying (32, 202).

25. Chandler, "A Personal Word." As with other continuationists, Chandler tries to maintain a distinction between Scripture, which he affirms is authoritative, inerrant, infallible, and inspired, and modern prophetic revelations, which have none of those qualities. However, Scripture makes no such distinction. Scripture has those qualities not because it is old, written down, or given through apostles and prophets. Scripture has those qualities because its source is God. God can't speak a nonauthoritative, errant, or fallible word. If revelation comes from God, then it must be authoritative, inerrant, and infallible by virtue of the fact that He spoke it. Continuationists have created a category of revelation that is fallible, errant, and unintelligible and yet has God as its source. To be clear, continuationists don't blame God for the error, failure, or unintelligibility. They suggest these things are the fault of the recipient of the revelation. In other words, God is *trying* to communicate clearly, but He can't overcome the limitations of His "prophets." That rescue device doesn't work since ultimately God is to blame for the fact that His revelation isn't received infallibly and inerrantly. If God is unable to give clear revelation today, then why should we have confidence He was able to when writing Scripture?

God Doesn't Try to Speak to His People

my head there's a picture of a ship, a pirate ship. And then there's like cannons on the pirate ship, and there's a shark chasing the pirate ship."[26]

Despite the silliness of this "word from the Lord" and without any idea what God might mean, Chandler persists with presenting the vision to his friend in the example: "I'm just going to go to Danny, and I'm going to be like, 'Hey, brother, you heard my sermon. I was praying. Danny, it was a pirate ship. There was a shark chasing it. There were cannons.'"[27] Chandler suggests that such puerile and senseless visions *may* be from the Holy Spirit and should be offered "in a great deal of humility"[28] in hopes that the revelation might make sense to the hearer.

Again, how is this an encouragement? Aren't there passages of Scripture to which Chandler could turn to offer encouragement? If there are, then why offer this nonsense instead? Is this clearer than Scripture? Is it better? Is it more profound and helpful? If not, then why seek or pass on such "revelations" or "words from God"? More importantly, why would we think that the source of this confusing palaver is God?

A BAD COMMUNICATOR?

We might expect a two-year-old to stammer, stutter, and blurt out incomplete sentences, two-word phrases, and stories about pirate ships, but should we expect the same from the Lord? Given the clarity, complexity, and perfection of written Scripture, why should we believe that the revelations described by Eldredge or Chandler are necessary or helpful? What do two-word phrases cloaked in confusion offer me that Scripture doesn't? What does a vision of a pirate ship provide that Scripture lacks?

Is God unable to speak clearly and articulately as He once did? The "communicating God" described by modern HVG advocates is nothing like the sovereign God of Scripture. The true God doesn't struggle to be heard or understood by those to whom He speaks. Without ever intending to malign God, His Word, or His power, many Christians inadvertently do that very thing when they describe what they think is the voice of God speaking to them. "I *feel* the Lord is telling me . . ." or "I *think* the Lord is possibly leading me to . . ." sounds spiritual to modern ears, but none of these sentiments or any-

---

26. Chandler, "A Personal Word."
27. Chandler, "A Personal Word."
28. Chandler, "A Personal Word."

God Doesn't Try

thing like them were ever uttered by those to whom the Lord actually spoke.

When God spoke, nobody ever doubted or wondered about the origin of the revelation. They were never uncertain about what they heard. They knew what they were to do in response to the message. They knew Who was speaking. Why? Because God doesn't *try* to speak. He doesn't struggle to be heard. He isn't *trying* to get our attention, get a message to us, or direct our steps. He doesn't need our attentiveness, quiet solitude, or humble posture. If He desires to speak, He has no problem ensuring that He is heard. There is no example in Scripture of God trying to speak and failing to be heard.[29]

Moses didn't walk away from the burning bush thinking, feeling, or sensing that perhaps the Lord might be trying to tell him something. Saul of Tarsus didn't get up off the Damascus Road with doubt regarding Who had spoken, what he had heard, or what he was to do. When God speaks, He doesn't utter enigmatic, monosyllabic, two-word statements or ambiguous platitudes like "My love" or "My heart."

No recipient of divine revelation had to nurture the ability, cultivate the discipline, or learn the skill. It is not a discipline anywhere encouraged in Scripture. No instructions are provided for how one might hear God. Nobody can be or needs to be taught how to hear the voice of God. The reason is simple: If God *isn't* speaking, you can't hear Him no matter how quiet you are or what disciplines you cultivate. If God *is* speaking, you can't miss Him no matter how busy, distracted, or uninterested you might be. God never tries to speak, attempts to communicate, or struggles to be heard. He doesn't lack the power to ensure He is heard and understood by anyone, including those least receptive to Him. God is able to speak clearly in complete and complex sentences and ensure He is heard.

---

29. The example of young Samuel mistaking the source of the voice he heard in the temple is often cited as proof that Samuel had to learn from Eli how to hear the voice of God (1 Sam. 3). The example of Samuel proves just the opposite. Samuel *heard clearly* what was said. He heard without ever learning how to hear from God or being told that he needed to listen. Samuel didn't know it was the Lord and didn't expect to hear God speak because "word from the LORD was rare in those days, visions were infrequent" (1 Sam. 3:1). Nobody told Samuel that he should expect to hear God, that God was always speaking, and that he could tune in to the frequency of Heaven. Samuel mistook the voice he heard for Eli's call (1 Sam. 3:1–14), but he heard and understood perfectly well what was said. Though using Samuel in this way is a tragic abuse of Scripture, that doesn't stop Charles Stanley from citing it (*How to Listen to God*) or Priscilla Shirer from writing an entire book based on that passage (*He Speaks to Me: Preparing to Hear from God*).

THE SAME BUT DIFFERENT

The continuationist must assert that God's voice today is *just like* what we find in Scripture, but at the same time, *nothing like* what we find in Scripture. To prove that God still speaks, they cite the instances of God speaking in the biblical record: Moses and the burning bush, Samuel called by God, Elijah and the still small voice, etc. That God gave direct revelation in the past is taken as an explicit promise that He'll do so for us today. Yet the alleged ways in which God speaks today are nothing like God's revelations recorded in Scripture.

HVG teachers believe God speaks through a myriad of different means, including impressions, promptings, random thoughts, inner voices, signs, fleeces, peace in the heart, other Christians, and, of course, Scripture. The category of "signs" is so broad that it can include nearly *anything*. John Eldredge claims God was speaking to him through hawks. Bill Hybels wondered if God was trying to speak to him through a Bud Light beer can floating by his boat.[30] Jack Deere claims God spoke to him through the lyrics of a country music song.[31] Robert Morris claims God revealed the name of a church he planted on a sign, a literal sign, advertising a shopping mall.[32] I could multiply examples of this from continuationists ad infinitum and ad nauseam.

While claiming that God's voice today is just like it was in Bible times, the methodology promoted is anything but biblical. Nobody exegeted a sign, a floating beer can, or song lyrics for the voice of God. Moses didn't get an impression, wait for a sign, and then confirm it by peace in his heart. Paul never suggested a random thought, followed by an internal nudge, and an open door might be the voice of God. Believers were never encouraged to write down dreams lest they potentially miss what God might be trying to say.[33] It never occurred to anyone in Scripture that believers needed to be taught a method for hearing the voice of God because nobody thought God was *trying* to be heard.

---

30. Hybels, *Power of a Whisper*, 107–8.
31. Deere, *Voice of God*, 128–29.
32. Morris, *Frequency*, chap. 5.
33. Jack Deere suggests this very thing in *Surprised by the Voice of God* (224).

WHAT'S WRONG WITH THEIR GOD?

What kind of god is unable to ensure that those to whom he is speaking are able to hear him?[34] What god needs us to be receptive and open, obedient and willing, before he is able to be heard? Robert Morris claims, "We need to tune in to the frequency of heaven and hear the voice of God" because "God is speaking all the time, but the only ones who hear are those who tune in to the right frequency through humility and obedience."[35] What kind of god speaks in monosyllabic words, truncated sentences, and incoherent phrases? What kind of god is less articulate than a three-year-old? What god speaks errantly, fallibly, and non-authoritatively? The god promoted by those who teach that he struggles to be heard.

This isn't the God of Scripture! God doesn't *try* to speak. He doesn't *try* to be understood. He doesn't *try* to direct His people or reveal His will. He doesn't need your assistance, submissive posture, or ready openness. God has a pretty good track record of speaking clearly to people who are hostile to Him, openly unreceptive, or not expecting to hear from Him. God was able to speak to Abraham, Nebuchadnezzar, Saul of Tarsus, and Cornelius. None of those men ever learned to hear the voice of God. None of them "tuned in to the frequency of Heaven," yet God was able to speak and ensure that He was heard and understood.

This blasphemy, promoted knowingly or unknowingly by those who teach the discipline of hearing the voice of God, has been tolerated far too long in Evangelicalism. It's taught under the guise of "intimacy with God" by men and women who claim to believe in the sufficiency and authority of Scripture. They claim to represent the God of the Bible while describing a god who *tries* to speak, longs to be heard, and struggles to communicate clearly. This isn't the God described in Scripture.

FOR THE SHEPHERDS

The precious souls committed to our oversight (Heb. 13:17) desperately need clarity on these issues. They're bombarded daily by bad doctrine, particularly regarding this subject. We must be very

---

34. I am intentionally referring to this deity as "god" rather than "God," since the god promoted in this theology has more in common with the mute idols mocked and derided in Scripture (Ps. 115:4–8; 135:15–17; Isa. 46:1–7) than with the true God Who made the mouth, the ear, and languages (Gen. 11:1–9; Ex. 4:11; Ps. 94:9; Prov. 20:12).

35. Morris, *Frequency*, chap. 7.

careful and precise when we speak of God's voice, God speaking, and how we hear Him in Scripture.

Never claim a "word from the Lord" or a "vision from God." God speaks in Scripture, not in your passions, emotions, or inclinations. Our passion for something isn't necessarily God's leading, guidance, or vision. It certainly isn't His voice. If we set the example of being led by feelings, thoughts, or circumstances, don't be surprised when those under our charge look to the same subjective and unreliable experiences for divine guidance. If you show by example that you trust your passions as reliable indicators of God's will, those in your fellowship will follow their passions into all manner of folly and evil.

We must use biblical language to communicate biblical truth. Distinguish between revelation and illumination. Don't describe the Spirit's work of granting understanding as the "voice of God." They are not the same. We can be convicted, encouraged, strengthened, enabled, emboldened, or empowered for service without ever hearing a voice. When the Lord graciously uses the truth of His Word in our hearts, lives, or ministries, He is not giving new revelation. Teach and encourage your people to use biblical language to describe biblical concepts.

To quote an old adage, "a mist in the pulpit is a fog in the pews." When we are unclear or imprecise in describing the works and the Word of God, our people will be confused. They live in a confused culture and hear conflicting messages all week. When you speak of hearing God, leave no doubt in the minds of your hearers that His voice is found in Scripture and Scripture alone.[36] Be clear regarding the nature of divine revelation and how it is to be understood (2 Tim. 2:15).

We must never say anything that disparages God's power, wisdom, or sovereignty. We should never speak of His revelation or guidance in a manner that suggests He is *trying* to speak, direct our steps, or be heard. God doesn't try to speak to His people.

---

36. This doesn't mean God speaks through words or phrases ripped out of context and assigned personal meanings foreign to the original author or audience. Rather, when the author's intended meaning is read and understood, the reader has "heard the Word of God." God's Word is found in the meaning of Scripture. The scriptural text doesn't *contain* the Word of God; the scriptural text rightly understood *is* the Word of God. Our goal in reading the text is to understand what the original author (including the divine Author, the Holy Spirit) intended by the inspired text. Any "message" from Scripture different from that intended by the Author is no more the Word of God than words found in a fortune cookie.

DISCUSSION QUESTIONS

1. Does your church experience include exposure to "hearing the voice of God" (HVG) theology? In what ways has this shaped your understanding of the will of God?

2. Is HVG teaching detrimental to Christian growth in holiness? Why or why not?

3. Should you be automatically suspicious of an HVG teacher in other areas of their teaching? Why or why not?

4. Have you believed things about "the voice of God" that dishonor His Word? In what ways do you think your views deny the sufficiency of Scripture?

5. How can we make our language more honoring to God? What does it mean to use biblical language to describe biblical concepts?

6. How does our use or interpretation of Scripture reveal our view of God's Word?

7. Why is the lack of specific guidance for everyday decisions not considered a deficiency in Scripture?

8. What is the significance of John's statement in John 10:6 that Jesus was using a figure of speech? What does it tell us about the Good Shepherd Discourse? Can you summarize the meaning of that passage?

9. Describe the difference between inspiration and illumination.

RECOMMENDED READING:

Decision Making and the Will of God by Garry Friesen and Robin Maxson

Guidance and the Voice of God by Phillip D. Jensen and Tony Payne

Charismatic Chaos by John F. MacArthur Jr.

One Foundation: Essays on the Sufficiency of Scripture by John F. MacArthur Jr., R. C. Sproul, and Dr. Jack MacArthur

God Doesn't Whisper by Jim Osman

To Be Continued?: Are the Miraculous Gifts for Today? by Samuel E. Waldron

Chapter 6:

God Doesn't Try to Provide for His People

6

God reveals Himself in His Word. One way He does so is through the use of images, metaphors, and similes. I would suspect that anyone reading a book like this would be familiar with several of them. Scripture compares God to a lion, an eagle, a lamb, a light, a fire, a fountain, a rock, a hiding place, a tower, a shield, a husband, a king, a builder, a shepherd, a physician, a potter, a door, and other created things. Each of these familiar images from creation communicates something true about God. A lion is powerful. A lamb is pure and used for sacrifice. Light illuminates. A fountain gives life. A tower protects. A potter creates. All these images give us insight into God's nature and interactions with His creation, especially His image-bearers.

GOD'S SURPRISING SYMBOL OF DESTRUCTION

One image used in Scripture may seem surprising at first: "With reproofs You chasten a man for iniquity; You consume as a moth what is precious to him; surely every man is a mere breath" (Ps. 39:11). David compares God to a moth. The same image is used in Hosea 5:12: "Therefore I am like a moth to Ephraim and like rottenness to the house of Judah." God "consumes as a moth" and is "like a moth to Ephraim." What is God telling us about Himself in these verses? There are times when God may act to destroy our material possessions (like a moth) for our chastening. This is His judgment on the unbeliever and loving discipline toward the believer.

God has the means to provide for the physical needs of His people and has promised to do so. Further, God has the means to provide far beyond our needs even though He has made no such promise. He may choose to provide moderately, abundantly, or superabundantly beyond our needs for anyone as He sees fit. But the moth imagery reminds us that God may also choose to reduce our wealth or worsen our health. Although He will never leave us, He may remove from our lives anything else to which we have looked for happiness, fulfillment, peace, or security. The mature Christian is content with whatever circumstances his Lord has ordained for him. He is free from the sins of worry and anxiety. He has a proper perspective on this life and an eager focus on the next. The mature Christian knows that God doesn't *try* to provide for His people as they sojourn here on Earth. He provides perfectly according to His power and will.

THE PROMISE: MEETING OUR NEEDS

And my God will supply all your needs according to His riches in glory in Christ Jesus. (Phil. 4:19)

Do not worry then, saying, "What will we eat?" or "What will we drink?" or "What will we wear for clothing?" For the Gentiles eagerly seek all these things; for your heavenly Father knows that you need all these things. But seek first His kingdom and His righteousness, and all these things will be added to you. So do not worry about tomorrow; for tomorrow will care for itself. Each day has enough trouble of its own. (Matt. 6:31–34)

It's a tremendous blessing to know that God will provide for the needs of His people. This frees us from worry and anxiety over material needs and allows us to focus our energy and resources on His Kingdom and righteousness. But if we presume upon God to provide beyond our basic needs, we commit the sin of blasphemy by claiming God has promised something He hasn't. Consequently, our faith may be shaken when God doesn't do something we thought He promised. We need to know what God meant when He said, "All these things will be added to you" (Matt. 6:33).

A ROSE GARDEN

When I (Dave) was an economics instructor, I taught a section on needs. The goal was to define the term *needs* and demonstrate that the transactions economists are interested in are choices and not needs. I would ask students what they need. I would write all their suggestions on the board. Their lists would normally include food, shelter, clothing, water, and air. Sometimes it included things like love, a nice pair of jeans, a phone, hope, music, a bed, etc. We would then define *needs*, and the class would always arrive at the same consensus in their definition: "those things without which life is impossible." I would then go back to the board and erase everything that didn't fit the definition. Lastly, I would consolidate the list down to two things: a jug of glucose per day and a blanket. Now, I have no idea if that would be sufficient for life. You would add air to that list, but air isn't scarce. It isn't something bought and sold and so doesn't fit in an economics discussion. The point was to show that we use terms like *needs* too broadly and without circumspection. We use terms that imply we have no choice to describe activities over which we do, in fact, have choice.[1] In other words, we vastly overestimate the resources that can be legitimately regarded as needs while formally defining *need* as "that without which we cannot live."

Often when people hear God's promises to meet our needs, they, like my economics students, have much more in mind than the basic human needs for survival. Most Christians speak as if God owes them perfect health, a perfect spouse, perfect children, a fun job with few demands, a maintenance-free house, two or three cars that never need repair, investments that always grow, consistently sunny seventy-five-degree days without drought, and a nice snow on Christmas morning. If anything is less than perfect, they are down, depressed, unhappy, ungrateful, angry, perplexed, and hurt. They find fault with God because God hasn't kept His promise according to their expectation. Their faith is damaged, their joy is suppressed, their esteem for God is diminished, and their sanctification is stalled.

A god who can't or won't keep his promises bears no resemblance to the God of the Bible. If in fact we worship a god who breaks his promises, that god is either a lying god or a trying god. Neither of those things can be said of Yahweh. God can't lie and God can't try.

So, is there a contradiction? Does God always keep His promise to provide for our needs? Either God keeps His promises, or He isn't

---

1. This way of thinking is endemic to modern Western society. We attribute to a constraint something that is a choice. We say we can't afford things instead of saying we made a choice to buy one thing instead of another. Imagine the person who needs something they can't afford. That's certain death! We say we don't have time instead of describing how we prioritize time. We "have anxiety" rather than sinfully worrying or being anxious, as if anxiety is a condition rather than an action we commit. We describe sexual perversion as something a person *is* rather than something that person *does*. People "identify" as something, claiming the action is just an expression of that identity. This insulates them from culpability for their actions. Tragically, it also inoculates them against eternal life and the abundant living that comes from repentant faith in Christ.

God. When we understand the true scope of God's promises, we will have confidence, even during the worst suffering or persecution, that God always keeps His promises. We question God's faithfulness only because we err in our understanding of the scope of the promise that God has actually made. What has God actually promised in the verses above? The positive promise of God regarding this life is only that He'll meet our needs. He enumerates those needs in Matthew 6:25. He has promised food ("what you will eat"), water ("what you will drink"), and clothing ("what you will put on"). If God were to provide a jug of glucose and a blanket (assuming again that that's sufficient for life), His promise would be fulfilled. We're promised nothing more than this and don't deserve even this! God has graciously promised to meet our most basic physical needs of food, water, and protection from the elements. We don't deserve even the meager provision He has promised to provide.[2]

But what about all the promises of God? Doesn't God promise temporal, material blessings to His people beyond just meeting basic needs? In a word, no.[3] Not in the way I've described above. We aren't promised material blessings in this life beyond these most basic needs. While God gives generously out of His grace, often far beyond our basic needs, such blessings are nowhere promised to us. We aren't promised an easy, prosperous, healthy life free from trials, challenges, conflicts, or scarcity. We're promised an abundant life of hope and peace, even joy, in the midst of trials, persecution, and war with our flesh. This is the sanctifying life described in chapter 4. We are sojourners, exiles, and aliens. We should expect in this life only what God has told us to expect as we anticipate our blessed eternal home in the presence of the One for Whom we exist, our perfect Master, Jesus Christ. Country singer Lynn Anderson never promised you a rose garden, and in this life, neither has God.

---

2. Indeed, even this provision can be removed from us if God determines to bring our physical life to an end.

3. There is much that could be said about the prosperity gospel (which isn't the gospel), and we address this heresy in chapter 9. Our good friend and faithful brother Justin Peters has sufficiently debunked the entire movement, and we would both highly recommend his YouTube channel and other resources. If your church has never hosted his *Clouds Without Water* seminar, you should do so soon. He has created a definitive work revealing the contradictions, buffoonery, hucksterism, debauchery, and heresy of the most well-known reprobates and charlatans in the Word of Faith movement. Other resources include MacArthur, *Charismatic Chaos*; and a concise and well-argued book by Jones and Woodbridge entitled *Health, Wealth, and Happiness*. For a repentant, converted insider's view of this movement, see Costi Hinn, *God, Greed, and the (Prosperity) Gospel*.

DO NOT WORRY

If you believe God is sovereign and good, you won't worry about His provision. God doesn't *try* to meet the needs of His people. You'll rest in the fact that God isn't trying to provide more or less than He has provided or will provide. The provision you currently have is always what God intends. In His sovereignty and goodness, He has provided perfectly for your current circumstances. Trusting the promise of God to meet your needs, you can rest in His sovereignty and goodness in every situation. A mature believer will, like Paul, learn to be content in any circumstance ordained by God (Phil. 4:11–12). He will live free from worry and be anxious for nothing.

BIBLICAL FEAR

The words *fear* and *afraid* appear in the NASB translation of Scripture over five hundred times. Most occurrences translate the Hebrew word *yārē'* or the Greek word *phobeō*. These passages teach us three important truths about fear.

First, we ought to fear God. There are about three hundred references to fearing God throughout Scripture. He is the proper object of our reverence and fear.

> The fear of the LORD is the beginning of knowledge; fools despise wisdom and instruction. (Prov. 1:7)

> The fear of the LORD is the beginning of wisdom, and the knowledge of the Holy One is understanding. (Prov. 9:10)

> And I saw another angel flying in midheaven, having an eternal gospel to preach to those who live on the earth, and to every nation and tribe and tongue and people; and he said with a loud voice, "Fear God, and give Him glory, because the hour of His judgment has come; worship Him who made the heaven and the earth and sea and springs of waters." (Rev. 14:6–7)

Second, we shouldn't fear men. About 180 references discourage the fear of man.

> But Moses said to the people, "Do not fear! Stand by and see the salvation of the LORD which He will accomplish for you today; for the Egyptians whom you have seen today, you will never see them again forever." (Exod. 14:13)

> Now when the attendant of the man of God had risen early and gone out, behold, an army with horses and chariots was

circling the city. And his servant said to him, "Alas, my master! What shall we do?" So he answered, "Do not fear, for those who are with us are more than those who are with them." (2 Kings 6:15–16)

The LORD is for me; I will not fear; what can man do to me? (Ps. 118:6)

Do not fear those who kill the body but are unable to kill the soul; but rather fear Him who is able to destroy both soul and body in hell. (Matt. 10:28)

Third, we should not fear circumstances or the unknown, but God alone. There are about fifty references that contrast sinful fear with trust in God's sovereignty and goodness.

God heard the lad crying; and the angel of God called to Hagar from heaven and said to her, "What is the matter with you, Hagar? Do not fear, for God has heard the voice of the lad where he is." (Gen. 21:17)

Then Elijah said to her, "Do not fear; go, do as you have said, but make me a little bread cake from it first and bring it out to me, and afterward you may make one for yourself and for your son. For thus says the LORD God of Israel, 'The bowl of flour shall not be exhausted, nor shall the jar of oil be empty, until the day that the LORD sends rain on the face of the earth.'" (1 Kings 17:13–14)

God is our refuge and strength, a very present help in trouble. Therefore we will not fear, though the earth should change and though the mountains slip into the heart of the sea; though its waters roar and foam, though the mountains quake at its swelling pride. (Ps. 46:1–3)

Are not two sparrows sold for a cent? And yet not one of them will fall to the ground apart from your Father. But the very hairs of your head are all numbered. So do not fear; you are more valuable than many sparrows. (Matt. 10:29–31)

Do not fear what you are about to suffer. Behold, the devil is about to cast some of you into prison, so that you will be tested, and you will have tribulation for ten days. Be faithful until death, and I will give you the crown of life. (Rev. 2:10)

Biblically, the only legitimate fear is the fear of God. Those at enmity with Him should fear His power, His wrath, and the judgment to come. Those reconciled to Him should live in reverent, loving fear as they seek to please Him. Fear of anything else, including death, natural disaster, your boss, your spouse, or loss of wealth is inappropriate. It is a sinful fear that results from a lack of faith in the sovereignty and goodness of God.[4] Sinful fear dissipates from the heart of one convinced that God doesn't try.

WORRY AND ANXIETY

> Be anxious for nothing, but in everything by prayer and supplication with thanksgiving let your requests be made known to God. And the peace of God, which surpasses all comprehension, will guard your hearts and your minds in Christ Jesus. (Phil. 4:6–7)

What would a biblical anxiety look like? Well, it wouldn't look like anything because its object would be . . . nothing. "Be anxious for nothing" is a command. Don't be anxious![5] The same command is repeated in different words by our Lord in the Sermon on the Mount. This was cited briefly above. Here is the longer passage from Matthew 6:25–34:

> For this reason I say to you, *do not be worried* about your life, as to what you will eat or what you will drink; nor for your body, as to what you will put on. Is not life more than food, and the body more than clothing? Look at the birds of the air, that they do not sow, nor reap nor gather into barns, and yet your heavenly Father feeds them. Are you not worth much more than they? And who of you by *being worried* can add a single hour to his life? And why *are you worried* about clothing? Observe how the lilies of the field grow; they

---

[4] I'm aware of 1 Pet. 2:18, where Peter says, "Servants, be subject to your masters with all fear" (LSB). In verse 17, Peter has told us to "honor all people, love the brethren, fear God, honor the king" (LSB). Peter doesn't tell us to fear the king but to honor him. It seems in verse 17 that Peter reserves that *phobeō* fear for God. So why would servants be told to fear their masters in the following verse? I think the best interpretation is that "all fear" in verse 18 is the same fear of God that Peter encourages in verse 17. We who are servants are to submit to our masters in obedience to God, in the fear of God.

[5] You'll see in our word study below that there are proper objects of concern. The Scriptures use the word translated as "anxiety" to express appropriate, righteous concern for the well-being of other people. The general command to "be anxious for nothing" is balanced by the acknowledgement that compassionate concern for others, in particular for other believers, is not sinful but commendable.

do not toil nor do they spin, yet I say to you that not even Solomon in all his glory clothed himself like one of these. But if God so clothes the grass of the field, which is alive today and tomorrow is thrown into the furnace, will He not much more clothe you? You of little faith! *Do not worry* then, saying, "What will we eat?" or "What will we drink?" or "What will we wear for clothing?" For the Gentiles eagerly seek all these things; for your heavenly Father knows that you need all these things. But seek first His kingdom and His righteousness, and all these things will be added to you.

So *do not worry* about tomorrow; for tomorrow will care for itself. Each day has enough trouble of its own.

Notice that *worry* and *worried* are mentioned five times. Don't worry!

Most occurrences of the words translated "worry" or "anxiety" in the Bible are the Hebrew *dā'ag* and the Greek *merimna*. A brief study of each will help us understand the Lord's attitude toward worry and anxiety.

The Hebrew *dā'ag* and its forms are generally translated "anxiety" and are always negative.[6] Here are a few Old Testament passages that use that Hebrew word.

> For I confess my iniquity; I am full of anxiety because of my sin. (Ps. 38:18)

> Anxiety in a man's heart weighs it down, but a good word makes it glad. (Prov. 12:25)

> Of whom were you worried and fearful when you lied, and did not remember Me nor give Me a thought? Was I not silent even for a long time so you do not fear Me? (Isa. 57:11)

> Blessed is the man who trusts in the LORD and whose trust is the LORD. For he will be like a tree planted by the water, that extends its roots by a stream and will not fear when the heat comes; but its leaves will be green, and it will not be

---

6. There are two possible exceptions in 1 Sam. 9:5 and 10:2, both of which refer to the "anxiety" of Saul's father over Saul's delay in his search for their donkeys. Another possible exception is in Josh. 22:24 where the half-tribe of Manasseh and two other tribes raise an altar out of "concern" (translators generally choose this word over "anxiety" in this case) that they would be excluded from the worship of Yahweh.

anxious in a year of drought nor cease to yield fruit. (Jer. 17:7–8)

Taken together, the usages of *dā'ag̱* in the Old Testament show that anxiety is a sinful lack of trust in God. The passage in Jeremiah is typical in that it contrasts trust in Yahweh with anxiety. These are opposites. To trust God's sovereignty and goodness is to be anxious for nothing. To be anxious or worry is to doubt either the sovereignty of God, the goodness of God, or both.

The Greek *merimna* is an extremely interesting word. Its root means "to draw apart, to separate, to divide and fracture." This vivid word describes a state of being pulled in different directions or having a divided mind. It's translated both as "worry" and "anxiety" in the New Testament.[7] It's heavily used in Jesus's teaching on worry in Matthew 6 and Luke 12. It's translated "anxious" in Philippians 4:6, quoted at the beginning of this section ("Be anxious for nothing"). Here are some additional New Testament verses revealing the Lord's view of anxiety:

> And others are the ones on whom seed was sown among the thorns; these are the ones who have heard the word, but the worries of the world, and the deceitfulness of riches, and the desires for other things enter in and choke the word, and it becomes unfruitful. (Mark 4:18–19)

> When they arrest you and hand you over, do not worry beforehand about what you are to say, but say whatever is given you in that hour; for it is not you who speak, but it is the Holy Spirit. (Mark 13:11)

> Be on guard, so that your hearts will not be weighted down with dissipation and drunkenness and the worries of life, and that day will not come on you suddenly like a trap. (Luke 21:34)

> Therefore humble yourselves under the mighty hand of God, that He may exalt you at the proper time, casting all your anxiety on Him, because He cares for you. (1 Pet. 5:6–7)

---

7. There's a single use of another word translated "worry" or "be of doubtful mind" or "keep worrying" in Luke 12:29. It's *meteōrizō*. It's obviously where we get our words *meteor* and *meteorite* and literally means "suspended in air." It gives the idea of vacillating, being uncertain or unsure, and not having sound footing. It's a great metaphor for the state of mind that we call worry or anxiety.

Merinma isn't always negative. It's often translated "concern" in the New Testament. It's used of the pastoral, loving concern Paul had for "all the churches" in 2 Corinthians 11:28. Paul and Timothy had concern for the saints in Philippi in Philippians 2:20. It's used of the concerns of married and unmarried people (1 Corinthians 7:32–34) and the general care of Christians for one another (1 Corinthians 12:25). These are positive "anxieties," indicating that the morality of anxiety of this type depends on its cause or the nature of the concern. While we're told to "be anxious for nothing," being concerned for the welfare of other Christians or for how we might please God are not unethical forms of concern. The account of Mary and Martha in Luke 10 is a perfect illustration of how *merimna* can either be misplaced and sinful or properly directed and laudable.

> Now as they were traveling along, He entered a village; and a woman named Martha welcomed Him into her home. And she had a sister called Mary, who was also seated at the Lord's feet, and was listening to His word. But Martha was distracted with all her preparations; and she came up to Him and said, "Lord, do You not care that my sister has left me to do the serving by myself? Then tell her to help me." But the Lord answered and said to her, "Martha, Martha, you are worried and distracted by many things; but only one thing is necessary; for Mary has chosen the good part, which shall not be taken away from her." (Luke 10:38–42)

Mary was concerned about worshipping and learning from Christ while He was physically there. Martha was distracted, concerned, and worried about good things, but not the best thing, which, in that moment, was learning from Jesus Christ, not preparing meals and accommodations for Him and His entourage. It's apparent from this account that *merimna* can be used of negative anxiety and worry or positive concern and care. The issue is whether it's concern for temporal, corruptible things or the eternal and incorruptible matters pertaining to God and His glory.

THE DISCONTENT OF THE PROUD

What causes our anxiety and worry, in particular about the things of this life that don't have eternal consequence? Why do we worry so much about relationships, money, car repairs, politics, and the latest headlines? We understand that this life is a mere moment in relation to eternity. It's a proving ground, a rehearsal stage, and a practice field getting us ready for our real life, our eternal life. So why so much angst over the temporal and secular?

I think it stems from two main sources. First, as emphasized above, we lack faith in or understanding of two great truths about God: He is sovereign and He is good. God doesn't *try* to provide. His provision is sufficient and perfect for you at this time and place. It is perfect for your sanctification and according to His will for you.

The second source of our sinful anxiety is our pride. We are concerned for our own relative position in the world's hierarchy. We are concerned with our reputation, what people think of us, and how they esteem us. In his book *The Pursuit of God*, A. W. Tozer writes,

> Think for yourself whether much of your sorrow has not arisen from someone speaking slightingly of you. As long as you set yourself up as a little god to which you must be loyal there will be those who will delight to offer affront to your idol. How then can you hope to have inward peace? The heart's fierce effort to protect itself from every slight, to shield its touchy honor from the bad opinion of friend and enemy, will never let the mind have rest. Continue this fight through the years and the burden will become intolerable. Yet the sons of earth are carrying this burden continually, challenging every word spoken against them, cringing under every criticism, smarting under each fancied slight, tossing sleepless if another is preferred before them.[8]

In contrast, the mature believer, whom Tozer calls "the meek man," has comprehended the sovereignty and goodness of God.

> The meek man cares not at all who is greater than he, for he has long ago decided that the esteem of the world is not worth the effort. He develops toward himself a kindly sense of humor and learns to say, "Oh, so you have been overlooked? They have placed someone else before you? They have whispered that you are pretty small stuff after all? And now you feel hurt because the world is saying about you the very things you have been saying about yourself? Only yesterday you were telling God that you were nothing, a mere worm of the dust. Where is your consistency? Come on, humble yourself, and cease to care what men think."

---

8. Tozer, *The Pursuit of God*, 112.

The meek man is not a human mouse afflicted with a sense of his own inferiority. Rather he may be in his moral life as bold as a lion and as strong as Samson; but he has stopped being fooled about himself. He has accepted God's estimate of his own life. He knows he is as weak and helpless as God has declared him to be, but paradoxically, he knows at the same time that he is in the sight of God of more importance than angels. In himself, nothing; in God, everything. That is his motto. He knows well that the world will never see him as God sees him and he has stopped caring. He rests perfectly content to allow God to place His own values. He will be patient to wait for the day when everything will get its own price tag and real worth will come into its own. Then the righteous shall shine forth in the Kingdom of their Father. He is willing to wait for that day.

In the meantime he will have attained a place of soul rest. As he walks on in meekness he will be happy to let God defend him. The old struggle to defend himself is over. He has found the peace which meekness brings.[9]

It is liberating to realize that we need fear no man, that the reputation and esteem in which we're held by others is of no consequence before the Lord. We serve Him alone! Only His estimation of us is relevant. Unless our relationships with others have a direct bearing on our relationship with God, they are immaterial and inconsequential.

Tozer writes,

Artificiality is one curse that will drop away the moment we kneel at Jesus' feet and surrender ourselves to His meekness. Then we will not care what people think of us so long as God is pleased. Then *what we are* will be everything; what we appear will take its place far down the scale of interest for us. Apart from sin we have nothing of which to be ashamed. Only an evil desire to shine makes us want to appear other than we are.[10]

Isn't that really the cause of our anxiety? We want others to think well of us. We want them to think better of us than we are. If we cared little of what others thought of us, if we thought of ourselves only as

---

9. Tozer, 112–14.
10. Tozer, 115–16 (emphasis in original).

God does and weren't ashamed to be regarded by others as God sees us, we would be completely free from sinful anxiety and worry. "Apart from sin we have nothing of which to be ashamed." There is no shame in honest work done diligently, no matter the pay scale. There is no shame in a true inability, disability, or lack of talent or resources in a particular area. There is no shame in any situation you may find yourself in that is not a result of sin. You needn't feel a sense of shame because you're not married or because you're unable to have children or because you're confined to a wheelchair. There is no shame in lacking musical talent, artistic ability, or teaching/preaching gifts, or in not measuring up to some shallow, earthly standard of beauty. Remember, statistically speaking, half of us are below average! Yet we are all God's image-bearers, and only in our sin do we fall short in a way that should make us feel ashamed.

CONCLUSION

God doesn't *try* to provide for you. If you aren't extremely wealthy, it isn't that God wanted you to be but was somehow thwarted in His efforts. If you aren't in poverty, it's not as if He wanted that for you but somehow by your own effort or determination you thwarted His will. He wants you to have exactly what you have in your bank account at this moment.

You needn't be anxious for the things of this world or worried about your position relative to other people. God has you where He wants you, and there is no shame in that. Both of the authors of this book grew up in relatively poor families. We grew up in America, so by global standards, we were rich, but we were considered poor by the standards of this country and our communities. Who cares? God had us in that condition according to His perfect will, and whatever the future may hold, we can rest in that enduring truth.

The Puritan Jeremiah Burroughs wrote a great little book entitled *The Rare Jewel of Christian Contentment*. He defined Christian contentment as "that sweet, inward, quiet, gracious frame of spirit, which freely submits to and delights in God's wise and fatherly disposal in every condition."[11] That's our desire for you. By resting in the profound truth that God's provision isn't a matter of chance, we can acquire this rare and precious jewel.

---

11. Burroughs, *Rare Jewel*, 3.

FOR THE SHEPHERDS

One thing we all want for the redeemed, beloved children of Christ under our care is the great freedom and peace of contentment. Too often, though, our people are unhappy, discontent, anxious, and depressed.

The world is accelerating downhill toward a disgusting septic lagoon of sinful madness. It's a sin-cursed asylum where the inmates are increasingly in charge. The world around us, particularly in North America and Europe, is morally decaying through intentional, open, and celebrated rebellion to a degree rarely seen in human history. We are setting new lows in intellectual futility and moral depravity with each new headline.

Not surprisingly, this postmodern decline of human civilization has resulted in unprecedented levels of unhappiness and discontentment. The mind can't make sense of the madness that it's being told it must affirm contrary to conscience. The cognitive dissonance is jarring and certainly not conducive to peace, happiness, or contentment. Gen Z (born 1997–2012) is the loneliest, most anxious, depressed, and stressed-out generation in history. They have more allergies, get less sleep, and have more diagnosed intellectual disabilities and psychiatric disorders than any prior generation.[12] They are glued to their phones when not on their laptops. They spend hours each day on social media, which, at best, presents filtered, heavily edited, and falsified versions of life which the honest person knows they can never achieve. Of course they can't because it's not real! At worst, social media offers up a smorgasbord of the absolute worst of human behavior, from gossip and slander to horribly stupid and ungodly philosophical, political, and theological ramblings to the worst extremes of sexual perversion. They're told that everyone is racist,

---

12. The data on this is ubiquitous. For example, Harmony Healthcare IT conducted a survey of more than one thousand Gen Zers and discovered that 42 percent had a diagnosed mental health condition (mostly anxiety or depression) and 31 percent rate their overall mental health as bad ("State of Gen Z Mental Health," September 15, 2022, https://www.harmonyhit.com/state-of-gen-z-mental-health/ [https://perma.cc/LVD5-TCVC]). Another study, published by the NIH, found Gen Z had the highest stress and the most mental health disorders and was the loneliest and most fatigued cohort in the study (Kaitlin Grelle et al., "The Generation Gap Revisited," https://doi.org/10.1007/s10804-023-09442-x [https://perma.cc/X36K-RUZN]). A study by Blue Shield of California found that Gen Zers spend on average nearly six hours *per day* on social media and nearly 90 percent face mental health challenges ("New Poll: Mental Health Challenges Prevalent Among Gen Z Youth; More Than Three in Four Have Discussed Their Struggles with Others," August 3, 2023, https://news.blueshieldca.com/2023/08/03/new-poll-mental-health-challenges-prevalent-among-gen-z-youth-more-than-three-in-four-have-discussed-their-struggles-with-others/ [https://perma.cc/ZQ5P-T6E5]).

that gender is unrelated to biology, and that we can eliminate police without repercussions. Math is white supremacy, marriage is malleable, body and mind are utterly disconnected, and nothing is true except the inviolable principle that truth doesn't exist. This is the untethered life of the postmodernist. The love for darkness has overcome the conscience and the remnants of the logical mind to the point that they may proclaim nothing is true, which is, of course, itself a statement of propositional truth. There is nothing to hold on to, nothing to hope in, nothing to live for. All they have is this unsatisfying and depressing life of sin and spiritual ruin.

It isn't surprising, then, that humanity in general and godless humanity in particular is riddled with anxiety. We have seen that trusting in the sovereignty and goodness of God gives contentment and freedom from worldly anxiety. There is, of course, no way for the unbeliever to enjoy this contentment. To enjoy the peace of God, one must have peace with God.

Unfortunately, our people are catching the world's disease. Worldly madness is rubbing off on Christians, especially in the form of denying responsibility for their actions. When it comes to anxiety, depression, and lack of contentment, Christians are attributing those sins to mental health disorders rather than accepting responsibility for their false beliefs, worldly attitudes, and sinful actions. You have many congregants who would say they "have anxiety" rather than saying "I am anxious." They would say "I have depression" rather than "I am depressed." We, as shepherds of the flock and undershepherds of Christ, must call sin what God calls sin. "Be anxious for nothing" and "do not worry" are commands of Scripture. We may no more claim that we need not obey those commands because of a mental health disorder than we may claim that we need not obey commands against sexual sin because we have an addiction, are homosexual, or have gender dysphoria. Some are more prone to sins of anxiety, depression, and discontent than others are. But anxiety is a sin, and happiness is a command (Phil. 3:1; 4:4). We are commanded to be content (Heb. 13:5). Constraints, real or imagined, don't exempt us from obedience to Christ.

What can you do about it? At the risk of redundancy, preach the Word! Preach the truth of Scripture, all of it. Don't shy away from any of its truth, as all of it is profitable for your people. Counsel the truth of Scripture. Show them God's ultimate triumph over all sin and evil. Lead your people in the knowledge that God is sovereign and good and that discontent, anxiety, and depression are sinful denials of both truths. You do them no service by allowing them to think that this is a normal or acceptable state of mind for believers. It isn't! We would never take that approach with murder, gossip, or pornography. You wouldn't deny that those things are sin or suggest that they are medical conditions for which secular treatment is needed. We wouldn't justify it with, "Well, we all murder sometimes," "We all gossip," or "We all look at pornography from time to time." You wouldn't if you're a shepherd. You would tell them to stop, repent, and obey the Word of God while providing them with help, encouragement, and accountability. And if they refuse to turn from their sin, you'd begin church discipline. We should do no less with these sins of anxiety and discontentment. I say that with a shepherd's heart for the people of God. Godliness with contentment is indeed great gain! Contentment is a rare and precious jewel that results in the peace of God, happy and joyful Christian lives, and better relationships for God's glory. Work hard, pastor, to help your people acquire contentment.

DISCUSSION QUESTIONS

1. In Philippians 4:11–12, Paul says he has learned the secret of contentment. What are some of the implications of contentment being a knowable secret?

2. Have you learned the secret of contentment? What are some ways you can help others learn it as well?

3. Have you experienced a time when you felt that God failed to provide for something you thought you needed? What lessons did you learn?

4. What kinds of sinful fear afflict you? What things are you tempted to fear? How does the sovereignty and goodness of God address that fear? What characteristic of God are you doubting in the moment of fear?

5. How much of your sinful worry stems from a concern for what others think of you? Discuss how the fear of man is a snare (Prov. 29:25). In what ways do you fall prey to the fear of man?

6. What does it mean to fear God? What kind of fear should we have of Him? How does fearing man differ from fearing God? Are they different kinds of fear or the same?

7. What is your estimate of yourself, your talents, and your duties? What is God's estimate of those things?

8. Discover and explain four Scriptures that demonstrate that anxiety is a sin and contentment a command.

RECOMMENDED READING

The Rare Jewel of Christian Contentment by Jeremiah Burroughs

Stressed Out: A Practical, Biblical Approach to Anxiety by Todd Friel

Why Are You Afraid? by Darrell Harrison and Virgil Walker

God, Greed, and the (Prosperity) Gospel: How Truth Overwhelms a Life Built on Lies by Costi W. Hinn

Health, Wealth, and Happiness: How the Prosperity Gospel Overshadows the Gospel of Christ by David W. Jones and Russell S. Woodbridge

Anxious for Nothing: God's Cure for the Cares of Your Soul by John F. MacArthur Jr.

Charismatic Chaos by John F. MacArthur Jr.

The Pursuit of God by A. W. Tozer

God Doesn't Try

Part 3

God's Infallible Work in the Church

Chapter 7:

God Doesn't Try to Build His Church

7

It's a tale as old as time: a struggling church got a new pastor.

The church considered it a fresh start. The pastor viewed it as a revitalization effort. He was aware of their recent history, and it wasn't flattering. The church had been slowly bleeding members for the last few years as young couples, families, and leaders left for various reasons. The previous pastor outlived his effectiveness and stayed longer than he should have. His unwillingness to receive correction and surrender control strangled the vitality of the church. The deacon board did nothing to provide direction for an increasingly discouraged congregation.

At first, everyone was excited about the new pastor. But before long, he felt pulled in a number of conflicting directions. Desiring a quick fix for their recent decline in attendance, the deacons started pressing for changes that promised rapid growth. Many of the former members now attended a trendy, flashy church that advertised its Sunday services as relevant, contemporary, and fresh. The new pastor wanted to center the worship services around expository preaching, but the deacons feared it would be more of the same. The previous pastor had fashioned himself an expository preacher, and, according to the deacons, that had almost killed a church once full of life and vitality. Their confidence in the sufficiency of the Word and its vital role in pulpit ministry was shaken.

Without being openly hostile to expositional preaching, the deacons started moving away from it. The denomination recommended church growth programs that promised success. Though never openly expressing it, a number of the leaders were jealous of the trendy church only a couple miles away whose Sunday services were the talk of the town. Attendance there was growing, and they were adding services to accommodate "the Lord's blessing."

When a few who had previously left heard about the new pastor, they returned to see if his preaching might satisfy their starving souls. They were refreshingly fed by his clear, doctrinal, and practical sermons but wondered how long he could endure under the pressure from those seeking to shape his priorities and preaching.

What's a pastor to do when the pressure to grow the church is palpable and people are impatient?

OUR FASCINATIONS WITH FADS

Celebrity pastors, church growth "experts," and marketing gurus aren't short on suggestions. The "solutions" come on the church scene as fast and frequently as *Christianity Today* can publish magazines and Christianbook can distribute catalogs. Each fad assaults the church with all the pomp and hype you might expect from the latest Marvel movie, and it lasts almost as long. Every current must-read found on the front page of the latest Christianbook catalog will, within twelve months, be relegated to the clearance section and shilled for a quarter of its original price. We're bombarded by an endless offering of programs, books, curricula, study guides, teachings, and videos promising intimacy with God, spiritual transformation, and church growth.

In twenty-five-plus years of pastoral ministry, I've watched more fads, fashions, and fascinations blow across the church scene than I care to count. In the late eighties, the seeker-sensitive movement was getting started while the Moral Majority was promising to "save America" with church-sponsored boycotts and voter information guides. In the early nineties, Gwen Shamblin's *Weigh Down Workshop* infiltrated thousands of churches only to be replaced by the Edenic diet, the Daniel diet, and eventually Ezekiel bread a couple of decades later. The *Fifty Day Spiritual Adventure* was promoted on Christian radio and used annually in thousands of churches. The nineties was the decade of "purpose," with *The Purpose Driven Life*, *The Purpose Driven Church*, and the *40 Days of Purpose* campaigns. The church suffered through the "What Would Jesus Do?" marketing fad, the Left Behind series of books and movies, and the Promise Keepers movement. *Experiencing God*, *The Prayer of Jabez*, and *Secrets of the Vine* all promised us success in life and ministry. *The 7 Laws of the Teacher* and *The Seven Laws of the Learner* changed preaching and teaching in the local church. The spiritual warfare movement offered deliverance from demons, healing from past sins, and broken bondages. Neil T. Anderson's *The Bondage Breaker* products were widely used for counseling and "spiritual warfare." The seeker-sensitive movement of the eighties spread relentlessly, boasting growing churches and "relevant" sermons. We see the fruit of that movement today, and it is a disastrous disappointment. With no self-examination or self-awareness, Evangelicalism moved on through the small group movement, numerous Charismatic revivals,[1] and the emergent church movement. Now the social justice movement is the new Evangelical fascination, and "woke Christianity" is all the rage.

Are you exhausted yet? I wish I could say the above is a comprehensive list of movements and methods that have plagued Evangelicalism. Unfortunately, it's only a representative sample. Most who read that survey of Evangelical fads won't recognize most of them, and that is to my point. They are forgotten. They disappeared from the church scene as fast as they arrived. The fruit of these passing fancies is as substantive and lasting as the morning dew. In a few cases, like the pragmatic, seeker-centered church growth movement or the Marxist social justice movement, the fruit will be a generational, spiritual, soul-destroying devastation perpetrated upon future generations. These fads were "clouds without water," "autumn trees without fruit," and "wandering stars."[2] Unfortunately, Evangelicalism's thirst for these short-lived fancies continues unabated.

What fuels the never-ending parade of pleasingly packaged programs? It is a function of supply and demand. The dearth of biblical exposition, clear theological preaching, and Word-centered church worship has created an increasingly undiscerning church community that longs for religious trifles and trinkets to adorn their Christian facade. For products to have the greatest appeal to the largest audience, they must be crafted for the masses. They are, by necessity, designed to be as banal, man-centered, and superficial as possible.

---

1. The Toronto Blessing, Brownsville Revival, Asbury Revival, and countless local manifestations around the country boasted millions of attendees but left a wake of undiscerning Christians and disillusioned false converts who had heard just enough truth to get inoculated against the true gospel.

2. These phrases are taken from Jude's description of false teachers (Jude 12–13) whose grandiose promises are never realized. Like dark storm clouds, these passing fashions promise food, life, and refreshment for a dry and weary soul. Eventually, the clouds pass and the land is as parched as before.

Clear theology and biblical exposition don't sell well in modern Evangelicalism. The spiritually immature and doctrinally vacuous Christian subculture demands products and programs that only cultivate even greater spiritual immaturity and doctrinal indifference. That paves the way for the next wave of products and fads that promise to scratch the itch. Unfortunately, these are just more of the same—spiritual poison oak.

Now, back to the new pastor. Like a new coach hired to revitalize a struggling franchise, he feels pressure to grow the church. No pastor wants the flock to shrink in size and influence. Naturally, the much-ballyhooed methods and movements can be appealing. It is tempting to think that we'll miss the work of the Spirit if we don't adopt the latest church growth strategies and marketing methodologies. Behind the endless stream of popular programs, fading fads, and marketing madness is the patently unbiblical and blasphemous assumption that Jesus is *trying* to build His church and needs our help.

JESUS'S PROMISE TO BUILD HIS CHURCH

> Now when Jesus came into the district of Caesarea Philippi, He was asking His disciples, "Who do people say that the Son of Man is?" And they said, "Some say John the Baptist; and others, Elijah; but still others, Jeremiah, or one of the prophets." He said to them, "But who do you say that I am?" Simon Peter answered, "You are the Christ, the Son of the living God." And Jesus said to him, "Blessed are you, Simon Barjona, because flesh and blood did not reveal this to you, but My Father who is in heaven. I also say to you that you are Peter, and upon this rock I will build My church; and the gates of Hades will not overpower it. I will give you the keys of the kingdom of heaven; and whatever you bind on earth shall have been bound in heaven, and whatever you loose on earth shall have been loosed in heaven." (Matt. 16:13–19)

Jesus's promise to build His church has been a source of encouragement, confidence, and strength to countless Christians over the centuries. Missionaries have faced daunting challenges and endured hostile environments convinced that their labor for the sake of the gospel and the ingathering of God's people was not in vain (2 Tim. 2:10; 1 Cor. 15:58). Many have rested in the assurance that God's purposes are being infallibly accomplished and His church built through their simple, faithful efforts. Jesus's words have been an impetus for missions, as thousands have sacrificed to take the gospel to unreached peoples with confidence that Christ cannot fail to fulfill His promise and accomplish what He intends.

This confidence is possible because Jesus's words are missing one short, simple word that would forever change the import of His promise: *try*.

"I will *try* to build My church."

"I *will* build My church."

There is a world of difference between those two statements.

If Jesus had said He would *try* to build His church, it would admit the possibility of failure. It would suggest He may not succeed despite His best efforts, resources, and desire to accomplish His goal. Failure would be a real possibility. Unforeseen circumstances or a lack of power or planning might thwart His intentions.

Since the Lord of the church doesn't lack power, wisdom, or resources to accomplish whatever He wills, failure isn't a possibility. If failure isn't possible, then Jesus doesn't *try* to build His church. He has ordained the end. He has ordained all the means to that end. He lacks no knowledge of past, present, or future things which might hinder His work. He lacks no wisdom to infallibly overcome all opposition, so no person or devil can outmaneuver Him. He lacks no power or authority (Matt. 28:18) to effectively conquer every resistance, every kingdom, and every enemy. He must and will get every last soul He intends. On the last day, the church will be faultless, complete, and perfect (Jude 24; Eph. 5:27). It will lack nothing. It will lack nobody. It will be the fullness of everything He has intended from eternity past.

Our temporal, limited perspective isn't a good vantage point from which to evaluate the work of our sovereign God in building His church. From our perch atop this cultural, political, terrestrial dunghill, the condition of the church can look pretty grim. We see her flaws. We see the unqualified leaders, ravenous wolves, cowardly shepherds, false teachers, apostates, compromisers, grifters, and craven opportunists that litter the church scene. We see the doctrinal compromises, aberrant theology, and spiritual lethargy. Some churches close and others divide. The church in our own nation is shrinking in numbers and sinking into doctrinal indifference, liberal theology, and in some cases, outright apostasy. The thoughtful observer has to wonder if we are on the threshold of some very dark days. These are just a sampling of threats *inside* the church.

The external threats are no less ominous. We've lived through a time in recent years when the government has used a "public health crisis" to shut down churches and silence Christians while promoting the open gathering of regime-approved political protests. Our culture is increasingly hostile to the Christian worldview and biblical truth. The true church is being attacked from without by government agencies, cultural institutions, educational establishments, and the entertainment industry. The levers of power and influence in our culture are turned against us. Faithful Christians, pastors, and churches are becoming targets of a death culture that hates God and seeks to extinguish any reference to Him from the public conversation. We feel the tide turning. We sense that difficult times are coming (2 Tim. 3:1–9).

Should we worry that Jesus might be having difficulty accomplishing His purposes for the church? Does He need help? Is our assistance crucial to the success of His endeavor? Is He *trying* to build His church, or is He succeeding in His purposes and accomplishing His will perfectly on schedule?

Despite threats both internal and external, Jesus is building His church. He will not fail. He cannot fail.

THE CHURCH: HIS PERFECT PLAN

The choosing, calling, and perfecting of those who belong to Christ wasn't an afterthought in God's plan. The church wasn't plan B among God's options for the redemption of sinners. Though the inclusion of gentiles as "fellow heirs and fellow members of the body, and fellow partakers of the promise in Christ Jesus through the gospel" is a mystery not revealed in the Old Testament (Eph. 3:5–6), those included in that body were chosen "in Him before the foundation of the world, that [they] would be holy and blameless before Him" (Eph. 1:4). God's plan for His church predates creation itself. Paul said in 2 Timothy 1:9–11 that He "has saved us and called us with a holy calling, not according to our own works, but according to His own purpose and grace which was granted us in Christ Jesus from all eternity, but now has been revealed by the appearing of our Savior Christ Jesus."

God the Father has chosen a people for His own possession (Titus 2:14). He has elected them "by the sanctifying work of the Spirit, to obey Jesus Christ and be sprinkled with His blood" (1 Pet.

1:1–2). They are a "chosen race" (1 Pet. 2:9), spanning the better part of two thousand years, comprised of men and women from every tribe and tongue and nation (Rev. 5:9; 7:9).

Those chosen by the Father have been given to the Son. Jesus expressly said that He came down from Heaven to fulfill the will of the Father—namely, to give eternal life to all those given to Him. Further, Christ came to secure their salvation and raise them up on the last day (John 6:35–40, 44). He has promised to gather all His sheep, lay down His life for them, and secure them everlastingly (John 10:11–18, 25–30). As our great High Priest, He uses His unlimited authority to give eternal life to those the Father has given Him (John 17:2), protect them from the world (John 17:14–15), sanctify them (John 17:17), and bring them to everlasting glory (John 17:24). Christ gave Himself up for His church "so that He might sanctify her, having cleansed her by the washing of water with the word, that He might present to Himself the church in all her glory, having no spot or wrinkle or any such thing; but that she would be holy and blameless" (Eph. 5:25–27).

This is the promised glory of the church: chosen by the Father from eternity past for eternity future, drawn to the Son in time, redeemed by the blood He shed for her, regenerated by the Holy Spirit, and kept by the intercessory work of her great High Priest. The bride of Christ will be presented complete, blameless, and perfect on the day of Christ Jesus. If one chosen soul should be lost, Christ would fail to accomplish what the Father sent Him to do. The intentions of the triune God in His redeeming work would be incomplete and His plan and purpose thwarted (Isa. 46:10; Job 42:2).

Individual believers are "living stones, . . . being built up as a spiritual house for a holy priesthood" (1 Pet. 2:5). Paul describes the bride of Christ as a building ("God's household"):

> So then you are no longer strangers and aliens, but you are fellow citizens with the saints, and are of God's household, having been built on the foundation of the apostles and prophets, Christ Jesus Himself being the corner stone, in whom the whole building, being fitted together, is growing into a holy temple in the Lord, in whom you also are being built together into a dwelling of God in the Spirit. (Eph. 2:19–22)

What will this spiritual house look like in eternity? Will it be incomplete, a paltry shell of its intended grandeur? Will it lack perfection and beauty? Or will it be exactly what the sovereign, omniscient, and all-wise God planned from eternity past?

Jesus said, "I *will* build My church."

NONE CAN STOP HIM

Christ is the Lord of the church, its authoritative Head (Eph. 1:22; 4:15; 5:23; Col. 1:18). He purchased every last one of His people with His own blood (Acts 20:28) and thus He owns us. We are His slaves (Rom. 6:18; Eph. 6:6; 1 Cor. 6:19–20; 7:22). He lacks no authority or power to fulfill His promise to build His church. The "working of the strength of His might" was put on display

> when He raised Him from the dead and seated Him at His right hand in the heavenly places, far above all rule and authority and power and dominion, and every name that is named, not only in this age but also in the one to come. And He put all things in subjection under His feet, and gave Him as head over all things to the church, which is His body, the fullness of Him who fills all in all. (Eph. 1:19–23)

All the demons of Hell, all the powers of the world, all the governments on Earth, all the kingdoms under the heavens, and all the rebellion of sinful men cannot thwart His purposes. They don't pose a hindrance or even the smallest obstacle to Him. When they collude together to overthrow His plan, oppose His work, and resist His will, "He who sits in the heavens laughs, the Lord scoffs at them" (Ps. 2:4).

John MacArthur offers this encouragement,

> No matter how liberal, fanatical, ritualistic, apathetic, or apostate its outward adherents may be, and no matter how decadent the rest of the world may become, Christ will build His church. Therefore, no matter how oppressive and hopeless their outward circumstances may appear from a human perspective, God's people belong to a cause that cannot fail.[3]

TRIUMPHANT VS. TEMPORAL

It would be helpful at this point to distinguish between the ultimate state of the church and its current temporal expressions. To

---

3. MacArthur, *Matthew 16–23*, 30.

affirm everything above is not to say that every local church is a perfect picture of the spotless bride promised in Ephesians 5. Even local congregations in the New Testament era had their share of problems. The Corinthian church was plagued by quarrels (1 Cor. 1:11–12), pride (4:18), immorality (5:1–2), drunkenness (11:21), and doctrinal confusion (7:1; 12:1; 15:12, 35). The Galatian churches were wooed by false teachers toward denying the very gospel that saved them (Gal. 1:6–7). The church in Ephesus was eventually taken over by self-seeking false teachers with whom Timothy had to contend (1 Tim. 1:3–4). Disunity and factions threatened the church in Philippi (Phil. 4:2) and Colossae (Col. 3:14–15). Even the church in Jerusalem had to face cultural and ethnic challenges that threatened to divide the brethren (Acts 6:1; 11:1–2; 15:1–7).

I'm not suggesting the church in its current state is a perfect and full "spiritual house." Actually, the analogy of a spiritual house is helpful in distinguishing between the church in its current state and the church in its perfect and eternal glory. Currently, we're "being built together into a dwelling of God in the Spirit" (Eph. 2:22). The building of His church is ongoing and incomplete while the elect are being gathered in and His sheep are being called to the Shepherd (John 10:16). We can acknowledge that the church is incomplete, imperfect, and inglorious without in any way doubting that the final product will be a complete, perfect, and glorious bride. It would be foolish to step onto a construction site of a new home and assess the final condition of the house based solely on what is visible while the workers are building. The scattered lumber, incomplete siding, and partial roof aren't representative of the finished product. The absence of trim, paint, cabinets, and carpet cast no aspersions on the character or competence of the craftsman at work.

So it is with the church. We don't yet see what it will be. While the Lord is building His church, we get a mere glimpse of its final form. We know it will be big, composed of innumerable millions of living stones. We know it will be diverse, including men and women from every tribe and nation. We know it will be righteous, sanctified, and glorified, being indwelt by the Holy Spirit. We know it will be complete and perfect, as our sovereign Lord will not do otherwise. When all the living stones are put in place and all His people are glorified, His work of building His church will be complete.[4]

---

4. Those already gathered in Heaven have overcome the world, the flesh, and the devil. They have been delivered from their bodies of death (Rom. 7:24) and await a perfect glorified

INDIFFERENCE OR CONFIDENCE?

The proper response to Jesus's promise is not indifference but confidence. We don't apathetically resign ourselves to whatever fate might bring. We don't neglect our responsibilities to evangelize, disciple, and serve in the church while using the sovereignty of God as a cover for our disobedience. The excuses for disobedience sound something like this: Why should I serve? Christ is going to build His church with or without me. Why should I evangelize if God is going to sovereignly save all He has chosen? Why should we support missions if building His church is certain and there is no possibility He can fail?

These and similar statements betray an immaturity in those who express them. They fail to distinguish between the end God has appointed and the means He has ordained to that end. God will accomplish all His purposes in spite of the disobedience of His people. Their ignorance and apathy pose no more hindrance to His purposes than the hostility and hatred of His enemies. Those who misuse biblical truth to excuse their disobedience will lose their reward and answer to the Lord (2 Cor. 5:10).

Instead, Jesus's promise should motivate us to faithful, diligent, and industrious labor in the gospel for His sake. Paul was convinced that Jesus Christ would build His church, and that conviction energized his faithful service (2 Cor. 5:11, 20–21). God's electing grace in eternity past motivated Paul to endure hardships and give his life for the gospel (2 Tim. 1:9–10; 2:10; 4:6–8).

We know Christ can't fail and that no purpose of His can be thwarted. We know whatever work He has called us to will accomplish what He has ordained. Those works which He has foreordained for us (Eph. 2:10) will bear the fruit that He intends, fruit for which we shall receive the reward. We can labor with certainty that our work in the Lord is not in vain. "Therefore, my beloved brethren, be steadfast, immovable, always abounding in the work of the Lord, knowing that your toil is not in vain in the Lord" (1 Cor. 15:58).

Jesus doesn't *try* to build His church. He is building it. He will build it. He will complete it. That glorious truth will motivate us to industry, fruitfulness, and loyalty, not indifference, fecklessness, and laziness.

---

body (Rom. 8:11, 18–25; 1 Cor. 15) raised in power and glory. All His sheep will be gathered as well and raised up on the last day (John 6:39–40, 44).

THE FRUIT OF FAITHFULNESS

Woe to the pastor who builds his own kingdom and fashions a church after his own image! Woe to the pulpiteer who imagines his clever campaigns, marketing manipulations, and shrewd strategies will be rewarded on the day of Christ. The Lord of the church will reprove the hirelings who foolishly suppose they can improve upon God's ordained means for shepherding His people.

Jesus Christ doesn't *need* us (Acts 17:24–25). He chooses to use us, and that is for our sake, not His. The Lord doesn't need our programs, talents, natural charisma, marketing prowess, clever ideas, cultural sensitivities, administrative successes, or leadership acumen.

The wisdom of man will build a "church" indistinguishable from a local business or Rotary Club. Those goat farms litter the landscape in America. Leaders are selected because they are successful in business, well-known in the community, possess natural leadership abilities, or give generously to the work. The style and philosophy of ministry are shaped by the culture, the fleshly desires of unbelievers, and social media trends. Pragmatism dictates the church's mission and leadership structure. The goals are set by men and women with little theological training and even less discernment. Without a doubt, the wisdom of man can build an appealing and polished facade.

Biblical wisdom begins with the fear of the Lord (Prov. 1:7; 9:10). The faithful servant begins with the instruction of Scripture and seeks to obey it faithfully. Scripture and Scripture alone must determine church structure (eldership), ecclesiology, philosophy of ministry, and approach to preaching (exposition). The fruit produced by the Spirit of God through our obedience will be abundant and eternal. Though the faithful shepherd may be unrecognized in this world, the Lord will abundantly reward his faithfulness in the one to come (1 Pet. 5:1–4).

The ills that plague modern Evangelicalism grow out of the fear of man. Man-fearers abandon exposition in favor of "contemporary" and "relevant" sermon series. Man-fearers avoid preaching through Bible books in long, in-depth, theologically robust, serial, expository series. Man-fearers plant churches that cater to niche demographics, whether cultural (cowboy church), economic (church for businessmen), or ethnic (black church[5]). Man-fearers invent clever ways to

---

5. Any attempt to cater the church's ministry to one particular ethnicity is a fundamentally unbiblical philosophy of ministry. Racial reconciliation has taken place through Christ's work on the cross and is best expressed when Christians gather around their fellowship in Christ and

observe the ordinances (clown Communion[6]). Man-fearers devise clever marketing strategies, book ideas, and publicity stunts (Ed Young's Sexperiment[7]) designed to appeal to the flesh and satiate an idolatrous heart.

Christ needs none of it. He doesn't bless it and won't reward it. Those who please men cannot be servants of Christ (Gal. 1:10).

CONCLUSION

There's nothing more anathema to most church leaders than being seen as foolish or out of touch in the eyes of the world. This cowardly craving for the world's approval among Evangelical leaders is a blight on the modern church. Too many pastors think their job is to make the church acceptable in the eyes of the world. To this end, they relentlessly court the approval of God's sworn enemies. They can't imagine the church flourishing without the praise of the world's power brokers and institutional gatekeepers. They minister as if the success of Christ's church rests upon their clever conventions and worldly wisdom. They have forgotten the somber warning of James 4:4: "You adulteresses, do you not know that friendship with the world is hostility toward God? Therefore whoever wishes to be a friend of the world makes himself an enemy of God."

God isn't trying to gain the world's approval. He is unconcerned with what worldlings think about His faithful and obedient people. He doesn't need the world's endorsement to accomplish His purposes. He calls His people out of the world and commands us to repent of our affections for it.

> Do not love the world nor the things in the world. If anyone loves the world, the love of the Father is not in him. For all that is in the world, the lust of the flesh and the lust of the eyes and the boastful pride of life, is not from the Father, but is from the world. The world is passing away, and also its

---

common communion in the Lord's death rather than according to ethnic identity. See Harrison and Walker, *Just Thinking: About Ethnicity*, and chapter 11 in this book.

6. This was a fad a few years ago. Some churches had their ushers dress in clown outfits to serve the Communion elements to their congregation. For an explanation and critique, see https://www.echozoe.com/archives/2064 (https://perma.cc/2HJC-98D9).

7. Ed Young challenged married couples in his church to engage in sexual intercourse every day for seven consecutive days. He turned this challenge into a church campaign and a book published by FaithWords. For more information, see the video entitled "Sexperiment—24 Hour Bed-In Recap," posted on Ed Young's YouTube channel (https://www.youtube.com/watch?v=9ijizXuH_Gs).

lusts; but the one who does the will of God lives forever. (1 John 2:15–17)

God isn't trying to make His ministers respectable in the eyes of the world. We should expect the world to regard the servants of Christ as foolish, weak, and ignorant (1 Cor. 1:18–2:5). We should gladly embrace their reproach rather than cravenly courting their respect (1 Cor. 4:10; Heb. 10:32–36; 11:24–26). Remember the exhortation in Hebrews 13:13–14: "So, let us go out to Him outside the camp, bearing His reproach. For here we do not have a lasting city, but we are seeking the city which is to come." This we do knowing we shall receive the reward for faithful service (2 Tim. 4:6–8).

God isn't trying to win as many as possible to His cause. There is no possibility He can fail to gather in all those for whom Christ died. Jesus isn't trying to be loved by the world. In fact, the world's rejection is exactly what every follower of Christ should expect (John 15:18–25).

Christ is building His church! He isn't *trying* to build His church.

FOR THE SHEPHERDS

Devote yourself to this glorious institution and fulfill your ministry. "But you, be sober in all things, endure hardship, do the work of an evangelist, fulfill your ministry" (2 Tim. 4:5). Love, serve, disciple, lead, protect, pray for, and feed the church. Eschew the frivolous Christian fads, fashions, and fancies. Devote yourself to the basics. Preach the Word. Observe the ordinances. Disciple the faithful and discipline the erring. Lift high the Word of God and find your satisfaction and glory in making Him known to His people.

Be ready and content to embrace the scorn the world will heap upon you as a faithful servant of Christ. Don't run from it. Don't seek the world's approval. Instead, be comforted by its disapproval. Know that the faithful shepherd will receive the reward (1 Pet. 5:1–4).

Finally, thank the Lord that by His good providence He has determined to use you for the advancement of His purposes, the building of His church, and the greatness of His name. Be humbled by it. It is a gift of God's grace not just that He has included you among His elect, but that He has chosen to use you to serve them by preaching His Word.

> O, when will Christians learn . . . that their puny, polluted offerings of works are not necessary to God? He permits them to work, as a favor, in order to do them good, personally,

because he loves them, and desires to honor them, not because he needs them.

Adoniram Judson[8]

DISCUSSION QUESTIONS

1. How do the truths explained in this chapter comfort and encourage you? How do they motivate you to service and diligent work for Christ and His purposes? Do you regularly evangelize your community? In what way, and by what means? Have you ever engaged in disciple-making? What role does prayer (corporate and private) play in these activities?

2. Have you ever been discouraged by the present state of the church? How does Jesus's promise encourage you?

3. How does a proper understanding of the future, glorious, ultimate state of the church inform how we treat others in this time of incompletion and imperfection?

4. Who is responsible to build the church? How does this inform the way Sunday morning worship is conducted? How does it inform our broader church ministry?

5. Which threats are more dangerous to the church—internal or external? Explain your answer.

RECOMMENDED READING:

The Missionary-Theologian: Sent into the World, Sanctified by the Word by E. D. Burns

A Supreme Desire to Please Him: The Spirituality of Adoniram Judson, chapter 4, by E. D. Burns

---

8. Wayland, *A Memoir*, 2:368, quoted in Burns, *The Missionary-Theologian*, 141. For a developed treatment of Judson's self-denying trust in God's providence, see chapter 4 in Burns, *A Supreme Desire to Please Him*. I highly recommend Burns's writings cited here.

This Little Church Went to Market: The Church in the Age of Entertainment by Gary E. Gilley

Just Thinking: About Ethnicity by Darrell Harrison and Virgil Walker

Ashamed of the Gospel: When the Church Becomes Like the World by John F. MacArthur Jr.

The Bleeding of the Evangelical Church by David F. Wells

No Place for Truth, or, Whatever Happened to Evangelical Theology? by David F. Wells

Courageous Churchmen: Leaders Compelling Enough to Follow by Jerry Wragg

Chapter 8:

God Doesn't Try to Organize His Church

8

Am I a pastor?

I (Dave) was at a conference of youth workers several years ago when the person on the platform asked all the pastors to stand for recognition. Should I stand or not? I was then, as I am now, recognized as a pastor in our church. I'm a pastor as Scripture defines the office, but I knew in that moment that I wasn't what the speaker and the vast majority of attendees would have considered a pastor. Most Evangelical Christians view "the pastor" as a seminary-trained single authority who preaches every Sunday. He is the CEO of the church, called by a pulpit committee, contracted to perform services, and compensated by the church. I am not that. I am not supported by my church nor seminary trained. I was never offered a contract, and I don't preach most Sundays. I am in no sense the CEO of my church. Someone has an incorrect definition of what it means to be a pastor, either Kootenai Church or most of Evangelicalism. Who's right? This chapter will lay out the biblical structure and qualification for eldership in a local church.[1]

Christians live in obedience to God. The Christian life is characterized by obedience (John 14:23–24). The Bible isn't merely a book of commands and principles comprising a handbook for Christian living. It is sufficient to answer all the ethical, theological, moral, and practical questions necessary to live God-honoring, obedient lives (2 Pet. 1:2–4). Paul reminds us that "all Scripture is inspired by God and

---

1. Don't get the wrong idea. It was great to sit and clap while Jim had to stand!

profitable for teaching, for reproof, for correction, for training in righteousness; so that the man of God may be adequate, equipped for every good work" (2 Tim. 3:16–17).

What's true for the individual Christian is also true for the corporate church body. God has revealed in His Word everything necessary to establish and organize His most treasured possession, His church. God's purpose for the church, individual believers, and all creation is His own eternal glory. His Word provides sufficient and clear instruction for the accomplishment of the church's God-ordained purpose. As the church obeys her sovereign Head, the Lord Jesus Christ, His rule and reign over His people through His Word is manifested in this world. God rules His church by His Word through the leaders that He calls and qualifies. We mustn't ignore His clear commands regarding the structure and organization of His church, thereby robbing His people of blessing, protection, and guidance.

In this chapter, we will examine the fundamental issue of the structure of church leadership and then address other aspects of church life and polity related to it. For any function of church life and ministry to align with God's Word, the proper structure and leadership must be in place. We must first have churches structured and led God's way. God didn't *try* to establish a good structure for His church, leaving us completely untethered and free to organize and qualify leaders according to our own preferences. He has given us clear, authoritative direction on how local church bodies are to be organized. Much of the impotence and insanity of modern Christianity is a result of willful ignorance of, and disobedience to, these important principles.

APOSTLES AND PROPHETS

In Ephesians 4, Paul turns his attention to the gifts God has given to the body of Christ and mentions four groups of gifted people: apostles, prophets, evangelists, and pastors.

> Therefore it says,
> "When He ascended on high,
> He led captive a host of captives,
> And He gave gifts to men."
> (Now this expression, "He ascended," what does it mean except that He also had descended into the lower parts of the earth? He who descended is Himself also He who ascended far above all the heavens, so that He might fill all

things.) And He gave some as apostles, and some as prophets, and some as evangelists, and some as pastors and teachers, for the equipping of the saints for the work of service, to the building up of the body of Christ; until we all attain to the unity of the faith, and of the knowledge of the Son of God, to a mature man, to the measure of the stature which belongs to the fullness of Christ. As a result, we are no longer to be children, tossed here and there by waves and carried about by every wind of doctrine, by the trickery of men, by craftiness in deceitful scheming. (Eph. 4:8–14)

Earlier in Ephesians, Paul gives a glorious description of the church, the bride of Christ, to whom these gifted men are given.

So then you are no longer strangers and aliens, but you are fellow citizens with the saints, and are of God's household, having been built on the foundation of the apostles and prophets, Christ Jesus Himself being the corner stone, in whom the whole building, being fitted together, is growing into a holy temple in the Lord, in whom you also are being built together into a dwelling of God in the Spirit. (Eph. 2:19–22)

The church is built on the foundation of the teaching of the apostles and prophets (Eph. 2:20). This designation encompasses the canon of Scripture we have today, both the Old and New Testaments. "Prophets" is shorthand for the Old Testament Scriptures. "Apostles" signifies the revelation of the New Testament given through the apostles and their close associates. There are no prophets or apostles in the church today.[2] Those were principal offices forming a completed foundation upon which Christ continues to build His church, Christ Himself being the corner stone. The church exists by the authority, power, and grace of its Lord, King Jesus, Who gave those gifted men their gifts and used them to transmit His Word to His body.

---

2. There are some within nominal Christianity who believe the office of apostle exists today. It clearly doesn't. The qualifications for apostleship in Acts 1 (in particular, the requirement that an apostle be an eyewitness to the risen Christ) unequivocally preclude the possibility of modern apostles. While all Christians are apostles in the sense of being "sent ones," the last person appointed to the office of apostle was Paul. Those who claim to be modern-day apostles are universally charlatans and generally heretics.

EVANGELISTS ("SHEEPDOGS")

Unlike apostles and prophets, evangelists, the third group listed in Ephesians 4, aren't "foundational" nor is there much further teaching on their role within the church. There are no qualifications given for evangelists and no direction on how the church is to use them generally. Apart from Ephesians 4:11, the word *evangelist* is only found two other times. The first is in reference to Philip in Acts 21:8: "On the next day we left and came to Caesarea, and entering the house of Philip the evangelist, who was one of the seven, we stayed with him."[3] Philip preached the gospel in Samaria with great success (Acts 8:4–8) and then shared the gospel with the Ethiopian official, leading to his salvation and immediate baptism (Acts 8:35–38). The second reference is in Paul's command to Timothy to "do the work of an evangelist" (2 Tim. 4:5).

While the lack of further teaching on the qualifications for, or the definition of, the evangelist role leads us to believe this isn't a church office, there is nothing to indicate that we won't continue to see individuals uniquely gifted as evangelists. In fact, throughout the history of the church, some people have been especially gifted at, and burdened with, sharing the gospel with unbelievers. While all Christians are given the ministry of reconciliation (2 Cor. 5:18) and the duty to proclaim the gospel to unbelievers, there are some to whom God has given a strong desire to evangelize along with the corresponding gifts. I heard one commentator[4] suggest that while elders serve the flock as shepherds, evangelists serve as sheepdogs. They bring wayward sheep out of the goatherds and into the flock where shepherds can protect and guard them. This is a fine analogy for the work of the evangelist and conveniently leads me to the work of an elder.

PASTORS: THREE DESIGNATIONS, ONE OFFICE

Ephesians 4:11 lists one more group of gifted people we haven't yet addressed: pastor/teachers. There is some debate about whether this is referring to two distinct roles or to one office of pastor that clearly includes teaching. We, along with most commentators, believe this describes one office, with the term *teachers* emphasizing

---

3. Philip the Evangelist is "one of the seven," a reference to the men chosen in Acts 6, a group regarded as the first deacons. It's interesting to note that Philip the Evangelist held multiple distinct roles in the early church.
4. I believe it was Todd Friel who made this comment on his excellent *Wretched* podcast. Todd is himself an exceptionally gifted evangelist, and we highly recommend his podcast, books, and other materials available at wretched.org.

the distinctive giftedness and activity of those who hold the office of pastor. This office is referred to in three different ways in the New Testament: elder, overseer, and shepherd. Each description is significant and tells us something important about the office of elder. Let's take a brief look at these three words.

The word translated "elder" is *presbyteros* and was generally used to refer to an older person, more specifically a leader in a Jewish synagogue or Christian church. When early Christians, mostly of Jewish background, first identified leaders in their churches, it was natural for them to use the familiar term for men who led a congregation.[5] Although no specific age requirement is listed in the qualifications (1 Tim. 3, Titus 1), it's clear that eldership requires a degree of spiritual maturity ordinarily possessed by those older in the faith. The term *elder* speaks of the maturity and wisdom necessary for spiritual leadership in the church.

The second word used for this office is *episkopos*, translated "overseer."[6] It is used as a noun in reference to the office in 1 Timothy 3 and Titus 1, the two books most focused on elders in the New Testament. It was used outside the New Testament to identify a supervising official who had responsibility and accountability for those under his watch. In the context of the church, it describes the necessity of vigilance and active concern on the part of the elder. The overseer is to pay attention to the life of the church, oversee its spiritual well-being, and lead for the benefit and blessing of those under his oversight.

The third word used to describe the New Testament office of pastor is translated "shepherd." The Greek word *poimēn* means "someone who tends and guards sheep." It's used of the shepherds in Luke 2. Christ applied it to Himself in the Good Shepherd Discourse (John 10) and used the verb form to command Peter to "shepherd [His] sheep" (John 21:16). Applied to the role of a church leader, the noun form is used only once, appearing in the aforementioned list of gifted people in Ephesians 4:11, where it is unfortunately transliterated "pastor."[7] The verb form is used in reference to the office

---

5. It's interesting to follow the usage of the word *elder* throughout the New Testament. In the Gospels and up through Acts 6:12, *elders* always refers to Jewish leaders. From Acts 11 onward, the usage is mixed, though it mostly refers to leaders of Christian congregations. In the Epistles, it always refers to leaders of Christian churches.

6. This is sometimes transliterated "bishop."

7. The English word *pastor* is found only once in the New Testament in the NIV, NASB, LSB, KJV, and NKJV, all in Eph. 4:11. While *poimēn* is used many times, it is only transliterated

twice. In Acts 20:28, the elders of the church at Ephesus were told to "shepherd the church of God which He purchased with His own blood." In 1 Peter 5:2, Peter exhorts elders to "shepherd the flock of God among you." The term is a beautiful metaphor for the work of the elder. As a shepherd of the sheep knows the sheep, provides for the sheep, lives among the sheep, and protects the sheep, so does a shepherd of the flock of God care for the saints under his oversight.

These three words (*elder*, *overseer*, and *shepherd*) all refer to a single office. They aren't three separate and distinct roles wherein some men serve as elders, others as overseers, and still others as shepherds or pastors. This is clearly proven by the way these words are used together in three different passages.

All three words are used of the same group of men in Acts 20:17: "From Miletus he [Paul] sent to Ephesus and called to him the *elders* of the church." Paul charges these elders in verse 28 to "be on guard for yourselves and for all the flock, among which the Holy Spirit has made you *overseers*, to *shepherd* the church of God which He purchased with His own blood." In that verse, Paul refers to the elders as "overseers" and encourages them to "shepherd" the flock.

In Paul's pastoral Epistle to Titus, he uses the terms *elder* and *overseer* synonymously:

> For this reason I left you in Crete, that you would set in order what remains and appoint *elders* in every city as I directed you, namely, if any man is above reproach, the husband of one wife, having children who believe, not accused of dissipation or rebellion. For the *overseer* must be above reproach as God's steward, not self-willed, not quick-tempered, not addicted to wine, not pugnacious, not fond of sordid gain. (Titus 1:5–7)

Peter exhorted the elders to "shepherd" and "exercise oversight" over the flock:

> Therefore, I exhort the *elders* among you, as your fellow elder and witness of the sufferings of Christ, and a partaker also of the glory that is to be revealed, *shepherd* the flock of

---

"pastor" this one time. The Latin word for "shepherd" is *pastor*, so the word *pastor* came to be associated with the office described as "shepherd" in Eph. 4:11. The verb form used in Acts 20:28 and 1 Pet. 5:2 was never transliterated "pastor" but always translated "shepherd." Transliterations can cause confusion, as the terms *apostle*, *bishop*, and *baptize* demonstrate. It's no less the case with *pastor*. Were this word consistently and correctly translated "shepherd" rather than "pastor," we would have a much clearer understanding of the role. The ESV is among few English versions that translate *poimēn* as "shepherd" in Eph. 4:11.

God among you, *exercising oversight* not under compulsion, but voluntarily, according to the will of God; and not for sordid gain, but with eagerness; nor yet as lording it over those allotted to your charge, but proving to be examples to the flock. (1 Pet. 5:1–3)

These passages are more than sufficient to demonstrate that we shouldn't make unbiblical distinctions in the church regarding this single office and ministry. A shepherd is an elder is an overseer.

PASTORS: A PERVASIVE PLURALITY

The New Testament consistently refers to multiple elders in individual churches. In the references below, notice how consistently the reference to "elders" (plural) is found with "church" (singular).

Luke refers to a plurality of elders in Judea: "And this they did, sending it in charge of Barnabas and Saul to the elders" (Acts 11:30). Likewise in the region of Lycaonia they "appointed elders for them in every church" (Acts 14:23). The church in Jerusalem enjoyed a plurality of elders: "The apostles and the elders came together to look into this matter" (Acts 15:6). This is the pattern seen in a passage we already cited: "From Miletus he sent to Ephesus and called to him the elders of the church" (Acts 20:17).

The New Testament Epistles reflect the same pattern of multiple elders in a single church.

In Crete: "For this reason I left you in Crete, that you would set in order what remains and appoint elders in every city as I directed you" (Titus 1:5).

In Philippi: "Paul and Timothy, bond-servants of Christ Jesus, to all the saints in Christ Jesus who are in Philippi, including the overseers and deacons" (Phil. 1:1).

In Judea: "Is anyone among you sick? Then he must call for the elders of the church and they are to pray over him, anointing him with oil in the name of the Lord" (James 5:14).

In Ephesus: "The elders who rule well are to be considered worthy of double honor, especially those who work hard at preaching and teaching" (1 Tim. 5:17).

In Asia Minor: "Therefore, I exhort the elders among you, as your fellow elder and witness of the sufferings of Christ, and a partaker also of the glory that is to be revealed . . ." (1 Pet. 5:1).

In Thessalonica: "But we request of you, brethren, that you appreciate those who diligently labor among you, and have charge over you in the Lord and give you instruction" (1 Thess. 5:12).

To the Hebrews: "Obey your leaders and submit to them, for they keep watch over your souls as those who will give an account. Let them do this with joy and not with grief, for this would be unprofitable for you" (Heb. 13:17).

The biblical pattern in the New Testament is that each church has a plurality of elders. No other model for church leadership is provided in Scripture. While Titus was commanded to appoint elders in the churches (Titus 1:5), this structure isn't given as an imperative generally to the church. However, the lack of an explicit command shouldn't be taken as permission to ignore the accounts of a universal biblical pattern. We are not free to regard this as one among many options for leadership structure in the local church. We may reasonably deduce from these accounts God's ordained pattern for church government. I can't understand how any reasonable, unbiased reader could suggest any other structure as a preferable or permissible option.

Opponents of this biblical pattern point to three apparent exceptions they say indicate that a plurality of elders is only one of many permissible models. First, James was the lone elder in the Jerusalem church. Second, apostolic delegates like Timothy and Epaphras served as single leaders of local churches. Third, each of the seven churches mentioned in Revelation had an "angel" or "messenger" that must be identified as the single elder presiding over the church. When examined, however, these examples fail to prove a God-ordained exception to the pattern.

First, James, the Lord's half brother, is a truly remarkable individual. He was a unique figure in the early church. He is referred to as an apostle in Galatians 1:19. He was definitely a key leader in the church at Jerusalem, but so were the apostles Peter and John. The church had two apostles and the Lord's half brother in leadership. We should be careful drawing conclusions from this for modern churches. At the very least, it's clear James wasn't a lone leader of the church in Jerusalem.

The second exception cited is the work of apostolic delegates like Timothy and Epaphras. Timothy was an evangelist and did pastoral work under the leadership of Paul. Normally, Timothy traveled with Paul and wasn't a local church elder. Epaphras had shared the gospel with the church in Colossae (Col. 1:7–8) and apparently in Laodicea and Hierapolis as well (4:13). He had traveled to Rome with Paul (4:12) and wasn't planning a return to Colossae (4:7–9). While these men may have served as teachers and briefly shepherded local flocks as they traveled, they weren't elders. They weren't appointed as elders in the churches. They weren't recognized from among the congregation and didn't live with those congregations. They were more like a modern traveling evangelist than elders. Even if they had served as elders for a brief time, there is no evidence that they did so as lone pastors in the church without the aid and accountability of other elders.

The third alleged exception is the seven churches in Revelation that are each said to have an angel (Rev. 1:20–3:22). The address to the church in Ephesus is typical: "To the angel of the church in Ephesus write: The One who holds the seven stars in His right hand, the One who walks among the seven golden lampstands . . ." (Rev. 2:1). The word translated "angel" generally means "messenger" and can refer to angelic or human messengers. There are good reasons to believe this refers to a human representative or messenger in each of the churches. Some suggest this refers to a person from each church who was given this letter by John to deliver to their congregations. Others see this as a reference to a leader within the church, likely an elder. The argument against plurality proceeds as follows: Since this was a single messenger, and since we can assume it was an elder, it must follow that there was a single elder in each church.

I agree that *angel* is most likely a human being and not an angelic spirit. Though it could refer to a spiritual leader, even an elder, from each church, that is not evidence that these churches had only one elder. A letter being addressed to *an* elder in a church doesn't prove that he was the *only* elder in that church. Plurality in eldership is the pattern for a local church in the New Testament, these three "exceptions" notwithstanding.

We might wonder, How does a plurality work? People in our church membership classes often ask something like, "Doesn't someone have the final say?" How can you run a church or any organization by committee? Doesn't it just devolve into arguments and schisms? Someone has to be in charge, don't they?

Before we can answer the practical question of how plurality works, we first have to briefly consider what Scripture requires of the men who are recognized to serve in that office.

PASTORS: QUALIFICATIONS

The qualifications for eldership are listed in 1 Timothy 3:1–7 and Titus 1:5–9. I won't deal thoroughly with all of the qualifications here, but I will mention a few that pertain to the functioning of a biblical eldership.[8] Elders are required to be of a certain character. Besides the qualifications regarding desire for the office, general moral conduct, and an ability to teach and lead others, Paul lists qualities that indicate a gentleness and stability of character. An elder must be temperate, sensible, respectable, considerate, peaceable, not self-willed, not quick-tempered, not pugnacious, and self-controlled.[9] To the extent that a congregation takes these qualifications seriously, spending time to examine a man's character to ensure they are present, the church will be blessed by able leadership who will bring the Word of God to bear on the life of the church. Qualified men aren't concerned about their status or getting their own way. This is so important. Compromise on these qualifications will cause trouble for the church more certainly than will a failure to follow the biblical structure. A plurality of elders with one or more unqualified men makes impossible the kind of shepherding the Spirit of God intends for His church. These biblical guidelines on eldership (plurality and qualification) are linked in two important ways. First, disqualified men will not function well in a plurality. Second, compromise on the biblical structure often results in compromise on the qualifications. A plurality of men qualified according to the standards in 1 Timothy 3 and Titus 1 is the New Testament model for the church.

PASTORS: PRACTICAL PLURALITY

With the importance of qualified eldership established, we can answer the question of how a plurality works. A plurality of elders functions because each man is determined to obey the Lord's will revealed in His Word. Qualified men, while sinners like the rest of us, won't seek their own but instead the glory of God and the good of the

---

8. Alexander Strauch defines biblical eldership, including exhaustive consideration of the qualifications, in his excellent and comprehensive book *Biblical Eldership*. We're deeply indebted to Strauch for his careful exposition of the relevant passages and recommend this book highly. Strauch's companion book, *The New Testament Deacon*, is also excellent. We also recommend his books *Acts 20* and *Paul's Vision for the Deacons*.

9. These qualifications are found in 1 Tim. 3 and Titus 1.

church under their care. Disagreements may arise due to different interpretations of a biblical text or the application of the text to a decision at hand. Even then, qualified men of the character described in 1 Timothy 3 and Titus 1 can come to a consensus in love and mutual respect. Biblical eldership isn't a committee of sin slaves warring against others to divide spoils amongst themselves. It is a plurality of regenerated men who are above reproach, determined to serve their common Master, familiar with the teaching of God's Word, and willing to work together in love and mutual respect. They are gospel men, Bible men, who understand their position before Christ, the Great Shepherd, Savior, and Lord. Such a group doesn't need a CEO, a final arbiter of each decision, or a tally of votes. They need the Word of God, shared hermeneutics, and a strong desire to obey what God has said about any particular issue that arises in the life of their beloved church.

Practically and biblically, this doesn't preclude the recognition of a leader among leaders. While all elders hold the same office, there will be natural leaders among them. Some elders will spend more time on the affairs of the church and bring more to the table when they meet to discuss the concerns of the church body. Though we all spend time doing the work of pastoring, our own church has an especially gifted, church-supported elder who devotes much more of his time to teaching, preaching, and administration than the rest. While I see no biblical support for formally ranking positions within the eldership (senior pastor, associate pastor, assistant pastor, etc.), it is apparent that there were leaders among equals in the New Testament. When the apostles are listed, we always see Peter first. James, John, and Andrew are always listed in the top four. Philip is always fifth, the first in the second group of four, which also includes Bartholomew, Matthew, and Thomas. James the son of Alphaeus, Simon the Zealot, and Judas the son of James are next. Judas Iscariot is always listed last, if at all. In the Gospels and Acts, Peter's leadership is more prominent than that of Simon the Zealot. It's reasonable to assume this "first among equals" pattern, not being condemned in Scripture, is something God may use in other settings where multiple people hold the same office. We observe this natural and informal leadership "ranking" among elders where biblical eldership is practiced, and it does not undermine the functioning of a plurality.

There is much to recommend the plural elder model described in the New Testament. Above all, this is the biblical pattern. While admittedly this structure isn't explicitly required by scriptural imperative, it is strongly suggested by its absolute ubiquity in the churches established by the apostles.

There are several practical benefits of this form of leadership. First, it prevents a concentration of power in the hands of one individual. Having all leadership decisions fall under the authority of one person is a recipe for corruption. While a careful qualification process will reduce the grave danger of having a single sinner in charge of an entire congregation, that concentration of power is still unwise. It's much better to have accountability among equals who may remove an erring elder, even the chief among them, in the case of a disqualifying event. This promotes accountability and care in the leadership of God's precious bride.

Second, while this structure prevents the concentration of power in one unaccountable individual, it allows for quick and efficient decision-making among a group of biblically minded, qualified men. Rather than running every decision through a congregational vote, a committee, or a church board, a biblical eldership can quickly apply the pertinent passages of Scripture and make an appropriate decision.

Third, it restores eldership to its proper role and function. This isn't a class, career, profession, title, or royal endowment. Eldership is work within the local church for the benefit of the body of Christ and the glory of God. An elder should serve as long as he desires the work and is biblically qualified for it. There is no shame in a man stepping down from the eldership role because of a disqualification, particularly if it isn't due to sin on his part. A man may become incapable of teaching because of illness or debilitation. That isn't shameful. He can and should step out of the elder role or be removed without any shame. He can be afforded love, respect, and gratitude for the time he spent serving in the work. If he has been dependent on the church for his income, the church could provide his income until other provisions can be secured. At the same time, eldership doesn't have term limits. Such man-made parameters are unbiblical limitations. An elder who is qualified, remains qualified, and continues to desire the work of the overseer should remain in that ministry. An elder recognized by the local church, unless he loses interest in the work or is disqualified, should remain an elder. If a man no longer desires the work, there is no shame. In fact, there is much honor in stepping down and leaving the work to those who desire it and will do it with excellence.

Contrast this with the completely unbiblical model of pastoral ministry practiced in modern American Evangelicalism. A person is mystically "called" to ministry by God Himself, gets a professional certification in seminary,[10] and is then "called" to a particular local church. He is now endowed with the title[11] of "Pastor" and must always and forever be the Pastor. This is not the biblical pattern!

The biblical pattern is men in the local church serving as shepherds who teach, preach, and care for the spiritual needs of the flock. They're recognized by the church and its other elders by the work they do in the body of Christ. They are tested, examined according to the biblical qualifications, and then recognized as elders/pastors by the congregation. As long as they desire the work and remain qualified for it, they should continue to serve. Titus wasn't told to appoint elders in every city based on transcripts of the graduates from Crete Theological Seminary. It is far preferable to have spiritual leaders rise up from within the congregation. Men who are known by the congregation, whose qualifications are manifest, will have a deep and abiding love for the flock. They will more effectively shepherd the sheep that comprise *their* church than a professional hired because of a flashy resume will.

---

10. Seminary training is a great thing, a terrific way to learn the Scriptures. I encourage anyone who desires the office of overseer to pursue as much formal education as they can in a sound biblical institution. However, Scripture doesn't require formal education for eldership in 1 Tim. or Titus. Elders can't be new converts, not because they lack education but "so that [they] will not become conceited and fall into the condemnation incurred by the devil" (1 Tim. 3:6). Titus 1:9 requires that an elder be "holding fast the faithful word which is in accordance with the teaching, so that he will be able both to exhort in sound doctrine and to refute those who contradict." There may be no better way to accomplish this than formal seminary training, but a degree is no substitute for the qualifications in 1 Tim. and Titus. The apostles were qualified for eldership but generally weren't formally educated beyond their normal Jewish upbringing. Paul was formally trained, but the others apparently were not. Peter, James, John, and Andrew were fishermen. Matthew was a tax collector. Luke was a physician. While the comparison here is somewhat tentative given the omniscience of the divine Person, even our Lord wasn't, in His humanity, formally trained beyond the norm for a Jewish man of His day.

11. This is another unbiblical and dangerous practice. The words used to define this role (*elder*, *overseer*, and *shepherd*) are never used as honorifics or titles for the men who hold the office. The New Testament doesn't describe the office that way. An elder is a qualified man from among the congregation serving in the congregation. These men would be known and addressed by their names. The use of "Reverend Smith" or "Pastor Jones" or "Bishop Jakes" is unbiblical and sets men above the church body. This isn't God's plan for the office. Biblical elders are undershepherds charged with the oversight and protection of a portion of Christ's church in their care. They aren't demigods or a priestly clergy class that mediates between God and His people.

Finally, this form of eldership provides for the sharing of burdens that accompany the work. Different men can lead in separate areas of ministry or address diverse questions according to their individual level of knowledge or expertise in various areas of theology. Each will have unique relationships with the members of the church and can minister accordingly. Elders deal with wolves, implement church discipline, make unpopular decisions, shepherd through disappointments and temptations, and bear burdens they can't ethically (and often legally) share outside of the eldership, not even with their wives. Elders need a group of peers with whom they can share burdens, discuss concerns, and pray for the sheep.

PASTORS: MALE ELDERSHIP

Biblical complementarianism[12] is under an egalitarian[13] siege in churches in the United States. There are other great resources on this issue.[14] I'll focus here on three key questions. First, does God's Word permit women to serve in the office of elder? Second, does God's Word permit women to teach or exercise authority over men in the local church? Third, who are "the women" in 1 Timothy 3:11? I'll address these in order, as the answers to the first two questions have bearing on the third.

First, does God's Word permit women to serve in the office of elder? This is an extremely simple question to answer with even the most cursory glance at 1 Timothy 3, without any appeal to other Scriptures. A consideration of all the relevant passages will ultimately affirm the conclusion drawn from a quick observation of the qualifications in 1 Timothy 3 and Titus 1.

1 Timothy 3:1: "It is a trustworthy statement: if any man aspires to the office of overseer, it is a fine work he desires to do." Does this disqualify women? Not necessarily. "Any man" translates a Greek word that can apply to either gender. A better translation choice would be "anyone." So far, so good for the egalitarian reader. The next verse, however, is a dagger to the heart of the egalitarian pipe dream. "An overseer, then, must be above reproach, the husband of

---

12. Complementarianism is the belief that while women are ontological equals to men, they have a subordinate role in the church and home. The Scriptures stipulate that maleness is a qualification for eldership.

13. Egalitarianism is the belief that there is no functional difference between men and women apart from the obvious physical characteristics. Egalitarians would argue that women may serve as elders and teach men in the church.

14. For a comprehensive study of biblical gender roles, see Piper and Grudem, *Recovering Biblical Manhood & Womanhood*.

one wife" (1 Tim. 3:2). The phrase "husband of one wife" is notoriously difficult to interpret as a qualification. Does it mean an elder may never have divorced, that he may not be or have been a polygamist, or simply that the man must be upright in his marital and sexual relationships? This is an important question in qualifying elders. We must get the qualifications right, but for our purposes here, what matters is that this unquestionably refers to a *man*. The phrase is *mias gynaikos andra* and literally translates to "one-woman man" or "one-wife husband." The fatal problem for an egalitarian interpretation of this verse is that *andra* unquestionably refers only to a male person. There is no honest translation or interpretation that could render that word "woman" or a genderless word like "person." This is not a "one-man woman" or a "one-person person." It's a one-woman *man*. Egalitarian interpreters don't even try to deny this fact. They simply nullify the force of the qualification by claiming it's a historical or cultural artifact referring to marital fidelity. To the egalitarian, this qualification only means that an elder, either man or woman, must be faithful to their spouse. To them, the gender is irrelevant while the moral uprightness is not. If the qualification is understood as a prohibition of prior divorce among elders, it can apply to either a man or woman. If it refers to marital fidelity, it can apply to men or women.

If the egalitarian view is correct, then the same argument applies to the male leadership in the home mentioned in the same context: "He must be one who manages his own household well" (1 Tim. 3:4). To be consistent, the egalitarian argument would extend to the home and so overturn the clear teachings of passages like 1 Peter 3:1–6:[15]

> In the same way, you wives, be submissive to your own husbands so that even if any of them are disobedient to the word, they may be won without a word by the behavior of their wives, as they observe your chaste and respectful behavior. Your adornment must not be merely external—braiding the hair, and wearing gold jewelry, or putting on dresses; but let it be the hidden person of the heart, with the imperishable quality of a gentle and quiet spirit, which is precious in the sight of God. For in this way in former times the holy women also, who hoped in God, used to adorn themselves, being submissive to their own husbands; just as Sarah obeyed Abraham, calling him lord, and you have become

---

15. See also Eph. 5:22–33 and Col. 3:18.

her children if you do what is right without being frightened by any fear.

All passages commanding male headship in the church and in the home would be viewed as merely limited cultural instructions on the general precept of submission. In order to claim a limiting historical context to 1 Timothy 3:2, the consistent egalitarian must claim that same limitation for 1 Timothy 3:4. Is it just as acceptable in the mind of God for a woman to lead the household with a submissive husband as for a man to lead the household with a submissive wife? If not (and clearly the Bible directs male headship in the home), then the egalitarian must admit that neither is male headship in the church a limited historical/cultural artifact.

May a woman serve as an elder in the church? The answer is clearly no. We can't dismiss all the Scriptures that have bearing on the question by claiming that they are limited to the first-century cultural setting.

Second, may a woman teach or otherwise exercise authority over men in the church? How does the egalitarian dismiss 1 Timothy 2:11–14? It reads,

> A woman must quietly receive instruction with entire submissiveness. But I do not allow a woman to teach or exercise authority over a man, but to remain quiet. For it was Adam who was first created, and then Eve. And it was not Adam who was deceived, but the woman being deceived, fell into transgression.

Clearly, Paul isn't appealing to any cultural convention in his instructions. He's stating a principle that transcends culture. His command is anchored in the order of creation. The creation order is a historical reality that trumps all cultures, traditions, and biases. Paul is presenting a theological argument grounded in historical realities, not cultural norms. The Holy Spirit says, through Paul, that a woman isn't allowed to teach or exercise authority over a man. The reason Paul gave was not a concern that female teachers would be offensive to the Ephesian culture. Nor was he narrowly concerned about one particularly domineering woman that he wanted silenced. He provides no cultural or situation-specific argument that would narrowly limit this clear prohibition. Paul prohibits women from these functions and roles because Adam was formed first and Eve was deceived.[16]

There are instances in Scripture where the cultural expression of a command is limited and time-bound though the principle is universal and timeless. Such is the case with the head coverings in 1 Corinthians 11 or the kiss of love in 1 Peter 5. Could the qualification that an elder be a man be another such example? Might it be merely a cultural relic of a bygone patriarchal society?

Unlike the passages that speak of head coverings (1 Cor. 11:1–16) and the kiss of love (1 Pet. 5:14),[17] there is no way to separate the principle of male headship from its expression. One can demonstrate biblical submission without a head covering in modern culture. One can express love and fraternal intimacy in church without kissing. There is no way to obey the command in 1 Timothy 2 and 3 regarding male headship in the church while women are teaching men and exercising authority over them. This absolutely precludes the possibility of interpreting Paul's words in 1 Timothy 3 and Titus 1 as merely cultural constraints.

Third, who are the "women" in 1 Timothy 3:11? In order to answer this question, we have to examine the context. At the risk of redundancy, below is the entire passage, with verse 11 in italics.

> It is a trustworthy statement: if any man aspires to the office of overseer, it is a fine work he desires to do. An overseer, then, must be above reproach, the husband of one wife, temperate, prudent, respectable, hospitable, able to teach, not addicted to wine or pugnacious, but gentle, peaceable, free from the love of money. He must be one who manages his own household well, keeping his children under control with all dignity (but if a man does not know how to manage his own household, how will he take care of the church of God?), and not a new convert, so that he will not become conceited and fall into the condemnation incurred by the devil. And he must have a good reputation with those outside the church, so that he will not fall into reproach and the snare of the devil.

---

16. There is no need here of further exposition of these verses, as the reader will find good treatments of these passages elsewhere if interested. See MacArthur, *1 Timothy*. See also Moo, "What Does It Mean Not to Teach or Have Authority Over Men?," in *Recovering Biblical Manhood & Womanhood*, ed. Piper and Grudem, 179–93.

17. See also Rom 16:16, 1 Cor. 16:20, 2 Cor. 13:12, and 1 Thess. 5:26.

> Deacons likewise must be men of dignity, not double-tongued, or addicted to much wine or fond of sordid gain, but holding to the mystery of the faith with a clear conscience. These men must also first be tested; then let them serve as deacons if they are beyond reproach. *Women must likewise be dignified, not malicious gossips, but temperate, faithful in all things.* Deacons must be husbands of only one wife, and good managers of their children and their own households. For those who have served well as deacons obtain for themselves a high standing and great confidence in the faith that is in Christ Jesus. (1 Tim. 3:1–13)

The word translated "women" in verse 11 is also the word for "wives" and is sometimes translated that way (e.g., in the KJV, NKJV, and ESV). There are three possible interpretations of who these women are:

First, the women are female elders. This interpretation can be dismissed because it contradicts the passages cited above.

Second, the women are female deacons. Given Paul's prohibition in 1 Timothy 2:11–14, these female deacons wouldn't be permitted to exercise authority over men, and the office and work of the deacon does involve an exercise of authority. This would, therefore, provide a limited role for female deacons as ministers of mercy to women and children only. This seems awkward but wouldn't violate any of the provisions or prohibitions above. It would, however, contradict the qualification for a deacon found in 1 Timothy 3:12: "husbands of only one wife." This is identical to the qualification for elders in 1 Timothy 3:2. In both cases, women are disqualified. Women can't be men or husbands as the verse requires (our culture's insane confusion about gender realities notwithstanding).

Third, the women are wives of deacons and/or elders. This interpretation wouldn't contradict the larger context or other passages in Scripture. It actually fits the context quite well. As a practical matter, these qualifications for the wives of the men in leadership would be extremely important. The church would be well served to analyze the qualifications of the man *and his wife* in light of this passage. A faithful elder must have a wife who is faithful, dignified, temperate, and able to maintain confidentiality. This is equally important for the faithful deacon, whose service would involve him heavily in the personal lives of people in need.

The reference to women seems strangely placed. Though an admittedly uninspired outline of the passage, the following breakdown of 1 Timothy 3 makes the meaning clearer:
- Qualifications for Elders (vv. 1–7).
- Qualifications for Deacons, Part 1 (vv. 8–10).
- Qualifications for Wives of Elders and Deacons (v. 11).
- Qualifications for Deacons, Part 2: Marital Lives (vv. 12–13).

I believe this third interpretation best fits the context. The qualifications for elders' and deacons' wives serve to protect interests of the church.

This doesn't mean women can't serve as ministers of mercy or teach women and children. A church is free to have ministry roles that are not defined as offices in Scripture, so long as their function doesn't violate biblical commands or principles. A woman may serve in any role within the church, so long as her work does not include teaching or ruling over men.

CONCLUSION

God has revealed a clear biblical pattern for the leadership structure of His local church bodies: a plurality of qualified elders. This is for His glory and the good of His people. He isn't *trying* to discover a good structure for church leadership. He doesn't need us to interpret away what He has clearly said regarding qualifications. We must not ignore His commands. Neither can we ignore principles clearly revealed or reasonably deduced from Scripture. The church is His. He has determined its organization and leadership structure. Ours is to submit to His direction.

FOR THE SHEPHERDS

In light of this teaching, here are four important questions every shepherd should answer. First, does your church have a biblical leadership structure? If your church has elders who aren't pastors, a board of deacons with oversight of the pastor, a single authoritarian pastor, or any other such nonsense, you don't have a biblical leadership structure. You must make every effort to teach your congregation about biblical elderships and biblical diaconates. Start with Alexander Strauch's two books mentioned earlier, *Biblical Eldership* and *The New Testament Deacon*. It may take some time and convincing, but in the end, we must encourage our congregations to live in obedience to Christ. The church has a prescribed function and a model structure to accomplish that function. We're without excuse before God if we ignore or disobey His will for the church. If you're a shepherd in a local church, you serve as undershepherd to your King. You are accountable for how closely you adhere to His commands and principles while serving Him.

Second, are you qualified? If you no longer desire the work or are otherwise unqualified, step down immediately from eldership with humility and grace. Let your last act as an elder be a memorable teaching moment showing the congregation the importance of having qualified elders who desire the work of ministry. Show them that God's Word must be obeyed at all costs.

If you're involved in a disqualifying sin issue, it should be made known as part of your separation from ministry. Repent and seek reconciliation. Don't hide from it. We're all sinners and have "an Advocate with the Father, Jesus Christ the righteous" (1 John 2:1–2). In your fall from ministry, teach by example what you didn't in word and deed. Don't leave the church but seek restoration and serve in a non-teaching role in submission to the remaining elders.

Third, are the other elders qualified? If not, lovingly approach them with 1 Timothy 3 and Titus 1 and point out their disqualification. If they are determined to reject truth for the sake of their position, work through the situation lovingly with the help of other elders. At some point, this could become a church discipline issue, but hopefully men who desire to obey the Lord will step down if confronted with a disqualification.

Remember, no one is entitled to eldership by experience or certification. It's not a lifetime appointment. It's a role, a function, a particular ministry within the context of the local church. A man who wanted to be a full-time teaching elder when twenty-one may change his mind later without shame or reproach.

Both eldership and disqualification may be temporary. A man may become disqualified and restored. It's also true that we often restore too quickly and thoughtlessly, so care must be taken. Multiple restorations of a disqualified elder are generally unwise. Some sins are permanent disqualifications because they irreparably damage credibility, rendering a man's leadership forever ineffective. It's possible, however, that a man may become temporarily disqualified and later be restored once the disqualifying condition is resolved.

Fourth, does your church have women in authority or leadership positions over men? It is a sad state of affairs when this has to be mentioned, but female eldership is prohibited. The Lord has made this clear in His Word, and to disobey is inexcusable. If your church has female elders, you must remove them lovingly and immediately. If you're a woman placed in the role of "elder," you aren't a "female elder." No such thing exists. You must submit to the Scriptures. If you do, you'll repent of your sin and step down from your leadership role. You will use your gifts in ways permitted in Scripture at the direction of the elders in your church.

Jim took Kootenai Community Church through a transition from an unbiblical form of church leadership to biblical eldership with a biblical diaconate over twenty years ago. If you're expecting the next sentence to be about the results of that transition, you've missed the point entirely. The results aren't what matters. Our church, including its elders, are, in this matter at least, living in obedience to the will of God revealed in His Word. That is what matters.

DISCUSSION QUESTIONS

1. What unbiblical ideas were corrected by this extended teaching on church leadership? Did you find it difficult to relinquish any of your previously held beliefs? Which ones and why? Is the structure of church leadership described in this chapter new to you?

2. How does a biblically correct leadership structure prevent sin and problems in the local church?

3. What role does or should a local congregation serve in the qualification, selection, training, and recognition of its own elders?

4. What do the Greek words for *elder* and *pastor* tell us about the work of their ministry?

5. Why are the qualifications given in Scripture essential to the success of the plurality leadership structure?

6. What are the two scripturally defined offices in the post-apostolic church? How do they complement one another?

7. Name the evangelists mentioned in the New Testament. What was their role? How does the role of an evangelist compare to the office of elder? How do they complement one another?

RECOMMENDED READING

The Master's Plan for the Church by John F. MacArthur Jr.

1 Timothy in The MacArthur New Testament Commentary series by John F. MacArthur Jr.

"What Does It Mean Not to Teach or Have Authority Over Men?" (chap. 9 in *Recovering Biblical Manhood & Womanhood*) by Douglas Moo

Recovering Biblical Manhood & Womanhood: A Response to Evangelical Feminism edited by John Piper and Wayne Grudem

Acts 20: Fierce Wolves Are Coming; Guard the Flock by Alexander Strauch

Biblical Eldership: An Urgent Call to Restore Biblical Church Leadership by Alexander Strauch

The New Testament Deacon: The Church's Minister of Mercy by Alexander Strauch

Paul's Vision for the Deacons: Assisting the Elders with the Care of God's Church by Alexander Strauch

Chapter 9:

God Doesn't Try to Prosper His Church

9

Things in this world are backward. I'm not talking about the fact that you can order a steak well-done in a restaurant. Or that there is someone in the kitchen with a conscience seared enough to actually make it that way. That's a travesty in its own right, and one about which we need to have a national conversation. As inexplicable as that is, I have something more perplexing in mind.

Does the bride of Christ occupy the place in this world you would expect given the Bible's teaching on the love of Christ for His church? In other words, if what Scripture says concerning the body of Christ is true, why are we so abandoned, persecuted, and deprived in this world? Why is the church rejected, scorned, and reproached? Is God unconcerned with this? If not, why does He allow it? Is He unable to provide for and protect us as He intends? Is He *trying* to prosper, protect, and provide for His bride?

THE GLORIOUS CHURCH OF CHRIST

The church is purchased with God's own blood (Acts 20:28) and comprised of individuals chosen in Christ before the foundation of the world (Eph. 1:4). Jesus referred to them as "My sheep" in John 10:25–30. They are predestined by the Father to be adopted into His family, having been redeemed at a very high cost—namely, the life of Christ (1 Pet. 1:17–19). The blood that purchased our redemption (Eph. 1:7) was shed by our God manifested in the flesh (John 1:1, 14). No greater price has ever been paid. No greater price could ever be paid.

In this case, the greatness of the payment doesn't reflect the worth of the object(s) purchased. We're sinners, ruined in our sin, lost, depraved, deserving only God's wrath and judgment. Our sin has merited eternal damnation. There is nothing lovely, alluring, or attractive about God-hating rebels. Any value we have is derived from the fact that God, for His own eternal glory and according to His own eternal purposes (Eph. 1:6, 12, 14), determined to glorify His holy name by redeeming rebels utterly unworthy of redemption.

These chosen people have been "blessed ... with every spiritual blessing in the heavenly places" (Eph. 1:3). They are likened to a "bride" (Eph. 5:22–33) and called the "body of Christ" (Eph. 4:12), a "holy temple," and a "dwelling of God in the Spirit" (Eph. 2:21–22). His "spiritual house" is "a chosen race, a royal priesthood, a holy nation, a people for God's own possession" (1 Pet. 2:5, 9–10).

Though He owns all men by right as their Creator, He owns the church in a very special sense as our Redeemer "who gave Himself for us to redeem us from every lawless deed, and to purify for Himself a people for His own possession, zealous for good deeds" (Titus 2:14). The Spirit of God indwells the church both individually (Rom. 8:9) and corporately (Eph. 2:22). Those who have been purchased by His blood are His slaves (1 Cor. 6:19–20), called into service and gifted (1 Pet. 4:7–11) to glorify Him through works He has foreordained for them (Eph. 2:10).

Our adoption into His family has secured our inheritance. We've been predestined to it (Eph. 1:5, 11). We're His children, "heirs of God and fellow heirs with Christ" (Rom. 8:17), "heirs of the promise" (Heb. 6:17) and "the grace of life" (1 Pet. 3:7). The inheritance reserved for us in Heaven is beyond our imagination (1 Pet. 1:3–5) and guaranteed by the Lord of the church (Col. 3:24). We'll receive the Kingdom (Luke 12:32) and reign on the Earth (Rev. 5:10).

We're "beloved by God" (1 Thess. 1:4), cherished (Eph. 5:29), and known by Christ (John 10:14–15). The Father has given us to His Son to redeem us and make us His own. There is no greater honor, privilege, or favor, and it was bestowed upon the most undeserving creatures.

If all that is true, and I'm convinced it is, why does the church suffer as she does? We might expect the church to occupy a more prominent position, experience more material blessings, and enjoy more favor in this world. It seems as if the church lacks the financial resources necessary to accomplish its task. This is often to blame for the closing of Christian colleges, the lack of missionaries on the field, and the paucity of church plants. Far too many pastors are bivocational out of necessity and not choice. Many are forced to leave ministry every year for secular employment. It seems that churches are closing faster than new ones are being planted. All too often, individual Christians are plagued by the same scarcity. The privation is particularly heart-wrenching outside the comforts of Western nations, where resources are plentiful compared to other countries around the globe.

The physical weaknesses and sufferings of the bride of Christ are constant and relentless. The wicked appear to escape the plagues common to mankind and enjoy good health, long life, and pain-free deaths (Ps. 73:3–5). The sharp pains of illness and the dull discomfort of bodily weaknesses, though not exclusively the lot and portion of the church, appear to afflict the righteous with disconcerting prejudice (Ps. 73:4–14).

This isn't even to mention the nearly ubiquitous reality of persecution that continually crushes many of our brethren around the world. Churches are burned. Pastors are imprisoned. Families are dispersed. Unbelievers oppress, enslave, torture, mutilate, and hunt Christians with impunity in some countries. In many nations, Christian believers aren't afforded the same liberties as unbelievers and are only allowed to worship within the confines of a regime-approved "church." In some places, the law actively discriminates against Christians, making the worship of God, obedience to His Word, and the evangelism of the lost extremely costly.

Around the world, it's difficult to find solid, doctrinally sound, biblical churches led by biblically qualified men. Even in our own nation, the "Christian West," biblical, expository churches are harder to find than a left-handed leprechaun. Some have to drive long distances to be part of the best church they can find, and even then, it isn't optimal. Others, because of physical ailments or disabilities, are unable to make the commute and instead stream distant church services to hear solid preaching. Their souls long for the fellowship and community that comes by in-person worship.

This ought not be! It's so tragic and heartbreaking! Why does the church have to endure this? The difficulties and deprivations endured by Christ's people seem entirely incongruous with Scripture's teachings regarding God's love, care, and concern for them.

If the Lord of the church lacks no resources, why do His people? If the Bridegroom has all authority, power, and provision and lacks no wisdom, knowledge, or love for His bride, why does He suffer her to endure such hostility from sinners and hardships in this world? The same apostle who said that Yahweh is not "served by human hands, as though He needed anything, since He Himself gives to all people life and breath and all things" (Acts 17:24–25) confessed of himself, "I have been in labor and hardship, through many sleepless nights, in hunger and thirst, often without food, in cold and exposure" (2 Cor. 11:27). If all we have comes from God, and we possess nothing we have not received from His gracious hand (1 Chron. 29:14–16; 1 Cor. 4:7), why does it seem as if the bride of Christ, for whom He shed His own precious blood, is deprived of the wealth of benefits at His disposal?

Is God *trying* to bless His church? Is He *trying* to provide the blessings He intends? Is there something in this world or in His church that stays His hand of grace? Is He *trying* to protect His church from persecution? Is He *trying* to prosper His bride? This tension is real and has been felt by saints through the ages.[1] Let's first dispatch a number of erroneous responses to this quandary.

DISPENSATIONAL AMERICANISM[2]

The latter half of the twentieth century witnessed the rapid spread and popularization of a "dispensational escapism" among Western Evangelicals. Riding the coattails of political movements like the Moral Majority[3] and coasting on the comforts provided by the capitalist system,[4] the American church enjoyed a measure of security,

---

1. Many saints in Scripture wrestled with the question, "Why do the wicked prosper?" That is the issue I've raised here. The dilemma is most pointedly addressed in Ps. 73, where Asaph asks and answers that question. See my (Jim's) book *The Prosperity of the Wicked*. We will return to Asaph's answer later in this chapter.

2. Note the order of these words. We're not calling this "American Dispensationalism." We don't believe that dispensational theology itself is to blame for the errors described below. Therefore, no form of dispensationalism, American or otherwise, should be misconstrued as support for the ideas critiqued here. We are both unapologetic pre-tribulational, premillennial dispensationalists. The critique in this section is offered against *some* in our own theological camp, broadly speaking.

3. Though we lament that we even have to say this, today's political climate forces us to draw clear and distinct lines. We do not object to the moral positions held by those on the "religious right." We are pro-life, politically conservative Christians who believe that abortion and homosexual conduct are sinful. We unapologetically affirm the Judeo-Christian worldview along with the ethical and moral standards derived from the Scriptures. But we object to political grifters using the church, the Scriptures, and moral issues to advance their party causes and fill their coffers while convincing believers that this constitutes the work of Christ in this world.

4. We do not object to capitalism at all. In fact, we are both committed capitalists. That system has created more wealth, freedom, and blessing than any other system. This is undeniably true, and our observation here is that it has benefited the church in America on the whole.

influence, and power unknown in other nations. The grifters of the "religious right" secured a seat at the table of political kingmakers. The power and financial resources leveraged by Christian leaders like Pat Robertson, Jerry Falwell, and Paul Weyrich tricked many Evangelicals into believing that the church in America could remain immune from persecution and suffering.

After the American-led victory of World War II, a spirit of religious patriotism and pride characterized our national identity. Humanly speaking, it was understandable. The "Christian West" had defeated some of the worst mass-murdering totalitarian regimes the world had ever seen. That indomitable spirit infiltrated the church and unconsciously crafted an eschatology to fit its own image. That eschatology is properly dubbed "Dispensational Americanism."

Though the label may be new, the teaching isn't. Undoubtedly, you've heard someone express the belief: "Before things get really bad in the world, the church is going to be raptured! Persecution can't come to the American church. We aren't appointed to wrath!" It was assumed that American Christians would ride atop their perch of cultural and political influence all the way to the pre-tribulation rapture, avoiding any of the persecutions, tribulations, and sufferings that have characterized the rest of Christian history.[5] In some circles, it was thought that the principles of American exceptionalism enshrined in the Constitution could be exported to the rest of the world through military occupation and/or American foreign policy. Christians overseas could enjoy the same perks of political power and influence if they would only adopt Western culture.

This teaching is quite insidious. It suggests that Western Christians have avoided suffering because we've done something right that believers around the globe haven't. Or perhaps God is sympathetic toward our unique American heritage and ideals. Eschatological escapism is oblivious to the sufferings of the church at large. Dispensational Americanism would craft a worldwide church after its

---

5. We believe in a pre-tribulation rapture (1 Thess. 4:13–18). We don't believe this guarantees any particular demographic of the church, either generational or national, a freedom from difficult times or suffering. Pre-tribulational teaching doesn't promise that Christians won't suffer, be persecuted, or live through difficult times. We acknowledge that conditions in our own nation could get really bad. We believe that things could get really, really, *really* bad before the Lord returns to take us home. We just don't believe that things will get "Revelation bad" before the rapture. We aren't promised freedom from the tribulations that characterize this life. However, we are promised deliverance from the Tribulation which brings the wrath of God on an unbelieving world. The point of this chapter isn't to defend a pre-tribulation or premillennial perspective but to critique an abuse of it.

own image, affluent and comfortable. Simply put, God's attempts to bless and prosper the church in America have been successful because of our constitutional form of government and capitalist free enterprise system. "We won't suffer persecution! We are America, baby!"

The answer offered by Dispensational Americanism to the perplexing question of whether God is trying to bless His church is "American" and not biblical. They think the church outside the US needs to embrace God's blueprint for success: capitalism, a constitution, and a pervasive, though nominal, "Christianity."

THE PROSPERITY GOSPEL ANSWER

For the sake of brevity, I'll lump together various related movements—the Charismatic movement, the Word of Faith movement, and the New Apostolic Reformation (NAR)[6]—under one umbrella: the prosperity gospel.

Word of Faith teachers claim that all sicknesses, even the smallest expressions of bodily illness, are outside the will of God for His people. Benny Hinn writes, "He promises to heal *all*—every one, any, any whatsoever, everything—all our diseases! That means not even a headache, sinus problem, not even a toothache—nothing! No sickness should come your way. God heals all your diseases."[7] He claims that "God's greatest desire for the church of Jesus Christ—is that we be in total and perfect health."[8] Hinn isn't outside the mainstream of the broader Charismatic movement. It isn't difficult to find the same ideas taught by Kenneth Copeland, Kenneth Hagin, Frederick Price, or Paul Crouch. The newer generation of Charismatic leaders have followed suit.[9]

Many in the Charismatic movement teach that it's always God's will for a Christian to be healthy and wealthy. Followers of Benny Hinn, Kenneth Copeland, and Creflo Dollar regard their lavish lifestyles, material prosperity, and inordinate wealth as evidence of God's blessing and favor. Allegedly, all God's children should expect

---

6. There are distinctives among these three movements not only in terms of leadership and theology but also their historical influence on American Evangelicalism. By lumping them together, I run the risk of painting with too broad a brush, but I believe I've accurately identified an area in which they share common ground.

7. Hinn, *"Rise & Be Healed!"*, 32 (emphasis in original).

8. Hinn, 65.

9. This isn't intended as a full critique of Charismatic doctrines or leaders. As mentioned in chapter 6, see Justin Peter's video seminar *Clouds Without Water* and visit his YouTube channel for more information on the false teachings of the Charismatic movement.

the same. God wants to bless His children with physical healing, unimaginable wealth, and spiritual power. All He lacks is our cooperation. He needs our faith, words, prayers, gifts, and permission. God is trying to bless, prosper, and protect His church, but His efforts are stymied by our lack of faith.

THREE ANCHORING TRUTHS

Sometimes God's providences eclipse His promises. The church is promised untold blessings, glories, and joys at God's right hand forevermore, yet we endure suffering and share His afflictions (Col. 1:24). The sufferings of the church in this world are real. Paul was sensitive to the possibility that believers who witnessed his suffering for the gospel might be discouraged by them. You can hear his pastoral concern in his words to the Ephesians: "Therefore I ask you not to lose heart at my tribulations on your behalf, for they are your glory" (Eph. 3:13). We aren't called to focus on our own afflictions, but to remember and reflect upon the sufferings of our Lord so that we might not lose heart. "For consider Him who has endured such hostility by sinners against Himself, so that you will not grow weary and lose heart" (Heb. 12:3).

We must be faithful to the end. We mustn't lose heart. Those who belong to Christ "are not of those who shrink back to destruction, but of those who have faith to the preserving of the soul" (Heb. 10:39). We have need of endurance so that we do not lose our confidence and our reward (Heb. 10:35–36). To that end, the afflicted bride of Christ must cling fast to three glorious and unchanging truths.

First, in this world, we will have tribulation. We shouldn't expect the approval of the world in this life. We can expect to bear the reproaches of Christ. There is no promise in Scripture of health, prosperity, or ease in this life. In fact, it is "through many tribulations we must enter the kingdom of God" (Acts 14:22). Jesus promised us the hostility of the world:

> If the world hates you, you know that it has hated Me before it hated you. If you were of the world, the world would love its own; but because you are not of the world, but I chose you out of the world, because of this the world hates you. Remember the word that I said to you, "A slave is not greater than his master." If they persecuted Me, they will also persecute you; if they kept My word, they will keep yours also. But all these things they will do to you for My name's sake,

God Doesn't Try

because they do not know the One who sent Me. (John 15:18–21)

He didn't hide the truth from us. "These things I have spoken to you, so that in Me you may have peace. *In the world you have tribulation*, but take courage; I have overcome the world" (John 16:33). There's no doubt as to the final victory. Though it has been secured, we don't enjoy it yet.

In this world, it isn't suffering that should surprise us, but success. We should expect the scorn of the world. Peter reminds us,

Beloved, do not be surprised at the fiery ordeal among you, which comes upon you for your testing, as though some strange thing were happening to you; but to the degree that you share the sufferings of Christ, keep on rejoicing, so that also at the revelation of His glory you may rejoice with exultation. If you are reviled for the name of Christ, you are blessed, because the Spirit of glory and of God rests on you. (1 Pet. 4:12–14)

Peter spent most of the first chapter of 1 Peter describing our inheritance, the glory reserved for us in Heaven, our salvation, and our ultimate eternal rejoicing. Interestingly, he doesn't see this as incongruous with the fact that we "share the sufferings of Christ" (1 Pet. 4:13). In fact, suffering is, for the believer, a source of great blessings. If we endure the hostility of sinners and suffer at the hands of the world, we are blessed. "If you are reviled for the name of Christ, you are blessed, because the Spirit of glory and of God rests on you" (1 Pet. 4:14). Suffering as a Christian for the cause of Christ brings great glory to God when we "suffer according to the will of God" and "entrust [our] souls to a faithful Creator in doing what is right" (1 Pet. 4:19).

The apostle Paul, whose sufferings for the cause of gospel ministry are legendary (2 Cor. 11:23–33), promised that "all who desire to live godly in Christ Jesus will be persecuted" (2 Tim. 3:12). He encouraged Timothy with these sobering words: "Therefore do not be ashamed of the testimony of our Lord or of me His prisoner, but join with me in suffering for the gospel according to the power of God" (2 Tim. 1:8).

Given that our Lord suffered to purchase the church and calls us to follow Him in this world, we shouldn't expect a smooth path, easy course, or carefree life. The gospel calls us to carry a cross, an instrument of death and suffering (Matt. 16:24; Mark 8:34; Luke 9:23).

Suffering is our calling; as Jesus said, "And he who does not take his cross and follow after Me is not worthy of Me" (Matt. 10:38). A faithful disciple and willing slave is prepared to suffer the loss of all things for the sake of his Lord (Luke 9:24) and count it gain (Phil. 3:8). Like Moses, the faithful follower of Christ is willing to forsake all the treasures and pleasures of this world for the reproach of Christ in order that he may gain an eternal reward:

> By faith Moses, when he had grown up, refused to be called the son of Pharaoh's daughter, choosing rather to endure ill-treatment with the people of God than to enjoy the passing pleasures of sin, considering the reproach of Christ greater riches than the treasures of Egypt; for he was looking to the reward. (Heb. 11:24–26)

That brings us to the second truth: we're promised an eschatological vindication, not a temporal one. In short, we know how the story ends. There will be final justice on the last day. Both God's judgment of the wicked and the reward of His righteous ones will be the final and full demonstration of God's promises and providences. We must fix our eye on the final goal, the glory that is to come. When our heart is set on future joys unspeakable, pleasures unending, and blessings unmixed, we will endure the suffering set before us. This is the example of Jesus, "who for the joy set before Him endured the cross, despising the shame, and has sat down at the right hand of the throne of God" (Heb. 12:2).

Biblical faith is a conviction that God exists "and that He is a rewarder of those who seek Him" (Heb. 11:6). Paul knew that having endured all things for the sake of those who are chosen, he could anticipate eternal glory. "For this reason I endure all things for the sake of those who are chosen, so that they also may obtain the salvation which is in Christ Jesus and with it eternal glory" (2 Tim. 2:10). With confidence, he said,

> For I am already being poured out as a drink offering, and the time of my departure has come. I have fought the good fight, I have finished the course, I have kept the faith; in the future there is laid up for me the crown of righteousness, which the Lord, the righteous Judge, will award to me on that day; and not only to me, but also to all who have loved His appearing. (2 Tim. 4:6–8)

God Doesn't Try

Writing to persecuted and suffering Christians, Peter spent the first chapter of his first Epistle reminding his readers that the inheritance reserved for them in Heaven is imperishable, undefiled, and unfading (1 Pet. 1:4). He assured them that they were being protected by God through faith so that they would not miss their inheritance. To persevere, they would need to diligently fix their mind on the final revelation of God's grace: "Therefore, prepare your minds for action, keep sober in spirit, fix your hope completely on the grace to be brought to you at the revelation of Jesus Christ" (1 Pet. 1:13).

There is a great glory yet to be revealed to the people of God. The promised glory isn't just the presence of God in the current Heaven. It's the glory and joys of the final Heaven. God will re-create (resurrect) this fallen creation. In the final conflagration of judgment, God will destroy with burning fire and intense heat all the elements of this present creation (2 Pet. 3:10, 12). That fiery judgment isn't the end, "but according to His promise we are looking for new heavens and a new earth, in which righteousness dwells" (2 Pet. 3:13).

His people will be vindicated. Their righteousness will be displayed in their bodily resurrection on the last day. Their works and service will be amply rewarded in the new creation. Their unjust suffering, labors of love, and patient endurance will be overwhelmingly compensated by the glory to be revealed. When we're convinced of yet-unseen realities and live as if they're true (because they are), we'll be strengthened, encouraged, and emboldened. We won't lose heart.

There is another aspect to this final vindication. We take heart and courage not just from the promise of glory for God's people, but also from the promises of God's judgment and vengeance upon His enemies. Many Christians are uneasy with the idea that we should take courage from the promises of God's eschatological judgments on the wicked. However, Scripture mentions these judgments with the purpose of encouraging God's people to hold fast to the end.

This is all over the Old Testament. The Scriptures describing the destruction of God's enemies shouldn't cause us to blush, apologize for God's justice, or shy away from boldly proclaiming the truth of divine judgment.[10] The judgment of God is a grand theme of Old Testament worship. The Psalms are replete with imprecations. References to God's justice, righteousness, triumphs over His enemies,

---

10. See Hamilton, *God's Glory in Salvation through Judgment*.

and past judgments (the flood, Sodom and Gomorrah, Babel, the exodus, etc.) are causes of great celebration, worship, and adoration in the Psalms.

The prophetic books are filled with promises of God's coming judgments. Because God is truthful, just, righteous, holy, and pure, He must judge His enemies who persecute His people. Often the eschatological judgments upon the nations are described in terms intended to encourage Israel in their state of exile, subjugation, or oppression. A cursory reading of the Old Testament prophets is sufficient to demonstrate this. Israel could take comfort and consolation in the ultimate vindication of God's righteousness through eschatological judgment.

Paul didn't shy away from this when writing to the Thessalonians to encourage them in the midst of their sufferings. He knew the young church in Thessalonica, with whom he had spent only three weeks, was suffering persecution at the hands of the same Jews who had run him and his traveling companions out of town (Acts 17:1–11). His encouragement to the church didn't consist of happy talk, fluffy sentiments, and "Chicken Soup for the Persecuted Soul" platitudes. He reminded the Thessalonians of God's coming judgment upon their persecutors, saying,

> For you, brethren, became imitators of the churches of God in Christ Jesus that are in Judea, for you also endured the same sufferings at the hands of your own countrymen, even as they did from the Jews, who both killed the Lord Jesus and the prophets, and drove us out. They are not pleasing to God, but hostile to all men, hindering us from speaking to the Gentiles so that they may be saved; with the result that they always fill up the measure of their sins. But wrath has come upon them to the utmost. (1 Thess. 2:14–16)

The Thessalonian Christians were to remain faithful in the midst of persecution and demonstrate God's righteousness by their faithfulness in suffering. Paul's second Epistle to that young church encouraged them with an even more graphic description of eschatological judgment.

> We ought always to give thanks to God for you, brethren, as is only fitting, because your faith is greatly enlarged, and the love of each one of you toward one another grows ever greater; therefore, we ourselves speak proudly of you among the churches of God for your perseverance and faith

in the midst of all your persecutions and afflictions which you endure. This is a plain indication of God's righteous judgment so that you will be considered worthy of the kingdom of God, for which indeed you are suffering. For after all it is only just for God to repay with affliction those who afflict you, and to give relief to you who are afflicted and to us as well when the Lord Jesus will be revealed from heaven with His mighty angels in flaming fire, dealing out retribution to those who do not know God and to those who do not obey the gospel of our Lord Jesus. These will pay the penalty of eternal destruction, away from the presence of the Lord and from the glory of His power, when He comes to be glorified in His saints on that day, and to be marveled at among all who have believed—for our testimony to you was believed. To this end also we pray for you always, that our God will count you worthy of your calling, and fulfill every desire for goodness and the work of faith with power, so that the name of our Lord Jesus will be glorified in you, and you in Him, according to the grace of our God and the Lord Jesus Christ. (2 Thess. 1:3–12)

God's final judgment upon His adversaries and those who afflict His people is not something Christians should apologize for, be ashamed of, or lament. God will be glorified through that judgment. Christians should rejoice in His glory and the vindication of His name.[11]

God isn't *trying* to judge His enemies. Neither is He *trying* to protect and prosper His church. All the suffering and affliction He has appointed for His people is intended for their ultimate good and His ultimate glory. God isn't *trying* to glorify His church. In fact, He is working to bring exceeding glory to His church through the suffering, persecution, and deprivation that we currently endure. The afflictions on God's people in this age are not a glitch in the plan. It is His plan. This should be an encouragement to us "so that no one [is] disturbed by these afflictions; for you yourselves know that we have been destined for this" (1 Thess. 3:3). Though we are destined to afflictions in this life, in a grand plot twist that only God could write, "God has not destined us for wrath, but for obtaining salvation through our Lord Jesus Christ" (1 Thess. 5:9).

---

11. See also 2 Thess. 2:8–17, where Paul's description of judgment is intended to bring comfort and hope to the Thessalonian believers.

The bride of Christ is destined for affliction in this life and eternal glory in the life to come. The unbeliever is given fading glory in this life and affliction in the life to come. That is good news by itself, but it gets even better! This life is temporary and passing away, and the life to come is endless and eternal.

This is the perspective we find in Psalm 73 that resolves the vexing problem of the prosperity of the wicked.[12] When Asaph observed the comfort and abundance enjoyed by the wicked, he almost stumbled by denying his faith and questioning the goodness of God toward His people: "Behold, these are the wicked; and always at ease, they have increased in wealth. Surely in vain I have kept my heart pure and washed my hands in innocence; for I have been stricken all day long and chastened every morning" (Ps. 73:12–14).

Asaph reflected upon this inequity and confessed, "It was troublesome in my sight" (v. 16). But when he "came into the sanctuary of God," he "perceived their end" (v. 17). Asaph saw God's perspective on the ultimate end of the wicked.

> Surely You set them in slippery places;
> You cast them down to destruction.
> How they are destroyed in a moment!
> They are utterly swept away by sudden terrors!
> Like a dream when one awakes,
> O Lord, when aroused, You will despise their form. (Ps. 73:18–20)[13]

God will settle all His accounts. He'll right every wrong, punish every sin, and reveal every secret. No one will get away with anything. Nothing is hidden that will not be revealed. Every sin will be

---

12. For a thorough study of Ps. 73, see my (Jim's) book *The Prosperity of the Wicked*. Two psalms (37 and 73) deal with the question, "Why do the wicked prosper?" Ps. 73 answers it by looking at the future eternal judgment of the wicked. Ps. 37 answers it by looking at the future eternal blessing of the righteous.

13. Ps. 37 describes the end of the wicked: "destroyed," "perish," and "cut off" from the land (vv. 9–10, 20, 22, 28, 34, 38). Reference to "the land" does not merely mean the land of Israel in this age, nor are these verses only describing Jewish occupation of it dependent upon their obedience as per the Mosaic covenant. Though that is part of the meaning, the multiple references in Ps. 37 to the righteous inheriting the land anticipate the eschatological future for Israel when all the wicked will be purged from the land and God will fulfill the Abrahamic covenant by giving it—the entirety of what was promised—to restored Israel and resurrected Old Testament saints (Ezek. 36–37). The eternal possession of the righteous is the secure and glorious promised land (even in the new creation) and all the prosperity and blessings that attend it (Ps. 37:9, 11, 18, 22, 29, 34).

exposed, every evil deed judged, and every motive manifested. He'll reveal the secrets of men's hearts, try every mind, and judge every act so that He may give to every man according to their sins (Jer. 17:9–10). His justice will be thorough and His judgment complete.

Those righteous by faith in Him, God will raise on the last day, bring into His eternal Kingdom, and shower with glory, blessing, and joy forevermore. The righteous will enjoy a new creation untainted by sin and free from corruption. Their blessings will be unmixed, their joys undiluted, and their glory unimagined. Their lives will never end, while their intimacy with the Lord and each other will ever deepen.

Jesus Christ will return in great glory (Rev. 19:11–19), destroy the wicked (Rev. 19:20–21), resurrect the righteous (Ezek. 37:12–14; 1 Cor. 15:23, 50–58; Rev. 20:4), and establish His Millennial Kingdom (Rev. 20:1–6). He'll resurrect the wicked, pronounce their final judgment (Rev. 20:11–15), and create a New Heaven and New Earth for His people (Rev. 21–22). These glorious truths are enough to sustain even the most war-weary saint. We shouldn't be surprised by the sufferings of this age. Our vindication and glory are destined for the next. These first two truths come together into a third glorious reality.

Third, the church's current afflictions are *producing* her future glory. Paul says this in 2 Corinthians 4:16–18:

> Therefore we do not lose heart, but though our outer man is decaying, yet our inner man is being renewed day by day. *For momentary, light affliction is producing for us an eternal weight of glory* far beyond all comparison, while we look not at the things which are seen, but at the things which are not seen; for the things which are seen are temporal, but the things which are not seen are eternal.

We would never think to label our afflictions as "momentary" and "light," especially if we had endured those described by Paul later in the same Epistle (2 Cor. 11:23–33). However, our afflictions can be described as momentary and light when compared with the "eternal weight of glory" those afflictions are producing.

Paul says that the weight of glory is "far beyond all comparison." Ironically, the passage has a number of comparisons: the outer man with the inner man, affliction with glory, the unseen with the seen, and the temporal with the eternal. These ideas are set side by side for the sake of comparison, while the glory itself is said to be "beyond all comparison." We tend to put these things on a mental scale as if we can weigh the afflictions of this life against the glory of the life to

God Doesn't Try to Prosper His Church

come. That is to weigh the value of things seen against things unseen. We may presume to measure the impact or significance of our afflictions, but there is only one standard by which they can be measured: the "eternal weight of glory" which the afflictions produce. Since affliction is momentary and glory is eternal, the comparison is rendered useless.

Imagine a balance scale in front of you. Now, for every drop of water you place on one side, a brick of gold instantly appears on the other. Does it seem fair to compare one to the other? Further, imagine that in a couple hours the drop of water evaporates but the brick of gold remains. Every drop of water you add eventually evaporates into forgottenness while the gold bricks remain. How many drops of water would you like to see sprinkled on that scale?

So it is with the afflictions appointed for the bride of Christ in this age. Every bit of suffering, affliction, tribulation, trial, pain, loss, and sacrifice is *producing* for us an unimaginable weight of eternal glory, reward, and joy. The afflictions will not last. Like the water, they'll evaporate into distant memory as we stand before the Lord with unveiled faces and enjoy Him everlastingly. The sufferings will feel like shadows, while the eternal weight of glory remains. Thus, Paul could encourage the Roman believers, saying, "For I consider that the sufferings of this present time are not worthy to be compared with the glory that is to be revealed to us" (Rom. 8:18). As Randy Alcorn has said, "Not only will we see his face and live, but we will likely wonder if we ever lived before we saw his face!"[14]

The Lord isn't *trying* to keep us for that glory. He has destined us to it! He isn't trying to prosper us in this life. He has destined us to prosperity in the next. He isn't trying to protect us from affliction in this life since He isn't trying to protect us from the glory of the next. He isn't trying to rescue us from suffering. He is producing our eternal reward.

The church's afflictions in this life aren't evidence that God has difficulty providing for, prospering, or protecting her. Rather, our Lord takes from His church all that competes with Him and all that would distract us from Him so that He may give us more of Himself in this life and the next. Our hardships are the means He uses to store up the glory to come. By these momentary and light afflictions, the Lord gives to His people every good and lasting benefit—an eternal weight of glory.

---

14. Alcorn, *Heaven*, 172.

The sovereign Lord of the church has infallibly secured our salvation. He perfectly keeps His own through affliction for His eternal glory. All whom the Lord saves, He sanctifies. All whom He sanctifies, He secures. He'll lose none:

> Now to Him who is able to keep you from stumbling, and to make you stand in the presence of His glory blameless with great joy, to the only God our Savior, through Jesus Christ our Lord, be glory, majesty, dominion and authority, before all time and now and forever. Amen. (Jude 24–25)

FOR THE SHEPHERDS

Gentlemen, we need to prepare our people for suffering. The American church has long enjoyed a season of peace, prosperity, and comfort not afforded to millions of other believers around the world. We have no promise it will last. We shouldn't expect it to. Our shepherding task includes the work of preparing our people to face sufferings of various kinds.

We must prepare our people to face the sufferings that come from living in a fallen world. We have to prepare them to face illness, deprivation, pain, disease, and even death. Everyone in our congregations is either suffering through an affliction or watching a loved one do so. Preaching the Word without avoiding these difficult subjects will prepare them to think biblically about suffering and to embrace the afflictions appointed by God's sovereign hand.

We must also prepare our people to face the sufferings that may come from faithful living in a hostile world. That doesn't mean we preach nothing but negative sermons about our horrible circumstances or the possibility of persecution. However, a balanced spiritual diet will consist of occasional text-appropriate reminders of the reality of persecution and how we are called to handle it. If you have never done so, consider preaching through Acts or 1 Peter.

Teach them to suffer well and be prepared to do so yourself if called upon by the Lord.

DISCUSSION QUESTIONS

1. In what ways has prosperity hindered gospel growth in the West? In your own life? In what way is your thinking about persecution, suffering, or affliction affected by the comforts and conveniences of Western culture?

2. Does God's promise to judge the wicked for their treatment of His people comfort you? Do you struggle with rejoicing in that truth? Is it hard for you to rest in it?

3. How does an eternal perspective help us deal with suffering?

4. Is suffering for Christ in this world optional or a given? Use Scripture to prove your answer.

5. Why is the judgment of God on the unrighteous with final adjudication in the lake of fire something for Christians to celebrate?

6. Discuss how the afflictions of this life can be described as momentary and light (2 Cor. 4:17). Would you describe your own sufferings that way? How does your view of your afflictions need to change?

RECOMMENDED READING:

Happiness by Randy Alcorn

Heaven by Randy Alcorn

If God Is Good: Faith in the Midst of Suffering and Evil by Randy Alcorn

God's Super-Apostles: Encountering the Worldwide Prophets and Apostles Movement by R. Douglas Geivett and Holly Pivec

God's Glory in Salvation through Judgment: A Biblical Theology by James M. Hamilton Jr.

Defining Deception: Freeing the Church from the Mystical-Miracle Movement by Costi W. Hinn and Anthony G. Wood

Charismatic Chaos by John F. MacArthur Jr.

The Prosperity of the Wicked: A Study of Psalm 73 by Jim Osman

God Doesn't Try

Part 4

God's Infallible Work in Creation

Chapter 10:

God Doesn't Try to Control Creation

10

Christians generally agree with the teaching that God is sovereign over all things, at least in the abstract. They willingly confess His sovereignty over the conglomerate of "all things." But we need to break "all things" down into its component parts to understand the magnitude of this claim the Spirit has made for the triune God. Christians tend to be comfortable with claims of divine sovereignty so long as they are generic or abstract. We may even be OK with some specific claims, but balk at others. We need to thoroughly understand the teaching of Scripture regarding God's sovereignty so we may rejoice in the majesty of God's absolute sovereign power, find ultimate comfort in His dominion, and give Him glory for this defining attribute.

GOD DOESN'T TRY TO CONTROL NATURE

Does Scripture teach that God is sovereign over nature? Very clearly, yes. We needn't spend a lot of time on this because it's not terribly controversial to most Christians. I don't know any Christian who denies God's sovereignty over nature in general. One passage in Scripture extends a general claim of sovereignty to specific examples in the natural realm. "Whatever the LORD pleases, He does, in heaven and in earth, in the seas and in all deeps. He causes the vapors to ascend from the ends of the earth; who makes lightnings for the rain, who brings forth the wind from His treasuries" (Ps. 135:6–7).

God is sovereign over inanimate natural processes, weather, and natural phenomena. He works through, and sometimes over, natural processes to do His will and accomplish His purposes. He said, "'Let there be light'; and there was light" (Gen. 1:3). God brought floodwaters on the Earth, parted the Red Sea, and turned back the sun. Jesus calmed the storm, turned water to wine, walked on water, and multiplied loaves and fish. There are many more examples.

God is sovereign over inanimate nature. He's also sovereign over the activities of plants and animals. God brought the animals to Adam (Gen. 2:19) and then to Noah (Gen. 7:13–16). He caused the fish to swallow Jonah (Jon. 1:17) and the ravens to feed Elijah (1 Kings 17:4–6). He claims sovereignty over the minute details of the normal activities of animal life throughout Scripture. We see this in the Psalms (Ps. 29:9; 50:10–11; 104) and especially in Job (Job 38:39–41:34). In God's answer to Job, He claims to control every detail of nature, from the success or failure of a lion hunt to the timing of the birth of a mountain goat. He claims sovereignty over the smallest details of natural life.

God brought plagues on Egypt to bring about the exodus. He used water, blood, gnats, flies, frogs, locusts, hail, fire, disease, darkness, and death. He brought these things. He caused them to happen. He makes His sun rise on the evil and the good. He sends rain on the just and the unjust. He feeds the birds and clothes the lilies of the field. He knows every sparrow and has numbered the hairs of your head.

We cannot escape the clear teaching of Scripture: God is sovereign over all of nature and everything in nature. He's sovereign over large activities like the movements of the oceans, the precise acceleration of gravity, and the constant motion of Earth and other heavenly bodies. He controls small events like the flight of a gnat in Pharaoh's palace, the fall of an unseen sparrow, and the formation of a single snowflake. God's control over nature extends from the unfathomable reaches of the physical universe to the workings of minute biological machines and subatomic particles. There is nowhere that God's power doesn't reach, and nothing is outside His sovereign control.

The clear declaration of Scripture is that God is sovereign over everything. There are two important implications of that truth we must understand.

First, God brings the natural events we call "good" from a human perspective as well as those we call "bad." He uses nature to bring pleasure and happiness to people as well as pain and misery. Isaiah writes,

> I am the LORD, and there is no other;
> Besides Me there is no God.
> I will gird you, though you have not known Me;
> That men may know from the rising to the setting of the sun
> That there is no one besides Me.
> I am the LORD, and there is no other,
> The One forming light and creating darkness,
> Causing well-being and creating calamity;
> I am the LORD who does all these. (Isa. 45:5–7)

God said to Moses, "Who has made man's mouth? Or who makes *him* mute or deaf, or seeing or blind? Is it not I, the LORD?" (Exod. 4:11). Through Amos, God took credit for "natural disasters," saying, "I smote you with scorching wind and mildew; and the caterpillar was devouring your many gardens and vineyards, fig trees and olive trees; yet you have not returned to Me" (Amos 4:9).

God ordains everything that happens in nature. He sends the sunshine, rain, and snow when we want it, and He sends the sunshine, rain, and snow when we don't. He causes summer breezes and hurricanes, gentle rains and mudslides, a white Christmas and, sometimes in North Idaho where we live, a white Easter. He causes our hearts to beat and gives us pleasure. He causes our hearts to stop beating and gives us pain. He causes children to be conceived and can cause their death. He causes wounds to heal and cancers to metastasize. He's God over everything we would call "natural processes," both those that seem good to us and those that seem harmful.

Second, God's sovereignty over natural causes doesn't mean there aren't natural causes. We don't deny there are natural causes for natural events. When we say that God brings rain, determining the existence, timing, size, temperature, composition, velocity, and trajectory of each raindrop, we aren't denying there are real and discernable natural processes that cause the rain. This is the doctrine of concurrence. There may be more than one cause for any event. We know that God causes rain. We also know that rain is caused by certain natural conditions including humidity, temperature, condensation, and gravity. There are concurrent causes for rain. God is a cause of rain (He sends rain on the just and the unjust [Matt. 5:45]), and condensation of water vapor is a cause of rain. There is no contradiction. Nature acts naturally and according to the divine decree. Is God sovereign over nature? Yes. He claims sovereignty over great events and seemingly insignificant ones. He claims sovereignty over things that bring blessing and disaster to humanity. He can work supernaturally (outside of natural processes), though He ordinarily works through natural processes.

So far, I don't anticipate any major objections. As I said, most Christians willingly affirm God's claim to sovereignty over nature.

GOD DOESN'T TRY TO CONTROL HISTORY

Is God sovereign over human history? Does He cause wars, elections, cultures, explorations, invasions, etc.? Is He sovereign over the affairs of nations? Paul said to the men of Athens,

> The God who made the world and all things in it, since He is Lord of heaven and earth, does not dwell in temples made with hands; nor is He served by human hands, as though He needed anything, since He Himself gives to all people life and breath and all things; and He made from one man every nation of mankind to live on all the face of the earth, having determined their appointed times and the boundaries of their habitation. (Acts 17:24–26)

God controls the histories of nations and people groups. This necessarily implies that He controls the outcomes of wars, revolutions, and cultural movements (Dan. 2:21). It also means He controls the outcomes of elections, coups, and appointments. He decides who'll lead.

Nebuchadnezzar learned this the hard way, just as Daniel foretold:

> This is the interpretation, O king, and this is the decree of the Most High, which has come upon my lord the king: that you be driven away from mankind and your dwelling place be with the beasts of the field, and you be given grass to eat like cattle and be drenched with the dew of heaven; and seven periods of time will pass over you, until you recognize that the Most High is ruler over the realm of mankind and bestows it on whomever He wishes. And in that it was commanded to leave the stump with the roots of the tree, your kingdom will be assured to you after you recognize that it is Heaven that rules. (Dan. 4:24–26)

God is sovereign over human history. He ordains the events. He appoints kings, rulers, and authorities. He determines who leads, who follows, who wins, and who loses. God raised up the Assyrians against Israel and the Babylonians against Judah to execute judgment against His faithless people (Ezek. 23). God called Cyrus the Persian His shepherd (Isa. 44:28) and determined that he would send the people back to Israel after their captivity (Ezra 1:1–4).

Don't miss the implications of this. God caused Saul to be king (1 Sam. 9:17). God caused the Assyrians to invade Israel. God caused the Babylonians to invade Judah. God caused Nebuchadnezzar to be king, deposed him, and restored him. God caused Cyrus to be king and Nero to be Caesar. God caused Hitler to rise to power, as well as Stalin, Mao, Pol Pot, Saddam Hussein, and the Ayatollahs of Iran. To deny this is to deny God's absolute sovereignty.

Moreover, God causes the actions of these leaders and directs their heart to accomplish His purposes. "The king's heart is like channels of water in the hand of the LORD; He turns it wherever He wishes" (Prov. 21:1). God controls the thoughts of the king, his mind, affections, and *will*. God's control of the king's will is the means He uses to direct his actions as He sees fit. In other words,

> God's sovereignty is unhindered. God never experiences frustration or failure in his exercise of power in the governance of his creation and the achievement of his purposes. Whatever he pleases, he does. "Why should the nations say, 'Where, now, is their God?' But our God is in the heavens; He does whatever He pleases" (Ps. 115:2–3; cf. Ps. 103:19; 135:5–6; Prov. 21:1).[1]

GOD DOESN'T TRY TO CONTROL YOU

God is sovereign over nature, the great events of human history, wars, elections, and cultural movements. What about individual human choices? Is God sovereign over the thoughts, words, choices, and actions of individual people?

Saying that God is sovereign over nations, rulers, and any event involving human actors necessarily implies that He controls every decision of every single human being. If there are some decisions or acts of libertarian free will outside His sovereign control, then He couldn't effectively and unfailingly raise up His chosen leader. Human decisions result in certain leaders coming to power either by birth, political process, war, or revolution. If God isn't sovereign over human choices, He can't control the outcome of any event, much less the big events of history.

---

1. Sammons, *Reprobation and God's Sovereignty*, 27.

Remember the words of the apostle Paul. God is sovereign over all things. He "works all things after the counsel of His will" (Eph. 1:11). All things. That necessarily includes every single decision of human actors.

If there is even one thing over which God can't or doesn't exercise absolute control, then we can't say that He "works all things after the counsel of His will." There would be things that wouldn't be according to the counsel of His will: surprises, disappointments, events that aren't part of His plan. We can't affirm that God is sovereign if He controls only ninety-nine percent of His creation. Ninety-nine percent sovereign is 0 percent sovereign.

Romans 8:28 has been a great comfort to Christians for millennia: "And we know that God causes all things to work together for good to those who love God, to those who are called according to His purpose." If some human decisions are beyond His sovereignty and outside His control, how could Paul say this? How could we believe it? We couldn't. A god who isn't sovereign over something, like human decision-making, isn't sovereign over anything. His will would be thwarted and his plans frustrated. A couple of examples from Scripture will illustrate this.

The Lord assured Jeremiah, "Before I formed you in the womb I knew you, and before you were born I consecrated you; I have appointed you a prophet to the nations" (Jer. 1:5). God ordained that Jeremiah would be a prophet before his conception. What must this imply about God's control over human decision-making? God caused Jeremiah's parents (and all his ancestors) to meet and marry. He caused the natural processes of Jeremiah's conception and development in the womb of his mother. God caused his birth, his upbringing, and his training. He wrought in Jeremiah's heart the desire and courage to speak God's Word to the people. He directed an incalculable number of decisions that resulted in Jeremiah being a prophet: decisions made by Jeremiah, his parents, his siblings, friends, acquaintances, teachers, leaders, priests, and other prophets. Jeremiah became a prophet because God determined that he would, and He caused the human decisions and actions that resulted in Jeremiah serving God as a powerful mouthpiece to the nations.

That example demonstrates the necessity of God sovereignly controlling human decision-making. Scripture makes the claim directly. We are assured that "man's steps are ordained by the LORD"

God Doesn't Try to Control Creation

(Prov. 20:24) and "the mind of man plans his way, but the LORD directs his steps" (Prov. 16:9). Jeremiah said, "I know, O LORD, that a man's way is not in himself, nor is it in a man who walks to direct his steps" (Jer. 10:23).

We make our decisions and we make our plans. We do so freely, willingly, and without compulsion from God, but the Lord establishes and directs our steps. We plan, think, decide, act, and cause while God has planned, acted, and caused according to His will, concurrent with human activity. Just as the rain has natural causes and a divine cause (concurrence), so our actions have both human and divine causes. God's sovereignty over human decision-making doesn't mean we don't make real decisions or that our decisions don't have real impact. This isn't fatalism.

Scripture contains commands. God's commands imply choice—real choice among real alternatives. We can choose to obey or disobey. He presents the alternatives at times: "If it is disagreeable in your sight to serve the LORD, choose for yourselves today whom you will serve" (Josh. 24:15).

Scripture clearly teaches that our actions matter, our prayers matter, and our choices have real consequences. What we do changes things. Yet, at the same time, God has ordained every decision, every action, and every result.

If you are married, your decision to take a spouse had significant effects. Your decision changed your life and the lives of others. God planned it all and was sovereign over your decision. Does a storm have real effects? Does it cause trees to sway and lawn chairs to fall over? Yes, it has real impact. Did God plan the storm, cause the storm, and so cause trees to sway and lawn chairs to fall over? Yes. In the same way, your decisions matter. God uses them to cause history to unfold according to His will. He is sovereign over human decision-making. God causes our decisions, actions, and the outcomes of those actions. He establishes our steps to accomplish His purposes or countermands our designs to secure His own. To say otherwise is to deny the absolute sovereignty of God. If He can't control some human decisions, He can't control anything.

GOD DOESN'T TRY TO CONTROL SIN

Christians will generally affirm God's sovereign control. Nearly all Christians pray for healing from a sickness, safety in a storm, rain during a drought, or provision for a need. We pray for doctors to have wisdom and skill, for police officers, firefighters, and soldiers to do their jobs well and be protected from harm. We pray for our children to make wise and godly decisions. Christians, in their prayer life, demonstrate by practice a belief in the sovereignty of God over nature, events of history, and even human decision-making.

But ask most Christians if God is sovereign in salvation or over sin, and that's where you'll see balking and backtracking. God's sovereignty over salvation was defended thoroughly in chapter 3, but what about sin? God's sovereignty over sin is the aspect of His power we're most reluctant to acknowledge. But only by being convinced of the sovereignty of God over the sinful decisions of moral agents can one embrace Scripture's statements regarding the sovereignty of God over "all things" (Eph. 1:11).

So, is God sovereign over sin? What does the Scripture say about this? Let's face that issue squarely.

Sovereignty Over the Sins of Joseph's Brothers

> Then Joseph said to his brothers, "Please come closer to me." And they came closer. And he said, "I am your brother Joseph, whom you sold into Egypt. Now do not be grieved or angry with yourselves, because you sold me here, for God sent me before you to preserve life. For the famine has been in the land these two years, and there are still five years in which there will be neither plowing nor harvesting. God sent me before you to preserve for you a remnant in the earth, and to keep you alive by a great deliverance. Now, therefore, it was not you who sent me here, but God; and He has made me a father to Pharaoh and lord of all his household and ruler over all the land of Egypt." (Gen. 45:4–8)

Joseph believed God was sovereign over the events of his life. He told his brothers that God had caused him to be sold into slavery, saying, "God did it! God has made me a father to Pharaoh, lord of all his house, and ruler over all the land of Egypt. God used you to bring it about, though you acted willingly of your own accord and sold me into slavery." His brothers sinned by selling Joseph into slavery. They hated, lied, and acted violently toward Joseph. They were covetous and murderous. Yet behind their sinful actions were God's holy intentions. God sent Joseph to Egypt through his brothers' murderous and deceptive plot. God's Word says that He caused and ordained those actions to bring about a good end. Joseph saw God's sovereign control over his brothers' sinful deeds.

Sovereignty Over the Sins of Pharaoh

In the account of the exodus, we see clearly God's sovereignty over Pharaoh and his rebellion: "The LORD said to Moses, 'When you go back to Egypt see that you perform before Pharaoh all the wonders which I have put in your power; but I will harden his heart so that he will not let the people go'" (Exod. 4:21). The Lord did as He promised: "And the LORD hardened Pharaoh's heart, and he did not listen to them, just as the LORD had spoken to Moses" (Exod. 9:12).

There is no denying that the Lord hardened Pharaoh as He said He would. Yahweh's hardening caused Pharaoh to reject Moses's pleas on behalf of the Israelites in the midst of the terrifying demonstrations of God's power. But, one may object, didn't Pharaoh harden his own heart? Yes, he did. And God hardened Pharaoh. The one doesn't preclude the other. That's the point. God acted by hardening Pharaoh, and Pharaoh hardened himself. Both are true. Just as God causes rain, and the natural precipitation process causes rain.

Pharaoh's treatment of the Jews was sinful. He oppressed those poor slaves, held them against their will, mistreated them, threatened them, and even killed some. He stood in sinful, prideful opposition to God, even in the face of His judgments. Yet God caused the hardening of his heart. God kept Pharaoh from assenting to Moses's pleas. Though Pharaoh was responsible for his sin, God ordained it and was sovereign over it.

Sovereignty Over the Worst of Sins

In John 17:12, Jesus refers to Judas as the "son of perdition," saying, "While I was with them, I was keeping them in Your name which You have given Me; and I guarded them and not one of them perished but the son of perdition, so that the Scripture would be fulfilled." Judas's betrayal was ordained by God. He used Judas's sin, which He foreordained, to accomplish His plan—namely, the salvation of our souls.

What about the Jewish leaders, Pilate, and everyone complicit in the crucifixion of Christ? Luke answers this question in Acts where he records the prayer of the early church:

> And when they heard this, they lifted their voices to God with one accord and said, "O Lord, it is You who made the heaven and the earth and the sea, and all that is in them,

who by the Holy Spirit, through the mouth of our father David Your servant, said,

'Why did the Gentiles rage,
And the peoples devise futile things?
The kings of the earth took their stand,
And the rulers were gathered together
Against the Lord and against His Christ.'

For truly in this city there were gathered together against Your holy servant Jesus, whom You anointed, both Herod and Pontius Pilate, along with the Gentiles and the peoples of Israel, to do whatever Your hand and Your purpose predestined to occur." (Acts 4:24–28)

By crucifying the Lord Jesus, the guilty parties did whatever God's hand and purpose had predestined to occur! The events of the passion week were entirely subject to the sovereign control of God. There have never been greater sins committed. All involved in killing the pure and innocent Son of Man, God incarnate, are guilty of the most heinous of transgressions. It was the arch crime of history. Yet God ordained it. He was sovereign over every detail, every horrible betrayal, torture, and blasphemy, even the murder of our Lord. Do you see that? John Frame rightly observes, "The crucifixion of Jesus could not have happened without sin, for Jesus did not deserve death. For God to foreordain the crucifixion, he had to foreordain sinful actions to bring it about."[2]

Peter gives a more general statement regarding sin and the sovereignty of God:

This precious value, then, is for you who believe; but for those who disbelieve,

"The stone which the builders rejected,
This became the very corner stone,"

and,

"A stone of stumbling and a rock of offense";

for they stumble because they are disobedient to the word, and to this *doom* they were also appointed. (1 Pet. 2:7–8)[3]

---

2. Frame, *Systematic Theology*, 162.
3. Emphasis in original.

The word *doom* is in italics in the NASB because it's not in the original text. It was added by the translators for clarity. The ESV provides a better translation for verse 8 with: "They stumble because they disobey the word, as they were destined to do."[4]

They were destined to do what? They were destined to stumble, disobey, and sin. "They" refers to unbelievers, whom Peter says were destined to sin. The word translated "destined" or "appointed" is a common one. It means "to place, lay, [or] set."[5] They were assigned to this, put in place for it. The verse means what it says. They stumble and disobey. They were destined to do so. Disobedience to the Word is about as clear a definition of sin as you might find.

So, if God appoints people to disobedience, He must ordain it. He must control it and be sovereign over it.

GOD'S RELATIONSHIP TO SIN

We need to be delicate with this important truth. We must choose our words carefully so that we remain true to the Scriptures in answering difficult questions like: How does God relate to sin? Is God the author of sin? Is God to blame for sin? Does God cause sin?

The words from the Westminster Confession of Faith are helpful in answering these questions.

> The almighty power, unsearchable wisdom, and infinite goodness of God so far manifest themselves in his providence, that it extendeth itself even to the first fall, and all other sins of angels and men; and that not by a bare permission, but such as hath joined with it a most wise and powerful bounding, and otherwise ordering, and governing of them, in a manifold dispensation, to his own holy ends; yet so, as the sinfulness thereof proceedeth only from the creature, and not from God, who, being most holy and righteous, neither is nor can be the author or approver of sin.[6]

Noting that God's providence or sovereignty extends to the fall of man and all sins of both angels and men, the writers declare that God is not "the author or approver of sin." They seem to equate the term *author* with *approver*. The term *author* may imply blame and is

---

4. See also the LSB translation: "They stumble because they are disobedient to the word, and to this stumbling they were also appointed." This makes it clearer that the appointment is to "stumbling," and not only to the "doom" associated with judgment of their sin.
5. Thomas, *Hebrew-Aramaic and Greek Dictionaries*, Strong's G5087.
6. Westminster Confession of Faith, in Grudem, *Systematic Theology*, 1182.

rejected for that reason. God isn't chargeable for sin. Always in Scripture, blame for sin is assigned to the morally responsible human actor. God is never blamed for sin, though Scripture declares that He ordains all that comes to pass.

John Frame strikes the balance well:

> God does bring about sinful human actions. To deny this, or to charge God with wickedness on account of it, is not open to a Bible-believing Christian. Somehow, we must confess both that God has a role in bringing evil about and that in doing so he is holy and blameless.[7]

Peter Sammons notes regarding God's providence,

> His providence is exercised in such a way that nothing happens without his involvement. Now that does not mean God forces everything that happens, thereby violating natural law, or the will of creatures, or exercising some universal meticulous dominion where the properties of creation are upended. Rather, providence is God's working with the properties of creation directing them to act as they do.[8]

Luke 22:22 records these words of Christ regarding Judas and his egregious sin: "For indeed, the Son of Man is going as it has been determined; but woe to that man by whom He is betrayed!" (See also Matt. 26:24 and Mark 14:21). Judas's sin was ordained by God. God determined, controlled, and directed his betrayal. It was caused both by God and sinful men. Yet God isn't to blame for the sin. Instead, "woe to that man by whom He is betrayed." The blame, accountability, and punishment belong solely to the sinful moral actor, Judas.

I repeat: we have to be precise with our terms. *Author* isn't acceptable because it implies blame. Likewise, there are other ways of describing God's relationship to sin that do not accurately represent the Bible's teaching on the matter. We will now examine some of those.

Does God Allow Sin?

Is it right to say that God permits or allows evil and specifically sin? It's technically correct, but it doesn't go far enough. It's too weak and doesn't accurately describe His relationship to sin and evil. When we say God permits sin, it suggests that He doesn't cause it. This

---

7. Frame, *Systematic Theology*, 294.
8. Sammons, *Reprobation and God's Sovereignty*, 25–26.

God Doesn't Try to Control Creation

denies that He is active in it. This suggests that God merely allows people to do what He doesn't want them to. It's a way of getting God off the hook for sin, morally speaking.

If we say that God only permits but doesn't control or ordain sin, what does that imply about Him? It means He is either incapable of accomplishing His purpose (for lack of power or knowledge) or He has no purpose for the sin. If God permits that which He doesn't ordain, then it can't be said that He determines or controls the future. This is an unbiblical Arminian premise that leads to heretical process theologies like Open Theism. This idea that God permits something but doesn't control or ordain it must be rejected. While God certainly does permit sin, it isn't "bare permission." He also ordains it.

Does God Cause Sin?

Is it right to say God causes sin? This is the language we've used a few times in this chapter. This is a difficult word for theologians because it seems to imply blame, but that's precisely the issue. God does cause sin, but He isn't to blame for it. We must be able to divorce *cause* from *blame*. We can say both that God causes sin, and that He does so sinlessly and blamelessly. This is a necessary distinction when explaining these truths to others.

Does God Ordain Sin?

Is it right to say God ordains sin? In modern English, the terms *ordain* and *cause* really aren't that different in their implications. While *ordain* might be easier to swallow because it has a sense of authority and separateness, we can't suggest that God ordains sin without causing it. He isn't passive when it comes to sin. We're not Deists, believing that God is inactive in the affairs of His creation.

What language does the Bible use? Scripture uses words like "destined," "predestined," "appointed," and "decided" in relation to man's sin and evil events. It uses words that describe God setting the limits and boundaries of sin ahead of time or "appointing" sinful acts. Most often, the Scripture says that God did it. God raised him up. God sent a plague. God hardened Pharaoh. God sent the Assyrian army. God bestows power. God frustrates plans. God rules. God knows. God does. God claims active involvement in all the affairs of men in history, including sinful actions.

However we speak of this truth, we must affirm the absolute sovereignty of God over sin without assigning responsibility or blame to Him.

Is God a Chargeable Cause of Sin?

How does God cause sin without bearing blame for it? Scripture teaches this, but how is it possible? If a human causes something, he's responsible for it. Why isn't God?

There is a mystery to this, as John Calvin rightly notes:

> But how it was ordained by the foreknowledge and decree of God what man's future was without God being implicated as associate in the fault as the author or approver of transgression, is clearly a secret so much excelling the insight of the human mind, that I am not ashamed to confess ignorance.[9]

That God is sovereign over sin and yet not "implicated as associate in the fault" is beyond the insight of the human mind. Ultimately, we can't explain why or how God can do this. Scripture doesn't provide a clear and detailed explanation of how God can cause something without being morally responsible for the sin involved. That doesn't, however, imply that God isn't sovereign or that He isn't blameless. It only means that God hasn't given a comprehensive explanation for how these things are simultaneously true.

However, I do believe we can come to an explanation that will satisfy a worshipper of Yahweh if we will hear and accept the teaching of Scripture.

TOWARD THEODICY

Attempts to explain this apparent conundrum are called "theodicies." A theodicy is an attempt to demonstrate that God is both good and sovereign in light of the existence of evil in the world. The atheist will often present the argument triumphantly in this way: "If God is all-powerful and all-good, then evil wouldn't exist. God, being all-good, wouldn't want evil to exist. God, being all-powerful, wouldn't allow evil to exist. But evil does exist. Therefore, either God isn't all-powerful, God isn't all-good, God is neither all-powerful nor all-good, or God doesn't exist." It's an attempt to argue specifically that the God of the Bible doesn't exist.[10]

---

9. Calvin, *Eternal Predestination of God*, 124.
10. This "problem of evil" is presented as a conundrum for a biblical worldview, but the same "problem" exists for any theistic worldview. In contrast, an atheistic worldview has many of its own conundrums, including the notion of objective morality. How can an atheist identify what is good and what is evil? How can either be identified in a world without an objective standard? Why are human beings deserving of goodness, anyway? Why is evil bad? What makes something evil and how do we know? These are questions an atheistic worldview fails to answer.

God Doesn't Try to Control Creation

Theodicies take different forms, some of them entirely unbiblical. Some appeal to mystery and offer no biblical explanation for evil that would defend the goodness and sovereignty of God. Others deny the existence of evil altogether by describing it as "the absence of good," the negation of some good thing, or as an illusion. But evil is real. It exists and isn't denied in Scripture. Evil, particularly moral evil, is a main focus of Scripture. It's moral evil that necessitated the incarnation, life, atoning death, and resurrection of Jesus Christ.

There is a class of false theodicies that affirm God's alleged inability to conquer evil. They accept the atheist's premise that God can't, in fact, prevent evil, thus denying His omnipotence. One class of theodicies comes from the ancient, tired dualistic argument that good can't exist apart from evil. They claim that evil is necessary for the existence of good and vice versa. This puts the principle of duality above the power of God, making Him subject to an external governing principle. That teaching is entirely foreign to biblical Christianity. There was no evil prior to creation, and there will be no evil in the eternal state. Good existed in God always before creation and will exist in God and the new creation long after evil has been finally judged and conquered.

Another class of arguments denies critical aspects of God's character. They are referred to as "process theologies" and teach that God is in a "process of becoming." He isn't perfect in all aspects of His being and so isn't infinitely capable of overcoming evil. Socinianism and its modern equivalent, Open Theism, are examples of process theologies that deny God's omniscience. In this case, God is subject to the freedom of the human will. According to the Open Theist, since God can't intervene in the free choices of human beings, He can't know the future infallibly or control it sovereignly. Events are subject to the libertarian[11] will of man. They are inherently unpredictable and so can't be known in advance. Perfect prescience is impossible, even for God. Therefore, while God may wish to prevent evil, He isn't capable of doing so since He can neither control nor predict

---

11. The term *libertarian* in this context means that the human will is subject to absolutely nothing in its decision-making. Libertarian freedom means a person is capable of making decisions without being influenced in any way by history, desires, preferences, or God's work on their affections to determine or direct their will. The intellect (the faculty that thinks, reasons, and remembers) doesn't influence the will (the faculty that decides). In other words, a person who made decision A could, under exactly the same conditions, make decision B (not A). The presumption of libertarian free will is necessary to the Arminian belief in the supremacy of the human will over any influence from God, particularly in the decision to believe the gospel.

the decisions and actions of men. He's in the same boat as you and me in that His ignorance makes failure a possibility. Such a god can only try.

The more typical Arminian argument wouldn't deny God's *ability* to control human decision-making and evil but would suggest that God is *unwilling* to do so. He refuses to control the events in people's lives that determine preferences or constraints. He won't directly influence their affections or incline their hearts. The Arminian god wants the love of free[12] people and doesn't wish to gain their affections through "manipulation." This desire to protect human free will takes precedence over His desire to prevent evil.[13] There is no shortage of answers to the shortcomings of Arminian theology,[14] so we'll refrain from discussing them here except to point out that this doctrine denies the sovereignty of God in all things. God can't be said to control anything if He can't (or won't) control the decisions of moral agents.

You've likely heard this theodicy expressed this way: "God doesn't want sin and evil in this world. It's a result of man's will, not God's will. God has nothing to do with evil and will someday stop it." That explanation denies the sovereignty of God. It accepts the atheist's premise. Either God isn't all-powerful because He can't prevent sin and evil or He isn't all-good because, while He could prevent evil, He chooses not to. This "solution" doesn't actually solve the problem. Why didn't God, Who is all-powerful, prevent the sin of Adam in the first place? Why doesn't He prevent sin today? These attempts to get God off the hook for evil end up denying His essential attributes by implicitly agreeing with the premise of the "problem of evil" argument.

Another explanation uses the language of permission that we mentioned earlier, claiming that God doesn't ordain or cause evil but merely permits it, though He wishes it didn't exist. This explanation isn't an adequate theodicy for the same reason as the other sovereignty-denying arguments. For an all-powerful Being, to permit something is to ordain it. To permit is to positively cause something

---

12. I use *free* here in the libertarian sense. See footnote 11 for a fuller explanation.

13. This would also take precedence over His decree of election. God could not be said to choose His elect in any sense in which we would normally use the word *choose*. This was addressed in chapter 3.

14. Bruce A. Ware has done some excellent work in answering the arguments put forward by proponents of Open Theism. We recommend his books *God's Greater Glory*, *God's Lesser Glory*, and *Their God Is Too Small*.

God Doesn't Try to Control Creation

by the conscious act of nonprevention. A god who permits what he doesn't ordain can't be considered all-powerful.

Where does that leave us? If God is all-powerful and all-loving, why does evil exist? The Bible gives us several responses to that question.

EVIL EXISTS FOR GREATER GOOD

Romans 9 is the key chapter for understanding God's sovereignty over all human choices. Having established this doctrine earlier in the chapter, Paul raises the obvious question in verse 19, "You will say to me then, 'Why does He still find fault? For who resists His will?'" That is really the question we're asking here. How can a sovereign God not be at fault for human sin? How can God be totally sovereign and yet hold the sinner accountable for their sin? If God is the cause of sin, who resists His will? If none can resist His will, and He wills sin, how can He blame us for it?

John Calvin gives voice to the hypothetical questions in this way: "Why, then, they ask, should the thief be punished for robbing him whom the Lord chose to chastise with poverty? Why should the murderer be punished for slaying him whose life the Lord had terminated?"[15] In other words, why isn't this all God's fault? If He's sovereign over the affairs of men, why isn't He culpable for their sins?

Paul gives us the answer in verses 22–24:

> What if God, although willing to demonstrate His wrath and to make His power known, endured with much patience vessels of wrath prepared for destruction? And He did so to make known the riches of His glory upon vessels of mercy, which He prepared beforehand for glory, even us, whom He also called, not from among Jews only, but also from among Gentiles.

Only one answer is given: God wishes to demonstrate His wrath, power, and mercy for His own glory. That's the answer to the question. It denies an assumption behind the "problem of evil" argument. Do you see it? The atheist's argument assumes God, being all-good, can have no use for evil and would want it eliminated immediately and entirely. But God ordained evil for the greater purpose of His glory, which is achieved by the demonstration of His justice, wrath, holiness, knowledge, power, wisdom, love, mercy, and grace. These

---

15. Calvin, *Christian Religion*, 127.

attributes are demonstrated in the gospel, and the gospel is necessary for salvation because of sin. In a universe without sin, there would be no punishment, no forgiveness, and no salvation. The attributes of God displayed in the salvation of sinners would never be expressed.

Romans 5:8 tells us, "But God demonstrates His own love toward us, in that while we were yet sinners, Christ died for us." God demonstrated the depth and majesty of His love toward us when Christ died for sinners! Salvation shows that God's love is dramatically merciful and undeserved. He extends it to unworthy sinners, not perfect people. God is glorified when His attributes are displayed through His triumph over sin and evil. The purpose of all things, the glory of God, is accomplished.[16]

A DIFFERENCE OF INTENT

Another element of a biblical theodicy is the consideration of God's intent in ordaining and using evil. In a criminal court, intent has bearing on punishment. An accidental homicide carries a lesser punishment than an intentional one. One may even kill another for a "good" reason like self-defense or the defense of innocent life. Such a justifiable action would receive no punishment at all. In that case, the homicide had a good purpose. A police officer or soldier may, in the performance of his lawful duties and for a good purpose, take a life without culpability of any kind. In fact, the act may be considered heroic in some circumstances.

This is another argument the Bible gives for God's innocence in causing sinful acts. The Assyrians and Babylonians intended to invade Israel for their own reasons. God caused the invasion for different reasons. He used their sinful actions sinlessly, intending them as judgment on a faithless nation. Joseph acknowledged different intentions on the part of different actors in the sins perpetrated against him. His brothers "meant evil" but God "meant it for good . . . to preserve many people alive" (Gen. 50:20). His brothers were accountable to God for their sin (though Joseph forgave them), but God, though He intended the same events, wasn't accountable for sin.

---

16. This may sound similar to the dualistic argument (there must be evil for good to exist) refuted earlier. The argument from dualism is an assertion that good and evil must always coexist, that one can't exist without the other because of a law that governs all actions, realities, and even God Himself. The greater good argument is quite different. To say that God chose to ordain evil so that good may come from it is not to say that good cannot exist without evil, that evil must always exist, or that evil exists apart from God's choice to ordain it. He isn't subject to laws or principles outside Himself.

God committed no sin while ordaining a sinful act because His intention for the act wasn't at all sinful. He intended good for Joseph and his brothers by saving the entire family through Joseph's slavery in Egypt.

This argument clearly has merit since God is said to have good intent for sinful acts that He ordains. It must be the case that intent matters. This isn't, however, a complete theodicy in and of itself, as an all-powerful God *could have* chosen a sin-free method of accomplishing the same end. He could have prevented the famine or placed Joseph in Egypt without his brothers' actions. This simply demonstrates that intent does relate to culpability and is part of a biblical explanation for God's lack of culpability for sin.

PROXIMITY OF CAUSE

Chief among historical Reformed theodicies has been the acknowledgment of different levels and types of causation. God is the ultimate cause of everything. His decree makes all things that happen necessary, and by it He causes all that is. This statement affirms the comprehensive sovereignty of God. When it comes to sin, the person who commits the sin is the efficient cause, the most immediate agent and actor. There may be other secondary human causes, whose culpability is determined by their proximity to the act. For instance, a gang leader who orders a member to commit a crime bears some blame. The parents of the man who commits the crime may have guilt depending on their own proximity to his actions. We can think of less proximate causes in that last example, as ancestors further removed from the perpetrator could not be rightfully blamed. We establish guilt based on the proximity of causality. In a gang murder, the shooter (efficient cause) is guilty. The gang leader (secondary cause) is also guilty. The person who sold the gun (depending on knowledge and intent) may bear some guilt. The gun manufacturer's culpability is debatable. Even further removed, the man working an oil rig that extracted the oil which was refined into the gas that powered the truck that brought the materials to the gunmaker wouldn't be considered guilty at all.

Similarly, this theodicy argues that God, as ultimate cause, isn't considered culpable because He isn't the immediate proximate cause. It's true that God isn't the immediate proximate cause of sin. It's also true that He is not culpable for that sin, nor is He a chargeable cause of sin. But while I agree there is benefit in understanding the difference between ultimate and efficient causality, it doesn't answer the question of why One with ultimate causality isn't culpable. God causes all of the steps and is sovereign over all of the causes, from His decree all the way down to the thoughts and deeds of the moral actor most responsible (and chargeable) for the sin. In that sense, God is not like the moral actor who has distance from the act through a series of causes. God has no such distance.

THE TRANSCENDENCE OF GOD

So what is a biblical answer? Why, according to Scripture, is God, Who is unquestionably sovereign over sin and evil of all sorts, not a *chargeable* cause of evil? We have examined some partial answers above, but the most direct biblical response to the question is found in Romans 9:20–21:

> On the contrary, who are you, O man, who answers back to God? The thing molded will not say to the molder, "Why did you make me like this," will it? Or does not the potter have a right over the clay, to make from the same lump one vessel for honorable use and another for common use?

There is the direct answer to the questions posed in verse 19 ("Why does He still find fault? For who resists His will?"). The answer: God is transcendent above man. We mere men have no right to question God. We can't hold Him to any standard. He holds Himself to the standard of His own character. His immutability and holiness govern all He does. We creatures can't hold Him accountable. We're not smart enough, wise enough, or powerful enough to do so. We appear ridiculously foolish for even asking the question. We're mere clay in the hands of the Potter. We have no right to expect Him to defend Himself or His actions. We are out of line for suggesting He needs to. God is accountable to nothing and no one outside Himself.[17]

The book of Job is one long, foolish attempt to defend God from His own actions. It sounds like a group of theologians of various stripes sitting around and trying to get God off the hook for His actions

---

17. Barbara Ehrenreich, in her article "God Owes Us an Apology," applies the "problem of evil" argument to the Indian Ocean tsunami of 2004 that killed over 225,000 people. She says, "If we are responsible for our actions, as most religions insist, then God should be, too." This is the central and unspoken assumption behind the objection: that God is responsible (to us) for His actions, just as we're responsible to Him. This assumption is presumptuous, unjustified, and unbiblical.

God Doesn't Try to Control Creation

against Job. Job and his friends were doing exactly that. God wasn't pleased with their efforts.

> Then the LORD answered Job out of the storm and said,
> "Now gird up your loins like a man;
> I will ask you, and you instruct Me.
> Will you really annul My judgment?
> Will you condemn Me that you may be justified?
> Or do you have an arm like God,
> And can you thunder with a voice like His?" (Job 40:6–9)

God's reproof continues in this vein through chapter 41, repeatedly challenging Job and revealing the infinite gap between the wisdom of man and the wisdom of God. There are some things that we can't fully comprehend. This question is one for which we don't, ultimately, deserve or receive a fully satisfactory answer. We aren't entitled to one.

God has graciously revealed that there is a greater good that comes from sin, including the display of His mercy, love, and grace toward His elect. He has explained that intent matters for culpability, and His ultimate intent is always good. Ultimately, and most clearly, we're warned about digging too deeply into matters that are above our station.

Why doesn't God explain why He isn't culpable for sin? Because He's under no obligation to do so. We don't need to know. He doesn't have to explain Himself to us.

John Frame puts it this way:

> The very transcendence of God plays a significant role in biblical responses to the problem of evil. Because God is who he is, the covenant Lord, he is not required to defend himself against charges of injustice. He is the Judge, not we. Very often in Scripture, when something happens that calls God's goodness into question, God pointedly refrains from explaining. Indeed, he often rebukes those human beings who question him. Job demanded an interview with God, so that he could ask God the reasons for his sufferings (Job 23:1–7; 31:35–37). But when he met God, God asked the questions: "Dress for action like a man; I will question you, and you make it known to me" (38:3). The questions mostly revealed Job's ignorance about God's creation: if Job doesn't understand the ways of the animals, how can he presume to call God's motives into question? He doesn't

even understand earthly things; how can he presume to debate heavenly things? God is not subject to the ignorant evaluations of his creatures.[18]

Martin Luther concurs, saying,

> God is that Being, for whose will no cause or reason is to be assigned, as a rule or standard by which it acts; seeing that, nothing is superior or equal to it, but it is itself the rule of all things. For if it acted by any rule or standard, or from any cause or reason, it would be no longer the *will of* GOD. Wherefore, what God wills, is not therefore right, because He ought or ever was bound so to will; but on the contrary, what takes place is therefore right, because He so wills. A cause and reason are assigned for the will of the creature, but not for the will of the Creator; unless you set up, over Him, another Creator.[19]

In the parable of the workers in the vineyard, the landowner pays each laborer the same wage regardless of the time or effort expended. Jesus quotes the landowner as saying, "Is it not lawful for me to do what I wish with what is my own?" (Matt. 20:15). That is God's fullest answer to the question. How can God be sovereign over sin and not be blamed? Is He not free to do what He wishes with His own? We're responsible for our sin. We choose it willingly. We're subject to God and accountable to Him. He is our God, Creator, Master, and King.

God isn't to blame for anything. He isn't accountable to anyone, because there is nothing and no one greater to whom He must give an account. There is no higher rule, standard, cause, or reason above His will. He has no master, king, or creator. God is, lives, acts, plans, and purposes. His activities aren't subject to the approval of His creation. God doesn't stand trial in human court. He does as He pleases. Everything He does is good by definition. Job's confession immediately after the tragic loss of his possessions, servants, and children was correct: "Naked I came from my mother's womb, and naked I shall return there. The LORD gave and the LORD has taken away. Blessed be the name of the LORD" (Job 1:21). He even reproved his wife for her foolish response to the tragedy: "Then his wife said to him, 'Do you still hold fast your integrity? Curse God and die!'

---

18. Frame, *Systematic Theology*, 299.
19. Luther, *Bondage of the Will*, 154 (emphasis in original).

But he said to her, 'You speak as one of the foolish women speaks. Shall we indeed accept good from God and not accept adversity?' In all this Job did not sin with his lips" (Job 2:9–10).

God is sovereign over all things. He is sovereign over nature, men, angels, and all decisions and actions, even sinful ones. Yet He isn't to blame for sin. Blame falls to the sinful moral actor.

GOD'S SOVEREIGNTY OVER SIN APPLIED

Why do we need to learn this? First, it's a truth taught in Scripture and, frankly, one many believers either haven't or won't confront. To deny this truth is to diminish God's glory by denying His absolute sovereignty. We ought to cherish God's glory.

Second, if God isn't absolutely sovereign, we can have no basis for confidence or peace. If God doesn't control everything, He doesn't control anything. A universe outside His control is fearsome indeed. The late R. C. Sproul said,

> If there is one maverick molecule in the universe, one molecule running loose outside the scope of God's sovereign ordination, then ladies and gentlemen, there is not the slightest confidence that you can have that any promise that God has ever made about the future will come to pass.[20]

What is true of molecules is true of thoughts, choices, actions, sin, and evil. Sovereignty is all or nothing. Either God is in absolute control of everything, as His Word clearly teaches, or He is in control of nothing at all.

We can rest with confidence in God's control of everything. No matter what may happen to us—whether it's a natural event like illness, disease, fire, or flood, or heartache, harm, or trauma caused by human sin—we can rest in two undeniable truths: God is good and God is sovereign. And that is enough! We agree with John Calvin when he said, "Ignorance of providence is the greatest of all miseries, and the knowledge of it the highest happiness."[21]

FOR THE SHEPHERDS

This is a chapter about the providence of God. I didn't use the term *providence* much, instead preferring the term *sovereignty*. Providence connotes a narrower expression of God's sovereignty—namely, His goodness toward His people. I wanted to be clear that

---

20. Sproul, "No Maverick Molecule."
21. Calvin, *Christian Religion*, 132.

we're speaking broadly of God's sovereignty in everything. In a chapter focused on His control over sin, it seemed appropriate. However, I would encourage every preacher and teacher to sing the praises of providence. Christians often overuse the word *miracle*, and we're sometimes unimpressed by the unmiraculous but equally gracious broader class of God's work in history and our lives, referred to as "providence." Healing is just as amazing if it happens slowly through the normal physical healing process. It is a gift of God we take for granted. We get hurt or sick, and we heal. That's a gift for which we ought to be grateful. We only seem to appreciate the providence of God when He uses extraordinary, supernatural, or unusual means. We should teach our people to identify and appreciate God's providential control over all things, as it is worthy of our attention and admiration.

I hope this chapter has helped you to be bold about God's sovereignty. We needn't make any effort to excuse God for the things He has done. We must preach and teach the truth around this topic as it is presented in Scripture. We affirm three scriptural axioms.

First, the sovereign King of the universe causes everything. He has a good reason for all He does. If the reason has been revealed, proclaim it and praise Him for it. If it hasn't, we must refrain from assuming to know God's motives, a common but entirely unbiblical and dangerous practice.

Second, while certainly a cause of sin, God never sins and is never a *chargeable* cause of sin. God is never to blame for sin.

Third, God never need explain Himself. John MacArthur wrote,

> If God has limited power or doesn't have complete knowledge, the universe is out of control at the most crucial point. And if God is not truly omniscient, how can anyone know for certain whether He will ever accumulate the knowledge He needs to curb the effects of evil and conquer it once and for all? Why would anyone prefer a God who is *trying* to get control of evil rather than a God who is completely in control of it?[22]

Indeed, no one convinced of God's goodness would want anything other than His complete sovereignty over all things, especially evil, both moral and natural. We must give our people the truth that

---

22. MacArthur, *None Other*, 53–54 (emphasis added).

will allow them to rest in the sovereignty of God and enjoy His peace. We rest in the peace of a God Who doesn't try.

DISCUSSION QUESTIONS

1. Why is an understanding of God's sovereignty crucial to a stable and productive Christian life?

2. Do you or have you struggled with the implications of God's sovereignty? What aspect of sovereignty is or was most troubling and why?

3. How do you disciple yourself and others to delight in God's sovereignty and experience joy?

4. Have you ever had your view on God's goodness and sovereignty tested by difficulties or tragedy? How did you hold up?

5. How does the doctrine of concurrence help you reconcile God's sovereignty and human responsibility?

6. What do we learn from Joseph's statements regarding the sins of his brothers? How can such a perspective help you forgive others?

7. Balance the sovereignty of God over sin with the clear lack of responsibility for that sin. Can man, through reason alone, reconcile these two things?

RECOMMENDED READING:

If God Is Good: Faith in the Midst of Suffering and Evil by Randy Alcorn

Commentaries on Election and Predestination by John Calvin

Concerning the Eternal Predestination of God by John Calvin

Institutes of the Christian Religion by John Calvin

Freedom of the Will by Jonathan Edwards

Systematic Theology: An Introduction to Christian Belief, chapters 8–11 and 14, by John Frame

Systematic Theology: An Introduction to Biblical Doctrine, chapter 16, by Wayne Grudem

Reforming Free Will: A Conversation on the History of Reformed Views on Compatibilism (1500–1800) by Paul Helm

"Kingly Office of Christ" (pt. 3, chap. 11), in *Systematic Theology,* Vol. 2, *Anthropology* by Charles Hodge

On the Bondage of the Will by Martin Luther

None Other: Discovering the God of the Bible by John F. MacArthur Jr.

Biblical Doctrine: A Systematic Summary of Bible Truth, chapters 3 and 6, by John F. MacArthur Jr. and Richard Mayhue

Behind a Frowning Providence by John Murray

The Sovereignty of God by A. W. Pink

Reprobation and God's Sovereignty: Recovering a Biblical Doctrine by Peter Sammons

God's Greater Glory: The Exalted God of Scripture and the Christian Faith by Bruce A. Ware

God's Lesser Glory: The Diminished God of Open Theism by Bruce A. Ware

Their God Is Too Small: Open Theism and the Undermining of Confidence in God by Bruce A. Ware

Chapter 11:

God Doesn't Try to Execute Justice

11

Our world is filled with a mind-numbing amount of evil. The disobedience of Adam and the consequent curse on creation (Gen. 3:1–19; Rom. 8:19–22) has unleashed upon his descendants a hellscape of death, disease, and destruction. This world teems with moral evils, vexing tribulations, and grave injustices. A world full of sinners makes for a world full of sin. The cause of those evils lies within the human heart. Man, in his natural state, is a moral monster. He is darkened in his mind (Rom. 1:21; Eph. 4:18) alienated from God, hostile to His truth (Rom. 8:6–8; Col. 1:21), and madly in love with darkness (John 3:19–21). Such a creature will inevitably fill his environment with evils of every variety.

The proofs of man's rebellion against and alienation from God litter our headlines every day. They scroll across the chyron under talking heads every night on the evening news. Reports of murders, rapes, thefts, riots, stabbings, shootings, divorces, adulteries, wars, and rumors of wars pour forth from media outlets like water from a fire hose. Past generations were spared the exposure to evil that saturates us. Two hundred years ago, news of a deadly earthquake killing thousands might take months to reach a distant land, if it made it there at all. The spread of information was extremely limited, especially compared to the instant and continuous barrage we endure today. We have instant visible and audible access to nearly every detail of a tragedy or crime hundreds or thousands of miles away. Seeing horrors played out in all their gory detail on our TV or the screen in our hand makes evil feel imminent and personal. Never-ending news flashes make every tragedy feel as if it were happening in our backyard.

Unbelievers, though they recognize evil exists, have no standard to quantify evil or account for its origin. The unbeliever has no capacity to understand or assess the nature of evil in this world. They don't have divine revelation or the wisdom imparted through the mind of the Spirit (1 Cor. 2:10–16). They seldom regard themselves as contributing factors to rampant evil. Instead, they see themselves as victims of something external to them.

The redeemed understand evil, its origin, and its consequences. Our understanding is informed by Scripture. We see sin for what it truly is—rebellion against an almighty and benevolent King. Scripture reveals the evil of sin. Sin is an affront to God. It's an assault against His truth, a rejection of His rule, His Word, and His authority. Though others are affected by our sin, our transgressions are first and foremost against God Himself. David confessed, "For I know my transgressions, and my sin is ever before me. Against You, You only, I have sinned and done what is evil in Your sight, so that You are justified when You speak and blameless when You judge" (Ps. 51:3–4).

Believers grieve sin and its destruction in this fallen world. We feel the weight of sin's curse, having known both slavery to sin and freedom from its power. We know the guilt of iniquity and the joy of forgiveness. We understand God's righteousness and man's sinfulness. When Scripture informs our thinking on sin and evil, we will feel its vexation and grief to a greater degree than we did as unbelieving rebels who lived, breathed, and drank iniquity (Job 15:16).

Equally troublesome is the reality that justice for these evils is seldom realized in this life. Roughly one-third of homicides in the United States go unsolved each year. That accounts for at least two hundred thousand murders from 1960 to 2015.[1] And even in the case of homicides where a likely perpetrator is identified, justice can still be elusive. Often there is insufficient evidence to issue a warrant for arrest or pursue a conviction. Guilty murderers walk on legal technicalities or procedural missteps. In the small percentage of cases where a guilty party is identified, arrested, tried, and convicted, their

---

1. Martin Kaste, "Open Cases: Why One-Third of Murders in America Go Unresolved," NPR, March 30, 2015, https://www.npr.org/2015/03/30/395069137/open-cases-why-one-third-of-murders-in-america-go-unresolved (https://perma.cc/BK7K-B6ZW). Of course, this doesn't include the sixty million unborn children who have been killed through legalized abortion in the United States since the Roe v. Wade decision in 1973.

sentences are far more lenient than their crimes warrant. Some criminals get off with time served. Others pull strings through political connections and avoid justice entirely. In short, the judicial system fails to satisfy justice.

The same is true of other crimes like rape, child abuse, theft, larceny, fraud, assault, and blackmail. If only a small fraction of murderers are caught, tried, and "brought to justice," how much worse is it for other crimes? Our nation is increasingly characterized by institutional injustice. Our legal institutions have been seized by a demonic spirit of the age. They are now weapons of a leftist, Marxist political machine that targets citizens of certain religious or moral convictions. Pro-life pastors are raided, tried, charged, and harassed by "law enforcement" while horrible violence and property damage is excused as "expressions of free speech." Certain privileged social classes, sexual preferences, or ethnicities are deemed marginalized or oppressed and afforded an immunity from prosecution and justice not enjoyed by others who don't share the same political philosophy. Rioters and looters assault citizens, burn down city blocks, and pillage stores with impunity because of their skin color, sexual preference, or political affiliation. Those responsible for enforcing the law and punishing evildoers aren't interested in pursuing justice. The most basic and fundamental function of government is neglected.

Further, we sense that some crimes are committed for which there can never be adequate justice in this life. In some cases, justice can't be satisfied in this fallen world. Is justice served by giving a child-abusing serial rapist and violent murderer a prison cell with three hot meals a day, a comfy cot, and taxpayer-funded health care? Even the death penalty for such crimes leaves us feeling unsatisfied. The homeless on the streets of Los Angeles have far worse living conditions than the convicted violent felon. After all the evil Hitler perpetrated, do you feel that justice was satisfied when he died in the arms of his mistress?

THEODICY AND GOD'S JUSTICE

A robust theodicy[2] must incorporate the biblical teaching of God's justice, particularly eternal justice, if it is to explain His goodness in light of present injustices. In the previous chapter, we showed that God has morally sufficient reasons for evil to exist. He uses sin

---

2. A theodicy is an attempt to demonstrate that God is both good and sovereign in light of the existence of evil in the world. See the previous chapter for an explanation of God's sovereignty over evil events, people, and actions.

sinlessly to accomplish His holy purposes, including the good of His people and the glory of His name. Our subject here is related to that theme. God will bring glory to His name and good to His people by executing perfect justice for sin and evil.

God's justice upon sinners and evildoers will be meticulous, complete, and eternal. God isn't *trying* to work good from sin. He isn't struggling to overcome evil. He isn't attempting to satisfy the demands of justice. God is a just God, and every demand of His justice will be fully satisfied in His perfect timing.

Questions regarding God's goodness or power in light of present evil only have traction because the objection assumes that nothing more will be done about evil than what happens in this world. However, the ultimate vindication of God's goodness is in His righteous wrath poured out on recalcitrant and impenitent sinners for all eternity. The ultimate vindication of His righteousness is the full and final triumph over sin and the complete destruction of all His enemies. Just as God raised up Pharaoh to demonstrate His power through the judgment on Egypt (Exod. 7:3; 14:4; Rom. 9:17–18), so He has decreed sin that He might vindicate His goodness, wisdom, and power before all creation by the execution of justice. The judgments of Hell and the death of Christ on the cross ensure that every sin ever committed will be fully punished.

Here we shall consider some of what the Scripture teaches concerning God's justice and how it is satisfied. These things have direct bearing in the modern church as many are confused about divine justice. Modern Evangelicals give little thought to the theology of God's righteous judgments and how it should inform our thinking and church life.

THE JUST JUDGE

These days of injustice will come to an end. The eternal and unchanging nature of God makes that certain. From the first words of Genesis to the end of Revelation, Scripture unequivocally and unapologetically affirms that God is just. Ultimately, His perfect and unchanging justice will be satisfied.

Abraham negotiated with God to spare the righteous in the cities of Sodom and Gomorrah. He appealed to God's justice and righteousness, saying, "Far be it from You to do such a thing, to slay the righteous with the wicked, so that the righteous and the wicked are treated alike. Far be it from You! Shall not the Judge of all the earth deal justly" (Gen. 18:25)? While Abraham emotionally wrestled with

God Doesn't Try to Execute Justice

God's revelation of wrath against Sodom, he knew God could be trusted to "deal justly" with all the inhabitants of the Earth. Even the instant destruction of cities full of hundreds, if not thousands, of wicked rebels was righteous.

Yahweh's authority, power, and sovereignty are founded upon His righteousness and justice. These are the foundation of His rule, as Psalm 89:14 declares: "Righteousness and justice are the foundation of Your throne; lovingkindness and truth go before You."[3] A throne is a seat of authority. He who sits on the throne wields the scepter, rules his kingdom, and exercises authority over his subjects. Some thrones are founded upon bloodshed and tyranny. Some are established by wars and intrigue. Some are usurped or gained by treachery. Some kings rule their subjects with injustice, partiality, violence, intimidation, corruption, and fear. God rules in righteousness, justice, faithfulness, and uprightness. As Moses sang in Deuteronomy 32:4, "The Rock! His work is perfect, for all His ways are just; a God of faithfulness and without injustice, righteous and upright is He."

God doesn't execute justice to satisfy a standard extrinsic to Himself. Justice isn't a principle that exists outside God and independent of His nature. Justice is an aspect of God's nature revealed in Scripture and written on our conscience. We can recognize and appreciate the principle of justice because we are created in the image of God (Gen. 1:26) and His law is written on our hearts (Rom. 2:12–16).[4] When God executes justice, He isn't conforming to some moral standard imposed upon Him by another. Rather, God executes justice because He is just and righteous. He is the definition and standard of perfect justice. All God's ways are just because He is just. He can never be unjust because He is perfectly righteous and entirely blameless. God is righteousness, justice, and truth.

In fact, God loves these virtues because they perfectly express His own nature. The psalmist describes Yahweh, saying, "He loves righteousness and justice; the earth is full of the lovingkindness of the LORD" (Ps. 33:5) and "the strength of the King loves justice; You

---

3. See also Ps. 97:2: "Clouds and thick darkness surround Him; righteousness and justice are the foundation of His throne."

4. We don't see justice pursued by the animal kingdom. The animals of the Serengeti don't hold court and put lions on trial for chasing down and killing the weakest zebra in the neighborhood. Animals don't contemplate moral standards, violations of property rights, or the value of animal life. Only human beings have the capacity to understand and desire justice because only they have been made in the image of God.

have established equity; You have executed justice and righteousness in Jacob" (Ps. 99:4).

Sin has invaded God's creation. Sinners have rebelled against His benevolent rule and trampled His truth underfoot. He must judge sin and sinners to satisfy the just demands of His righteous and holy nature. Scripture warns us of this coming judgment. "For He is coming to judge the earth. He will judge the world in righteousness and the peoples in His faithfulness" (Ps. 96:13).[5]

There is no court higher than God's, no justice more perfect, and no standard more equitable. He must and will hold court to ensure that all crimes are punished thoroughly. He alone is infinitely wise, powerful, and knowledgeable. No creature is unchanging and eternal, unbiased and impartial, or truthful and trustworthy.[6] Therefore, none is more qualified to be "Judge of all the earth" than Yahweh our God (Gen. 18:25). As Psalm 50:6 says, "And the heavens declare His righteousness, for God Himself is judge."

Against the backdrop of that Old Testament teaching, Jesus's claim in John 5 would have infuriated the Pharisees of His day.

> For the Father loves the Son, and shows Him all things that He Himself is doing; and the Father will show Him greater works than these, so that you will marvel. For just as the Father raises the dead and gives them life, even so the Son also gives life to whom He wishes. For not even the Father judges anyone, but He has given all judgment to the Son, so that all will honor the Son even as they honor the Father. He who does not honor the Son does not honor the Father who sent Him. (John 5:20–23)

Jesus Christ, the Divine Son, is the appointed mediator of Yahweh's salvation and the One through Whom the entire world will be judged (Matt. 25:31–46; Rev. 19:11–18; 20:11–15). Since Christ will

---

5. See also Ps. 98:9: "He is coming to judge the earth; He will judge the world with righteousness and the peoples with equity."

6. God is infinitely qualified to be a perfectly impartial and just judge. Though Elihu misapplied this truth in his accusations against Job, and though he didn't get much else right, he spoke rightly when he said, "Therefore, listen to me, you men of understanding. Far be it from God to do wickedness, and from the Almighty to do wrong. For He pays a man according to his work, and makes him find it according to his way. Surely, God will not act wickedly, and the Almighty will not pervert justice" (Job 34:10–12). Peter affirmed God's impartiality, saying, "I most certainly understand now that God is not one to show partiality" (Acts 10:34). See also Rom. 2:11: "For there is no partiality with God."

judge all men, "God is now declaring to men that all people everywhere should repent, because He has fixed a day in which He will judge the world in righteousness through a Man whom He has appointed, having furnished proof to all men by raising Him from the dead" (Acts 17:30–31). "It is a great honour put upon Christ; he who was himself judged, shall be judge: he who once hung upon the cross, shall sit upon the throne of judgment."[7] The perfect God-man is able to execute Yahweh's justice since "He is the image of the invisible God" (Col. 1:15), possessing all the attributes and fullness of Deity (Col. 2:9) manifested in the flesh (1 Tim. 3:16). "The exaltation bestowed upon him is the highest exaltation conceivable . . . and this exaltation will be verified and consummated in the judgement of the whole world."[8]

All God's vengeance against sin and sinners will be accomplished by and through Jesus Christ. He is the Savior to any and all who call upon Him for forgiveness and life. He is the just Judge of all the world, executing Yahweh's vengeance[9] upon evildoers and all who will not heed the summons of God's gospel. Paul promised the Thessalonian believers,

> For after all it is only just for God to repay with affliction those who afflict you, and to give relief to you who are afflicted and to us as well when the Lord Jesus will be revealed from

---

7. Watson, *A Body of Divinity*, 311.
8. Murray, *Collected Writings*, 2:415-16.
9. The infinitely righteous God has every right to take vengeance on those who have rebelled against His benevolent rule and assaulted His chosen people. When Scripture speaks of God's vengeance, it is not describing an uncontrolled, petty vindictiveness that we commonly associate with vengeance in the human realm. God's vengeance is the just retribution on rebels for their trespasses against His holy law. It is never uncontrolled, arbitrary, or impulsive but always an expression of His perfect nature. God says of Himself in Deut. 32:35, "Vengeance is Mine, and retribution." It is appropriate for Yahweh worshippers to long for and pray for the day of God's vengeance, just as the psalmist does in Ps. 94:1, saying, "O LORD, God of vengeance, God of vengeance, shine forth!" Even God's cataclysmic eschatological judgments will be met with praise and worship by the righteous.
After these things I heard something like a loud voice of a great multitude in heaven, saying,
"Hallelujah! Salvation and glory and power belong to our God; because His judgments are true and righteous; for He has judged the great harlot who was corrupting the earth with her immorality, and He has avenged the blood of His bond-servants on her." (Rev. 19:1–2)
It's comforting for God's people to know and affirm that "the LORD takes vengeance on His adversaries" (Nah. 1:2). Jesus comforted His disciples by reminding them that God will "bring about justice for His elect who cry to Him day and night" (Luke 18:7). Affirmations like this cut against the grain of modern Evangelicalism and the feel-good, sloppy sentimentality that characterizes most preaching, but they are true nonetheless.

heaven with His mighty angels in flaming fire, dealing out retribution to those who do not know God and to those who do not obey the gospel of our Lord Jesus. These will pay the penalty of eternal destruction, away from the presence of the Lord and from the glory of His power, when He comes to be glorified in His saints on that day, and to be marveled at among all who have believed—for our testimony to you was believed. (2 Thess. 1:6–10)

ALL HIS ATTRIBUTES

All God's attributes work in harmony, ensuring that the justice, righteousness, and vengeance He has promised will be thorough, meticulous, and perfect.

Yahweh's omniscience ensures that every last crime against His law will be fully and finally punished. Every deed done in darkness will be brought into the full light of truth. Every sin, every transgression, and every violation of His law is known by Him. He knows the hearts of all men, sees their motives, and knows their thoughts (1 Sam. 16:7). Everything God knows, He knows infallibly. He can't be mistaken about anything. He knows every thought you've ever had, every motive of your heart, and every deed you've done. He knows every action, affection, desire, lust, intention, yearning, and craving (Ps. 44:21). He isn't fooled by appearances or deceived by our self-deceptions. He is intimately acquainted with every detail of our existence from the moment of our conception to our last heartbeat (Ps. 139:3).

Since God's knowledge is thorough and perfect, He can't be in error about anything we've ever done. He can't forget anything.[10] Most sins committed by the wicked have passed from their memory. I doubt that your average, garden-variety pagan could make a list of one hundred lies they've told in the last year. However, on the day of judgment, every lie will bear witness against them in the court of God's perfect justice. God can't, nor will He, forget even one. Just

---

10. Scripture does use the language of God remembering our sins no more: "For I will be merciful to their iniquities, and I will remember their sins no more" (Heb. 8:12; see also Jer. 31:34; Heb. 10:17). This is a promise for those who are in the new covenant, whose sins have been forgiven in Jesus Christ. It is not that God forgets our sins in the sense of becoming unaware they were committed. Rather, God chooses to deal with us not on the basis of those sins but according to the righteousness merited by His Son, the Lord Jesus Christ. God refuses to call our sins to mind, hold them against us, or factor them into His loving relationship with His people.

one lie would be sufficient to justly damn them eternally (James 2:10). They shall be tried for, convicted of, and punished for every last one.

The thought of God's wrath being poured out against even one sin for all eternity is terrifying. But it isn't just one sin that God will punish. Nor is it just one kind of sin that God will punish. It is all kinds of sins and every last one of all the various kinds of sins. Justice will be satisfied when *every last sin* is thoroughly and exhaustively punished.[11] If even one sin should go unaccounted for in eternity, then God would fail to execute perfect justice. Every sin must be punished for justice to be done.

God's infallible knowledge means no sin will escape His notice or be lost to faulty memory. God's eternality guarantees that no sinner will escape justice by outliving Him. God's infinite power assures that no transgressor will escape justice by eluding Him, overpowering Him, or escaping from His hand. God's wisdom ensures that no rebel will outwit Him and gain acquittal. God's immutability guarantees that justice and righteousness will always be the foundation of His throne and that His holy, righteous indignation against sin and sinners will never subside or change (Ps. 55:19; Heb. 13:8; James 1:17).

Steven Lawson has put it well:

> Every one of God's dealings with man is marked by impeccable justice. Every verdict reached in His divine courtroom is the right decision. Every punishment or exoneration is the proper execution of equity. Every acquittal is perfectly pronounced. When the divine gavel comes down, every crime of cosmic treason against Him will be condemned and punished to the fullest extent of the law.[12]

TREASURE AND TERROR

This truth should terrify the unbeliever and comfort the one who trusts Christ. We are comforted not because we delight in the suffering of the wicked, but rather we know that God's justice, once satisfied in Christ, will never fall on us (Rom. 8:1). Believers escape God's wrath not because He ignores the just demands of His law, perverts justice, or compromises His standards. We escape the wrath of God because He has fully satisfied the demands of His law by extinguish-

---

11. Scripture consistently teaches that Hell is eternal: "These will go away into eternal punishment, but the righteous into eternal life" (Matt. 25:46; see also Rev. 20:10, 15). See the Recommended Reading section at the end of this chapter for more resources on the subject.
12. Lawson, *Show Me Your Glory*, 224.

ing His wrath on His Son. Christ has borne the penalty of sin on behalf of His people as our Substitute.[13] The one whose sins have been laid upon a substitute, whose price has been paid and debt discharged, possesses the blessed certainty that no further payment can be demanded for their sin. Christ is the satisfaction (1 John 2:2) of divine justice for all those in whose place He has died.

No further payment for sin can be required by God's holy justice. Christ has paid the full price for every last sin of all Yahweh's elect from the beginning of time to the last day. The full cup of the Father's wrath has been poured out on Him. He has absorbed the penalty for us. It would be *unjust* for God to punish the believer for even one of their many transgressions since the cost of their forgiveness and righteousness was the perfect and infinite sacrifice of Jesus Christ. He stood in their place on Calvary's tree. This is precisely Paul's point in Romans 8:31–34.

> What then shall we say to these things? If God is for us, who is against us? He who did not spare His own Son, but delivered Him over for us all, how will He not also with Him freely give us all things? Who will bring a charge against God's elect? God is the one who justifies; who is the one who condemns? Christ Jesus is He who died, yes, rather who was raised, who is at the right hand of God, who also intercedes for us.

Having been declared righteous through faith, the believer is at peace with God (Rom. 5:1). Christ has forever removed the enmity between Yahweh and His people, an enmity our sins created (Col. 2:13–15). With the cost of our transgressions fully paid, the believer will never face condemnation (Rom. 8:1). Thus, we can never be separated from the Father's undeserved love (Rom. 8:35–39). We can say with David in Psalm 32:1–2, "How blessed is he whose transgression is forgiven, whose sin is covered! How blessed is the man to whom the LORD does not impute iniquity, and in whose spirit there

---

13. We affirm the substitutionary nature of the death of Christ. Jesus didn't merely die to make men savable, nor to pay a potential penalty for sin, nor simply to demonstrate the love of God. Christ died to bear God's wrath against sinners by taking on Himself all the punishment for all the sins of all who believe on Him. The sins of Old Testament saints were punished on Christ as their Substitute (Isa. 53; 1 Pet. 2:21–25). Jesus Christ, the final sacrifice, has done what all the animal sacrifices of the old covenant could never do—namely, to put away sin through His death on the cross (Heb. 9:23–10:18). Those who lived prior to the death of Christ placed their faith in a sacrifice that was yet future. We place our faith in the One Who has come and made the sacrifice on our behalf.

is no deceit!" The perfection of God's justice guarantees that He'll never demand a double payment for crimes committed against His law. He cannot punish Christ for your sin and then demand payment from you for the very same transgressions. For the believer, God's justice means freedom from condemnation.

The perfection of God's knowledge ensures that He will never forget me. He will never forget you. He will never forget that He has satiated the demands of His justice on the head of your Substitute. He will never forget that His wrath against you has been extinguished. He knows fully all your sins and has exhausted His wrath against them on His Son.

His perfect immutability means His standard of justice will never change. Therefore, further payment will never be required. Since God is unchanging, His righteousness is unchanging. He gives us His own righteousness, an imperishable, never-fading, perfect righteousness that avails for all whose sins have been forgiven. That righteousness can never fade because it is Christ's perfection, and He is immutably righteous. Our eternal High Priest never ceases to make intercession for us (Heb. 7:23–25), guaranteeing that His sacrifice on our behalf is forever credited to our account. He preserves us in His righteousness forever.

God's justice for the sins of His people has been fully satisfied through the death of Christ on their behalf. His justice against the sins of those who will not repent and believe will come in the everlasting punishment endured in Hell. Therefore, in the end, every last sin will be fully accounted for and justly punished. The sins of the righteous (God's elect) are fully paid in Christ. The sins of the wicked (those passed over) are forever punished in Hell. God isn't *trying* to execute justice against sins committed in this world. He is sovereignly doing so in His way and on His timetable.

THE PUSH FOR "JUSTICE" IN THE CHURCH

These truths need to be affirmed afresh in the modern Western church. An insidious worldview is spreading like gangrene within Evangelicalism. It is a worldview, Marxist in its origins and manifestations, that denies the sufficiency of God's justice against sin. It seeks to revive the ethnic hostilities, class distinctions, and sinful animosities which the death of Christ and His payment for sin has put away. While hijacking gospel language, they promote ideologies and worldviews completely antithetical to the biblical gospel. "Woke" preachers and others in the social justice movement use words like *justice* and *righteousness* while promoting unjust and unrighteous standards within the church. This worldview has been referred to as woke Christianity, the social justice movement, or critical theory.[14] It is all poisonous fruit from the same rotten Marxist tree.

The social justice movement destroys unity in the church by promoting a view of justice that is patently unbiblical. Proponents advocate for "structures of justice" within the Christian community as if the gospel requires them. They "re-problematize"[15] grievances from past sins committed by people of previous generations and demand they be re-adjudicated. The ethnic, social, and class hostilities that characterized previous eras are reintroduced into our own time, and reparations are demanded. This has the disastrous effect of fomenting resentment, intensifying ethnic hostility, and promoting bitterness between brethren who have been reconciled by the work of Christ on the cross.

This ideology denies the sufficiency of God's work in executing justice His way. The lie of the social justice movement is very simple: justice has not and will not be done, therefore we must right those wrongs on God's behalf. They assume God is trying to right past wrongs by building a more just society. Their notion of social justice rests upon the assumption that divine justice isn't sufficient. They deny in practice that God is the only One Whose justice must and will be satisfied. They establish their own standards of justice and insist that their demands be met. It is difficult to imagine a more high-handed act of impudence by mere creatures.

THE GOSPEL IS JUSTICE

When God reconciles men to Himself, He reconciles them to one another. Ethnic reconciliation[16] is accomplished in Jesus Christ as

---

14. It's beyond the scope of this chapter and the purpose of this book to give a full critique of this movement. See Strachan, *Christianity and Wokeness*; and Baucham, *Fault Lines*. We highly recommend the *Just Thinking Podcast* with Darrell Harrison and Virgil Walker, as well as their book *Just Thinking: About Ethnicity*. Kootenai Church hosted an Equipping Conference on the subject featuring Darrell and Virgil. These sessions are archived on our various media platforms linked at https://kootenaichurch.org.

15. I first heard this term from Darrell Harrison, who borrowed it from a paper by Dr. E. San Juan Jr. entitled "From Race to Class Struggle: Re-Problematizing Critical Race Theory." To re-problematize an issue is to take something that isn't a modern issue and treat it as if it has never been resolved. Social justice proponents approach modern society as if there has been no improvement within social structures or on social issues. Re-problematizers lament race relations in America as if conditions haven't improved for minority groups since 1865.

16. The term *racial reconciliation* is widely used in our culture. We reject the Darwinist notion that humanity can be divided up into races. There is only one human race, comprised of various ethnicities, nationalities, skin colors, and other physical features. Scripture says that

He reconciles people. Races cannot be reconciled; only people can. The only ground for true reconciliation between peoples is the work of Christ, Who paid for sin and brought men and women from every tribe, tongue, class, and social status into one body. Those in Christ are one church, one people.

Hostility is always the result of sin. People sin against other people. People commit crimes against other people. This is true for every skin color, ethnicity, social class, nationality, background, and pedigree. It is true in every age, on every continent, and among all peoples. Every sin we commit against a fellow image-bearer reveals our hatred for the God in Whose image we are created. Jesus said, "For out of the heart come evil thoughts, murders, adulteries, fornications, thefts, false witness, slanders" (Matt. 15:19). Sinful men are at war with one another because they are at war with God. When God removes the hostility of sinners by changing their hearts and affections (Ezek. 36:26) and reconciling them to Himself through the work of Christ (2 Cor. 5:17–20; Rom. 5:1), they can be at peace with one another.

This is the very thing Paul was dealing with in Ephesians 2. The perpetual hostility that existed between Jews and Gentiles was deep-rooted, perdurable, and resilient. Yet even that abiding division was eliminated when God brought all ethnicities together in one church. Once "separate from Christ, excluded from the commonwealth of Israel, and strangers to the covenants of promise," Gentiles had no hope and were "without God in the world" (Eph. 2:12). Though they were in such a hopeless, destitute state of spiritual and ethnic alienation, God brought Gentiles near to Himself by the blood of Christ (Eph. 2:13). Where hostility once reigned, peace must now govern relationships within the body of Christ (Col. 3:15).

Men are at war with one another because they are at war with God. Being at peace with God, men must be at peace with one another.[17] Paul said in Ephesians 2:14–16,

---

God "made from one man every nation of mankind to live on all the face of the earth, having determined their appointed times and the boundaries of their habitation" (Acts 17:26).

17. The radical reconciliation accomplished at the cross affects every area of life and social structure. The cross transforms marriage relationships (Eph. 5:22–33), parental relationships (Eph. 6:1–4), and master-slave relationships (Eph. 6:5–9). Scripture must inform every dynamic of our interaction with and relationship to other people regardless of sex, ethnicity, or class. The regular act of coming to the Lord's Table in self-examination and unity forces believers of every background and social class to acknowledge that all people are accepted by God on the same basis. God shows no partiality. The slave and the master are equals at the Lord's Table. It was entirely possible in the early church for a man to be a slave at home while

> For He Himself is our peace, who made both groups into one and broke down the barrier of the dividing wall, by abolishing in His flesh the enmity, which is the Law of commandments contained in ordinances, so that in Himself He might make the two into one new man, thus establishing peace, and might reconcile them both in one body to God through the cross, by it having put to death the enmity.

Christians must be content with God's satisfaction of justice for their sin and the sins of others committed against them. The certainty that justice will be done for every sin ever committed frees the believer to rest in God's unfailing promises. Every wrong will be righted and every evil punished. Every sin committed against us is primarily a sin against God.[18] God's plan for executing justice must satisfy us if it satisfies Him. We aren't more righteous than He so as to hold higher standards by which He should judge. We aren't more knowledgeable than He that we should be disappointed with the scrupulousness of His justice. We aren't holier than He that we should be more incensed by violations of His law. If we won't rest in God's justice as He sees fit to execute it, we make ourselves His judge, critiquing His ways and scrutinizing His works. This is the height of conceit from a proud heart.

For believers, the Father has satisfied the just demands of His law by laying the sins of His people on His Son. For those outside His saving purposes, the just demands of His law will be executed in Hell as sinners are punished eternally under God's wrath. We must rest in this.

The Evangelical church's preoccupation with racial reconciliation and social justice is entirely unbiblical, misguided, and contrary to the gospel. The social justice movement, empowered by critical race theory, divides Christians in the body of Christ by resurrecting sins, re-

---

an elder in the church. The slave who must submit to his master's authority in one context might have the responsibility to shepherd his master's heart and give him spiritual instruction in another.

18. When David confessed his sin, he said in Ps. 51:3–4, "For I know my transgressions, and my sin is ever before me. Against You, You only, I have sinned and done what is evil in Your sight, so that You are justified when You speak and blameless when You judge." David had sinned against Bathsheba and Uriah. He had also sinned against his wives, his children, and, as the leader of Israel, the entire nation. Though all those people were affected by David's transgression, and though all were harmed by it and the effects of it in some measure, David's sin was ultimately against God, Who had shown him such grace and favor. It was a violation of God's law. David's most intense guilt came from that realization.

problematizing grievances, and re-adjudicating offenses. It suggests that the work of Christ on the cross that brings men and women from different ethnicities together is insufficient. We are encouraged to host Racial Reconciliation Sundays, a popular virtue-signaling exercise of the Southern Baptist Convention as of late. We are "wokescolded" if we aren't having conversations about race in the church or if we don't have proper "racial representation" among church leaders. It's assumed that congregations of homogenous skin color must be doing something wrong—an accusation always leveled against "white churches" and never against "black churches." As Darrell Harrison has pointed out, none of the social justice warriors ever say that the "black church" needs to be more white.

The cessation of hostilities between men and women of different ethnicities has already been effected through the death of Christ. One in His body, there remains no basis for ethnic division. Those who deny this are denying a glorious gospel truth. They are refusing to walk in gospel reality, rejecting God's answer to ethnic hostility. Christ has put to death that hostility. No longer enemies of God, believers have no grounds to be at enmity with each other. The hostility has been removed. Those who nurse grievances over race, economic status, or class are undermining the work and fruit of the gospel they claim to espouse.

Outside the true church of Jesus Christ, there are no grounds for reconciliation. There can be no true peace between peoples who have not first been reconciled to God. The hostility will remain since the heart of God's enemy remains unchanged. A government program can't change this. Public school anti-bullying campaigns won't bring peace. No measure of progressive religious genuflecting can bring lasting peace between ethnicities or cultures. The best we can expect from all these efforts is a perpetual grievance culture that swaps one victim group for another as grifters and opportunists fleece well-intentioned but naive sheep.

Christians preoccupied with establishing societal justice in this world have missed the mission. They organize ministries to achieve something that can't be accomplished in this age. We live in an imperfect world, and it is naive at best, and foolish at worst, to expect perfect justice in an inherently imperfect world. God isn't trying to make the world more just or establish an earthly kingdom from the corrupt political and societal structures of this age. He is calling sinners to repent and trust the once-for-all sacrifice of His Son that has satisfied His justice for all who believe. We aren't called to pursue racial reconciliation. We are called to announce that reconciliation has been accomplished in Christ.[19]

PERSONALLY CONTENT WITH GOD'S JUSTICE

The truth about God's justice has direct bearing upon the life of the believer in a number of ways.

First, you can rest in your free and full justification. If you're in Jesus Christ, you needn't fear any condemnation. This is the ground of your assurance: The Father, Who has emptied the cup of His wrath upon His Son, has saved back none for you to bear. The Father receives you with all the affection and joy that He has for His own beloved Son. You can be assured of your acceptance with the Father because of the work of the Son. He has clothed you with an unblemished, imperishable, and infinite righteousness that doesn't depend on your works, acts of service, or spiritual strengths. All your labors and sacrifices in gospel service should be done from a grateful heart. You couldn't be any more loved by God than you already are. His perfect love has removed all fear (1 John 4:18). With no debt to pay and no punishment to anticipate, you have no cause for fear.

Second, you can grant forgiveness to those who have wronged you. We have no grounds to take personal vengeance. Since every sin committed against us will receive full punishment, we can graciously forgive others. If the sin against us was committed by a believer, then the full punishment for that sin was paid by Jesus Christ. How can I demand a payment from that person when God Himself has refused to do so? If God has satisfied justice for the sin committed against me, then I can be satisfied that the wrong has been properly righted through the death of Christ. If an unbeliever has sinned against me, then I have no justification for vengeance since vengeance belongs to the Lord (Deut. 32:35; Rom. 12:19; Heb. 10:30). He will exact a perfect payment for that sin in the judgments of Hell. In short, the full punishment for every sin against me will be

---

19. Paul does describe his ministry as a "ministry of reconciliation" in 2 Cor. 5:18. He goes on to say, "Therefore, we are ambassadors for Christ, as though God were making an appeal through us; we beg you on behalf of Christ, be reconciled to God. He made Him who knew no sin to be sin on our behalf, so that we might become the righteousness of God in Him" (2 Cor. 5:20–21). He is not speaking of racial reconciliation but God's work of reconciling sinners to Himself through Christ. We are ambassadors for Christ who proclaim that reconciliation between God and men has been accomplished through the finished work of Christ. Reconciliation between men of different ethnicities is the fruit or by-product of reconciliation with God. "Be reconciled to God" is the heart of the gospel. "Be reconciled to your fellow man" is the fruit of the gospel.

fully paid. I don't need to receive any payment since, ultimately, the payment is not mine to demand at all.

Third, we don't need to be anxious or frustrated over the injustices of this world. Resentment, bitterness, anxiety, frustration, and anger over the inequities and injustices of this age are inappropriate responses for those who understand what God's justice entails. Though the short and momentary triumphs of the wicked are vexing to the believer (Ps. 73:1–14), the ultimate judgment upon the wicked will affirm God's goodness and glory (Ps. 73:15–28).[20]

This doesn't mean we shouldn't do what we can to promote true goodness in this world for the good of our neighbor. Men and women are created in the image of God and flourish in cultures and nations where criminals are punished and those who do good are rewarded. That is the biblical role of government (Rom. 13:3–4). We should never promote injustice, excuse sinful behavior, or turn a blind eye to the oppressed. We aren't advocating apathy and indifference toward the evils of society. Those things that harm image-bearers should concern us. We don't commend a negligent approach to social, political, or cultural involvement. Christians should live biblically, bringing God's Word to bear in every area of our lives and in every arena in which God has placed us. We do this for the glory of God and the good of our neighbor. But we aren't seeking to build a utopia. We aren't here to help God execute justice. He isn't *trying* to do so.

FOR THE SHEPHERDS

Gentlemen, we should never apologize for the biblical doctrine of Hell. God will be glorified in the damnation of sinners; therefore, we should not hide the truth from either God's people or the lost, nor should we ever soften the doctrine. It's common to hear preachers tiptoe around the issue of eternal damnation. Never do that! We should speak about this subject with all the sobriety, earnestness, and bluntness with which Scripture does. We must warn sinners of their eternal damnation. We must tell them that God's justice will fall upon them and grind them to powder. If they are outside Jesus Christ, their judgment will mean the loss of everything they cherish.

Let's be clear in our gospel presentations. Avoid euphemisms for sin. Don't speak of mistakes, wrong things, and missteps. Men and women are liars, blasphemers, thieves, fornicators, adulterers, idolaters, and God-hating rebels in love with darkness. This is the

---

20. See my (Jim's) book *The Prosperity of the Wicked* for a full study of that Psalm.

language of Scripture. Use it. Avoid euphemisms for Hell. Don't just speak of separation from God and being outside Heaven. We must warn sinners that they are going to outer darkness where there will be weeping and gnashing of teeth, eternal judgment, and suffering under the wrath of God as He pours out His just judgment upon justly damned rebels.

Let's stop speaking of this world, this age, and the political systems that characterize them as if they are capable of being reformed for Christian purposes. This world, its political structures, and its leaders aren't interested in true biblical justice. They don't understand it. Instead, they will fall under it and be crushed by it. Never speak of Heaven, Hell, or this age in any way that suggests God is *trying* to accomplish His purposes for them.

DISCUSSION QUESTIONS

1. Have you ever experienced injustice? How did you respond to it? What specific role did the gospel play in aiding and enabling your response?

2. Do you long for the return of Christ so that justice will be done? Do you look forward to escaping this sin-cursed world?

3. Has someone you know and care about been influenced by the social justice movement? In what ways? What help have you offered them? How did they respond? Is there anything more you can or should do?

4. When was the last time you heard an entire sermon on the subject of Hell? How did it strike you? What did you learn?

5. Is it difficult for you to rest in your justification? Why or why not? When are you most tempted to doubt the truth of your righteous standing before God?

6. How does the work of Christ on the cross enable and motivate forgiveness between believers?

7. How can we rest in God's justice? Is it difficult for you to rejoice in God's righteous judgments? Why or why not?

RECOMMENDED READING:

Fault Lines: The Social Justice Movement and Evangelicalism's Looming Catastrophe by Voddie T. Baucham Jr.

Sinners in the Hands of a Good God: Reconciling Divine Judgment and Mercy by David Clotfelter

Just Thinking: About Ethnicity by Darrell Harrison and Virgil Walker

The Prosperity of the Wicked: A Study of Psalm 73 by Jim Osman

Hell on Trial: The Case for Eternal Punishment by Robert A. Peterson

Christianity and Wokeness: How the Social Justice Movement Is Hijacking the Gospel—and the Way to Stop It by Owen Strachan

A Gospel Primer for Christians by Milton Vincent

Chapter 12:

God Doesn't Try to Establish His Kingdom

12

Where is history going?

That's a million-dollar question! There are several ways to ask it. Why am I here? What should I be doing? What will come after me? Is time never-ending? Do we live in a random world where events, thoughts, and actions are merely molecules in motion, matter colliding in mayhem? Can humanity determine its own future? Is there a point to human existence? What is God doing in time? Does He have a plan?

Humans have a unique capacity to contemplate the future. We wonder about it, worry about it, and try to plan for it. We bet on it, speculate about it, and try to insure against its unforeseen elements. Animals may store food for winter months or embark on fantastic migratory journeys governed by the seasons, but those created in God's image have a capacity to contemplate and plan for the future in a way that is unparalleled in the animal kingdom. Your poodle doesn't plan dinner with his friends two weeks out.

Our culture is obsessed with the future. There's a reason the Left Behind series by Tim LaHaye and Jerry Jenkins was so popular. In the secular marketplace, The Hunger Games books and movies became a cultural phenomenon. Likewise, the Divergent series, portraying a dystopian future in an apocalyptic wasteland, captured the imaginations of millions. Humanity is fascinated by the future and what it might have in store.

CATASTROPHE AND CONVERGENCE

Oddly enough, our culture simultaneously entertains two entirely different visions for the future of humanity: the dystopian catastrophe and the utopian convergence.

We are constantly warned of the dystopian catastrophe certain to befall our planet if we don't change course. We are both over fifty years old at the time of this writing. We don't remember a time when we haven't lived under the constant drumbeat of apocalyptic environmental and humanitarian doomsday warnings from "experts" promising an irreversible catastrophe in our lifetime. We've been promised a worldwide famine, an ice age by the year 2000, water and food rationing in America by 1980, ozone depletion, planetary cooling, acid rain, regional droughts, rising sea levels, ice-free polar caps, overpopulation, mass starvation, declining food production, global shortages of gold, tin, oil, natural gas, copper, and aluminum, the death of the world's oceans and all sea life, severe air pollution, and global plagues. That's only a sampling of the ecodisaster doomsday predictions over the last fifty years.[1]

When I was in grade school, we were consistently informed by experts in white coats that by the year 2000 we would be in another ice age. The summers would be too cool and short to grow gardens in North Idaho. Today we are promised cataclysmic global warming on a scale that threatens the extinction of life. The solution is always the same: throw taxpayer money at special interests, researchers, and organizations that fashion themselves the saviors of humanity. Allegedly, our only hope of avoiding extinction is to tax and control everything that exists while giving unlimited power over our lives to our moral betters in the nation's capital. They will save us from destruction by flying around the world in private jets to climate-shame everyone into complying with their benevolent agenda.

With stunning cognitive dissonance, secularists also promise a glorious utopian convergence in which our hopes and dreams are realized, our potential fulfilled, and our problems solved. Every two years, Americans drive to the polls by the millions to vote for the candidate who best convinces them of their ability to solve all their problems. The amount of faith we place in our institutions, politicians, and

---

[1]. You can find a list of fifty such predictions with accompanying news articles in Mark J. Perry's blog post "50 Years of Failed Doomsday, Eco-pocalyptic Predictions; the So-Called 'Experts' Are 0–50" (https://www.aei.org/carpe-diem/50-years-of-failed-doomsday-eco-pocalyptic-predictions-the-so-called-experts-are-0-50/ [https://perma.cc/4TXZ-H5RN]).

their ability to rid our lives of all discomfort would mystify previous generations.

Political candidates promise to lower crime; fix broken families; improve education; heal the environment; solve inner-city degradation; legislate effectively; end wars; lower the cost of health care and prescription drugs; solve the energy crisis; cure cancers, plagues, and Alzheimer's; feed the hungry; clean the air; fix water systems and infrastructure; bring transportation into the twenty-first century; lower inflation; prevent recessions; bring peace to the Middle East; protect us from all enemies, foreign and domestic; fine-tune the economy; solve racism; eliminate poverty; end hate crimes; root out political corruption; eradicate inequality; defend democracy; unite the nation; and usher us into the golden age of American greatness.

What is required for such a perfect society? Well, it is simple really. Not surprisingly, it is the very same thing needed to protect you from the dystopian disaster they say threatens us all. They need your vote, your money, and your willingness to give them complete control over every facet of your life, the economy, culture, education, and technology. That's all. What could go wrong?

This secular utopia is within our grasp. Once our moral and intellectual betters can regulate business, censor the public square, and punish all dissent from their collectivist vision, the grand age of human progress will dawn. Our needs will be met by machines. Our physical and emotional afflictions will be healed by drugs. The dangers to our peace, prosperity, and health will be vanquished. The perfect and inevitable convergence of government power, scientific discovery, and technological advancement will usher in a utopia which previous generations could only imagine. This is a secular eschatology. The humanistic, secular religion of the current progressive dogmatists warns of the coming dystopian catastrophe (the secular version of Hell) so we'll be adequately motivated to forfeit anything and everything we hold dear to achieve their utopian convergence (the secular version of Heaven).

These two destinies form the secular eschatology of the progressive religion of our day. It is a false religion, an unbiblical worldview with an unbiblical eschatology. It offers its own answer to the question "Where is history going?" Unfortunately, it is an answer dreamed up by the devil himself.

A BIBLICAL ALTERNATIVE

The Bible gives a far more God-centered answer. History isn't headed toward humanity's extinction in a dystopian catastrophe nor toward its superficial liberation in a secular, atheistic utopian convergence of technology, government, and science. History is progressing inexorably toward a Kingdom. God is working through all human history to accomplish His ultimate purpose: His triumph over all His enemies, sin, and death for the glorification of His name and the good of His people, whom He will rule in a Kingdom of righteousness and holiness forever. God isn't *trying* to accomplish this. He is infallibly working to establish His Kingdom, ruled by the Lord Jesus Christ. The appointed Davidic King will reign over a redeemed humanity in a perfect, always expanding, never-ending messianic Kingdom.[2]

This Kingdom is the ultimate eschatological goal of God's creative purposes and redeeming works. It's a plan that can't be thwarted or overruled. The establishment of His Kingdom is as inviolable and inevitable as His accomplishment of redemption for His elect, their ultimate sanctification, and their future glory (Rom. 8:28–30). The judgment of the nations (Joel 3:2), the punishment of the devil (Rev. 20:10), and the fiery destruction of this creation (2 Pet. 3:7–12) are all certain and guaranteed future realities. God won't *try* to do these things. He isn't *trying* to direct all things toward that end. He is, at this very moment, inexorably carrying the entire creation toward that Kingdom. He has fixed a day for the judgment of the world (Acts 17:30–31). He knows infallibly the precise day on which He will judge the nations (Ps. 110:6; Isa. 2:4; Rev. 11:18), raise His people in glorified bodies (John 5:28–29), and establish the earthly Kingdom of the Son in fulfillment of the sure and certain promises to David (2 Sam. 7:8–17; Ps. 89; Rev. 20:1–6).

He knows and has determined all future events (Isa. 42:8–9; 43:9–12; 44:6–8; 46:9–11). No purpose of His can be thwarted (Job

---

2. It is beyond the scope of this book, and certainly this chapter, to expound upon the nature and timing of that promised Kingdom. Nor do we intend to defend or critique particular eschatological perspectives like premillennialism, postmillennialism, or amillennialism. We're both committed to premillennial eschatology. This is the doctrinal position of the church we pastor. We unashamedly preach and defend that doctrine and the hermeneutical methodology that inevitably leads to that eschatology. We believe Jesus and the apostles read and interpreted the Old Testament and understood its Kingdom promises in the same way the original readers of the Old Testament did. The Jewish rejection of their Messiah didn't cause Yahweh to redefine, allegorize, or spiritualize the Kingdom promises. Their rejection of Christ and the subsequent inclusion of Gentiles into the salvific blessings of the new covenant were part of God's plan from eternity past. The prophetic promises of a literal physical Kingdom for national Israel are not the least bit incompatible with that eternal plan.

42:2). He is the Sovereign Who reigns over all creation (Ps. 115:3; 135:6; Dan. 4:35; Rom. 9:19). God will accomplish all His good pleasure without fail (Isa. 46:10). Therefore, the fulfillment of His intention to establish His Kingdom, on His timetable, as He has promised, is certain.

DANIEL AND THE MESSIANIC KINGDOM

The book of Daniel is known to most as an Old Testament prophetic book featuring strange visions of weird animals, structurally unsound statues, odd prophecies about horns and long-forgotten kingdoms, and really exciting Sunday school stories. The refusal to eat the king's dainties, the fiery furnace, and the lions' den make for engaging morality tales certain to hold a kid's attention. However, these stories are intended to demonstrate that Yahweh Most High is to be praised and honored.

> For His dominion is an everlasting dominion,
> And His kingdom endures from generation to generation.
> All the inhabitants of the earth are accounted as nothing,
> But He does according to His will in the host of heaven
> And among the inhabitants of earth;
> And no one can ward off His hand
> Or say to Him, "What have You done?" (Dan. 4:34–35)

That is as clear and concise a statement of the absolute sovereignty of God as human language can form. You would be well served to memorize that passage and recite it aloud every time you use the phrase *God is trying to*. In that short description, God's power, authority, and complete control over all things is contrasted with "the host of heaven" and "the inhabitants of earth." No angel, man, or council of either can stop God from accomplishing all that is "according to His will." He is accountable to none. No one can charge Him with wrongdoing. He takes questions from no one. None can call Him to account or render judgment upon the appropriateness of His actions. All God does and all He wills is holy, righteous, just, and good. He stands before no higher court.

His absolute and unquestionable sovereignty is vividly on display in His dealings with the kingdoms and nations of human history. Daniel served in the court of Nebuchadnezzar, the king of Babylon. Babylon was the most dominant, powerful, and wealthy kingdom of its time. Daniel had a front-row seat to the machinations of human kingdom authority. By God's providence, he lived long enough to see the

Babylonian Empire rise to the pinnacle of military and economic greatness and then fall to the upstart Medo-Persian Empire.

Daniel watched as Babylon conquered nation after nation, colonizing and subjugating peoples, cultures, and tribes (including his own) and ruling vast expanses of land and natural resources. Then he watched Darius the Mede take all that Nebuchadnezzar had acquired (Dan. 5:30–31). The drama of rising and falling kings and kingdoms is the work of God. It serves to move history toward the inevitable establishment of God's messianic Kingdom (Dan. 2:44). That eternal Kingdom will be possessed by the "saints of the Highest One" (Dan. 7:18, 27). They will enjoy the benefits, blessings, and glory of God's rule and reign over them as His grateful and adoring subjects. The chaos of the world's kingdoms, the turbulences of political events, and the machinations of potentates only serve His unalterable purposes. They move us inexorably toward that eternal Kingdom. It can't be stopped, avoided, or delayed. God isn't *trying* to establish a Kingdom. He is!

The destruction of Judea by Nebuchadnezzar would have appeared to the Jews to be the fall and end of the Davidic Kingdom. God had promised David, "Your house and your kingdom shall endure before Me forever; your throne shall be established forever" (2 Sam. 7:16). After the death of David's son Solomon, the Davidic Kingdom gradually declined in power, influence, and wealth. In fact, it was immediately divided into a northern kingdom, Israel, and a southern kingdom, Judah (1 Kings 12:1–20).

The Northern Kingdom was conquered by the Assyrians in 721 BC. That destruction was regarded by Judah as the righteous judgment of God upon a rebellious nation steeped in idolatry and immorality. Further, they would have viewed it as divine confirmation that the blessing of God, and the continuation of the Davidic line, would fall to the Southern Kingdom comprised of just two tribes, Judah and Benjamin. When the Southern Kingdom was laid waste by Nebuchadnezzar in 586 BC, one singular question would have been at the forefront of every Jewish mind: "Is this the end of the Davidic line, the failure of God's promise?"

What about the kingdom promised to David? The last of the kings from David's line had been either executed or taken into exile to die under Nebuchadnezzar's oversight. Solomon's Temple was robbed of its riches, looted of its instruments, and deserted by its

God. The wall around Jerusalem was destroyed, and the once glorious kingdom was gone. The Davidic monarchy had come to an end.

What did this mean for the plan and purpose of God? David was promised a Son Who would sit on his throne to rule and reign forever. How could that promise be fulfilled if the Jews were the vassals of a wicked pagan king? Had God's promises failed? Had He changed His mind? Did the unfaithfulness of the Jews nullify God's promise of an eternal Davidic Kingdom?

The book of Daniel answers these questions. Nebuchadnezzar's vision of the statue (Dan. 2:31–45) was itself a prophecy of the series of kingdoms that would follow Babylon (Medo-Persia, Greece, and Rome). From the human perspective, this series of kingdoms appeared to be the fruit of human effort, military victories, and political intrigue, but behind the scenes, God was directing it all. Daniel said, "Let the name of God be blessed forever and ever, for wisdom and power belong to Him. It is He who changes the times and the epochs; He removes kings and establishes kings; He gives wisdom to wise men and knowledge to men of understanding" (Dan. 2:20–21).

Nebuchadnezzar's ascendency was no accident. He was appointed by God, Who sovereignly rules all things. Far from signaling the failure of God's promises, the rise of Nebuchadnezzar was necessary for the fulfillment of them. It would comfort the Jewish people to hear that the rise and fall of kings and kingdoms would ultimately end in the fulfillment of God's promise to David.

> In the days of those kings the God of heaven will set up a kingdom which will never be destroyed, and that kingdom will not be left for another people; it will crush and put an end to all these kingdoms, but it will itself endure forever. Inasmuch as you saw that a stone was cut out of the mountain without hands and that it crushed the iron, the bronze, the clay, the silver and the gold, the great God has made known to the king what will take place in the future; so the dream is true and its interpretation is trustworthy. (Dan. 2:44–45)

To demonstrate His absolute sovereignty, God judged Nebuchadnezzar by removing him from his position of authority (Dan. 4:28–33). He drove Nebuchadnezzar into the field to eat grass like a beast of the Earth for seven years "in order that the living may know that the Most High is ruler over the realm of mankind, and bestows it on whom He wishes and sets over it the lowliest of men" (Dan. 4:17). That was stated by the angel in Nebuchadnezzar's dream (v. 17) and affirmed by Daniel in the interpretation of the dream (v. 25) and by God to Nebuchadnezzar at the moment of judgment (v. 32). At the end of the seven years, Nebuchadnezzar had learned a very important lesson. He said of the Most High God, "His kingdom is an everlasting kingdom and His dominion is from generation to generation" (v. 3). He "blessed the Most High and praised and honored Him who lives forever," saying,

> For His dominion is an everlasting dominion,
> And His kingdom endures from generation to generation.
> All the inhabitants of the earth are accounted as nothing,
> But He does according to His will in the host of heaven
> And among the inhabitants of earth;
> And no one can ward off His hand
> Or say to Him, "What have You done?" (Dan. 4:34–35)

Belshazzar ignored the lesson taught to his father, Nebuchadnezzar, so the Lord wrote out His judgment decree on the palace wall before all his nobles and officials (Dan. 5:5–6). Belshazzar would learn the same lesson as Nebuchadnezzar. Before Daniel interpreted the writing on the wall, he reproved Belshazzar for his pride and blasphemy, saying,

> O king, the Most High God granted sovereignty, grandeur, glory and majesty to Nebuchadnezzar your father. Because of the grandeur which He bestowed on him, all the peoples, nations and men of every language feared and trembled before him. . . . But when his heart was lifted up and his spirit became so proud that he behaved arrogantly, he was deposed from his royal throne and his glory was taken away from him. He was also driven away from mankind, and his heart was made like that of beasts, and his dwelling place was with the wild donkeys. He was given grass to eat like cattle, and his body was drenched with the dew of heaven until he recognized that the Most High God is ruler over the realm of mankind and that He sets over it whomever He wishes. (Dan. 5:18–21)

God gave Nebuchadnezzar power and authority. Then He took them away. Then He restored them to Nebuchadnezzar. God gave power to Belshazzar. Then God took away the power and the kingdom and gave it to Darius the Mede. "That same night Belshazzar

God Doesn't Try to Establish His Kingdom

the Chaldean king was slain. So Darius the Mede received the kingdom at about the age of sixty-two" (Dan. 5:30–31).

After Daniel survived the night in the lions' den,

> Then Darius the king wrote to all the peoples, nations and men of every language who were living in all the land: "May your peace abound! I make a decree that in all the dominion of my kingdom men are to fear and tremble before the God of Daniel;
>
>> For He is the living God and enduring forever,
>> And His kingdom is one which will not be destroyed,
>> And His dominion will be forever." (Dan. 6:25–26)

In chapter 7, Daniel received a vision in which all the previous themes of the book converge:

> I kept looking
> Until thrones were set up,
> And the Ancient of Days took His seat;
> His vesture was like white snow
> And the hair of His head like pure wool.
> His throne was ablaze with flames,
> Its wheels were a burning fire.
> A river of fire was flowing
> And coming out from before Him;
> Thousands upon thousands were attending Him,
> And myriads upon myriads were standing before Him;
> The court sat,
> And the books were opened. (Dan. 7:9–10)

In this vision, Yahweh, the sovereign God, Who alone possesses life, immortality, and authority, gives an everlasting Kingdom to "One like a Son of Man."

> I kept looking in the night visions,
> And behold, with the clouds of heaven
> One like a Son of Man was coming,
> And He came up to the Ancient of Days
> And was presented before Him.
> And to Him was given dominion,
> Glory and a kingdom,
> That all the peoples, nations and men of every language
> Might serve Him.
> His dominion is an everlasting dominion

Which will not pass away;
And His kingdom is one
Which will not be destroyed. (Dan. 7:13–14)

This Kingdom will "crush and put an end to all these kingdoms, but it will itself endure forever" (Dan. 2:44). The end of the story is glorious for believers. The "saints of the Highest One will receive the kingdom and possess the kingdom forever, for all ages to come" (Dan. 7:18). Yahweh's saints have no true home in this world. We are ostracized and excluded, reproached and cast down, persecuted and oppressed for the Lord's sake by the kingdoms of this world. However, "the sovereignty, the dominion and the greatness of all the kingdoms under the whole heaven will be given to the people of the saints of the Highest One; His kingdom will be an everlasting kingdom, and all the dominions will serve and obey Him" (Dan. 7:27).

The book of Daniel answers a lot of pressing questions. Can anything thwart the establishment of God's eternal Kingdom and the glory He has promised for His people? Will the promises of God fail? Is there any authority in Heaven or on Earth that will prevent God from giving an earthly Kingdom to David's greater Son?[3] Clearly, the answer is no.

ISAIAH AND THE MESSIANIC KINGDOM

The glory of Christ's eternal Kingdom is foretold in the book of Isaiah. The birth, nature, and reign of the King is described. It's common around Christmas to read the familiar prophecy of the birth of Christ found in Isaiah 9:6: "For a child will be born to us, a son will be given to us; and the government will rest on His shoulders; and His name will be called Wonderful Counselor, Mighty God, Eternal Father, Prince of Peace."

Those familiar words mention a government resting on His shoulders. That is a figure of speech that describes bearing the burden, carrying the authority, and executing the office of a government.

---

3. It is our conviction that this messianic Kingdom described in Dan. 2 and 7 is the Davidic Kingdom revivified. Jesus is the rightful heir of the Davidic promises, and He will fulfill the Davidic covenant when He rules on David's throne in Jerusalem over a worldwide Kingdom. This is described in Rev. 20 and will last on this Earth for one thousand years. When the thousand years is complete, God will judge the living and the dead, destroy this present creation with an intense heat, and re-create (resurrect) it as a New Heaven and a New Earth. The throne of that eternal Kingdom given to the Son of Man will continue through the thousand-year earthly reign into the new creation. It will be an eternal and everlasting Kingdom. Though unbelievers will be present during part of the Millennial Kingdom, they will not continue to live in the Kingdom in the new creation. The glories of that eternal righteous reign in a new creation belong only to God's people.

The administration of an earthly Kingdom will rest upon His shoulders. He will rule and administer a Kingdom. This is what God promised David and what the Jews of Isaiah's day understood concerning the coming Messiah. He would rule and reign in an earthly Kingdom. The very next verse of Isaiah makes it even more clear.

> There will be no end to the increase of His government or of peace,
> On the throne of David and over his kingdom,
> To establish it and to uphold it with justice and righteousness
> From then on and forevermore.
> The zeal of the LORD of hosts will accomplish this. (Isa. 9:7)

God promised to seat the Messiah "on the throne of David and over his kingdom." That isn't a heavenly throne. That isn't a spiritual throne. It doesn't promise a spiritual reign. Jesus Christ will take the throne of David, receive the messianic Davidic Kingdom, and rule it "with justice and righteousness from then on and forevermore" (Isa. 9:7).

Gabriel's announcement to Mary concerning the Son she would bear identified Him as the fulfillment of that Old Testament hope. "He will be great and will be called the Son of the Most High; and the Lord God will give Him the throne of His father David; and He will reign over the house of Jacob forever, and His kingdom will have no end" (Luke 1:32–33).

How was it possible that a kingdom which "ended" over twenty-five centuries ago (586 BC) would be reestablished and given to the Son of Man? Let the reader understand; "The zeal of the LORD of hosts will accomplish this" (Isa. 9:7). He will not *try* to accomplish this. God doesn't try. He will!

THE PSALMS AND THE MESSIANIC KINGDOM

Yahweh's answer to the rebellious nations in Psalm 2 is a promise to establish His Kingdom and appoint His Son as the King Who will rule them in justice and righteousness.

> Why are the nations in an uproar
> And the peoples devising a vain thing?
> The kings of the earth take their stand
> And the rulers take counsel together
> Against the LORD and against His Anointed, saying,

> "Let us tear their fetters apart
> And cast away their cords from us!"
> He who sits in the heavens laughs,
> The Lord scoffs at them.
> Then He will speak to them in His anger
> And terrify them in His fury, saying,
> "But as for Me, I have installed My King
> Upon Zion, My holy mountain.
> I will surely tell of the decree of the LORD:
> He said to Me, 'You are My Son,
> Today I have begotten You.
> Ask of Me, and I will surely give the nations as Your inheritance,
> And the very ends of the earth as Your possession.
> You shall break them with a rod of iron,
> You shall shatter them like earthenware.'" (Ps. 2:1–9)

All the rulers of the Earth should stand up and take notice. They will be judged and crushed by this King if they will not take refuge in Him.

> Now therefore, O kings, show discernment;
> Take warning, O judges of the earth.
> Worship the LORD with reverence
> And rejoice with trembling.
> Do homage to the Son, that He not become angry, and you perish in the way,
> For His wrath may soon be kindled.
> How blessed are all who take refuge in Him! (Ps. 2:10–12)

According to Psalm 110, the most quoted Psalm in the New Testament, this messianic King is also a priest after the order of Melchizedek (Ps. 110:4; Heb. 7:14–17). The cataclysmic establishment of His Kingdom will mean judgment and destruction for all who refuse to find their refuge in Him and His priestly sacrifice for sin.

> The LORD has sworn and will not change His mind,
> "You are a priest forever
> According to the order of Melchizedek."
> The Lord is at Your right hand;
> He will shatter kings in the day of His wrath.
> He will judge among the nations,
> He will fill them with corpses,

He will shatter the chief men over a broad country. (Ps. 110:4–6)

The Psalms are filled with references to the Messiah-King and His Kingdom. Dozens of chapters in the prophetic books of the Old Testament are dedicated to describing the nature and form of the coming Kingdom. The Old Testament is a historical record of men failing to fulfill God's design for the Kingdom. It anticipates His ultimate triumph through His appointed Servant-King. The Gospels chronicle the life of this King and His ultimate rejection by the nation He came to rule. The Epistles give instructions to the church (the bride of the King) as she awaits His return to establish His Kingdom.

John Bright has rightly noted, "The Bible is *one book*. Had we to give that book a title, we might with justice call it 'The Book of the Coming Kingdom of God.' That is, indeed, its central theme everywhere."[4] Alva J. McClain says, "In the Biblical doctrine of the Kingdom of God we have *the* Christian philosophy of history."[5]

THE END OF THE WORLD AS WE KNOW IT

We must allow the following truths to govern the way we think and speak of this world.

First, when we speak of the injustices, evils, and rebellion of the nations, we should describe them in terms of the ultimate victory God will have over His enemies. The angst you feel over the current condition of the government in whichever nation you live is, in the ultimate sense, undue. Eventually, all the kingdoms of this world will be destroyed. They and their people shall become the kingdoms of our God and of His Christ. Canada, the United States, Japan, Germany, et al. will be judged and destroyed at the coming of our King. As empires crumble, and they will, Christians must rest in the truth that God raises up kings and takes down kings according to His will and for His purposes.

The rise and fall of nations should be a constant reminder that "our citizenship is in heaven, from which also we eagerly wait for a Savior, the Lord Jesus Christ" (Phil. 3:20). He "will be revealed from heaven with His mighty angels in flaming fire, dealing out retribution to those who do not know God and to those who do not obey the gospel of our Lord Jesus" (2 Thess. 1:7–8).

---

4. Bright, *The Kingdom of God*, 197 (emphasis in original).
5. McClain, *Greatness of the Kingdom*, 5 (emphasis in original).

A biblical response to the political machinations of the wicked is not hand-wringing, preoccupied political involvement in hopes of Christianizing America, reclaiming culture, or returning to the good old days. Instead, we must remind people that there is a coming Kingdom, a Kingdom of perfect righteousness and justice, sovereignly ruled by the One Who has been the object of their hatred and scorn.

> From His mouth comes a sharp sword, so that with it He may strike down the nations, and He will rule them with a rod of iron; and He treads the wine press of the fierce wrath of God, the Almighty. And on His robe and on His thigh He has a name written, "KING OF KINGS, AND LORD OF LORDS." (Rev. 19:15–16)

As ambassadors of Christ, we proclaim the good news of His completed redemptive work and His soon and coming judgment. God will use His gospel to call His people to Himself (Rom. 1:16). Our task is to plead with men to be reconciled to God through Jesus Christ before His wrath is executed on rebels. They must "do homage to the Son, that He not become angry, and you perish in the way, for His wrath may soon be kindled" (Ps. 2:12). Truly, "how blessed are all who take refuge in Him!" (Ps. 2:12)

Second, we should ignore the apocalyptic doomsday scenarios of the progressive secularist religion. Do not concede one inch of ground to their religion of Earth worship and environmentalism. This is a disposable planet. It isn't intended to last forever. It's under a curse, dying and destined for the ash heap of history. God will dispose of this world in a fiery conflagration. Until that time, mankind can't destroy it. Our carbon emissions cannot endanger the entire human race.

When Christians adopt the language, priorities, and worldview of progressive environmentalism, they pay homage to a false religious system and its pagan gods. Mankind is not going to destroy himself by burning too much fossil fuel, using too much energy, or producing too many pollutants. This world will continue as a habitable place for mankind until it is destroyed in judgment by God Himself. God isn't trying to clean up the planet. He isn't trying to save the environment.

We know where history is going. We know how this creation will end. We know its destiny. We know the goal of all of God's works. Therefore, we can rest in that knowledge, trusting in His purposes and His ability to bring to pass all that concerns His Kingdom and our place in it. "The zeal of the LORD of hosts shall accomplish this" (Isa. 9:7).

FOR THE SHEPHERDS

Pastors, remind your people regularly of God's ultimate triumph over evil. Scripture repeatedly encourages the people of God with that truth. As the West crumbles, persecution looms, and the true church is surrounded by false professors and apostates, the people of God need to hear His promises concerning the destruction of evil, His judgment on the wicked, and His victory over all the nations. We would encourage you to make this a regular aspect of your preaching ministry, as Scripture often points to the return of Christ as motivation for the work of sanctification (1 Pet. 1:7; 4:7; 5:4; 1 John 2:28; 3:2–3).

We regularly preach and counsel with these truths. They embolden the sheep, encourage the fainthearted, and strengthen the weak. Let's encourage the ambassadors of Christ toward fearless, triumphant hope!

DISCUSSION QUESTIONS

1. Is God's Kingdom physical or spiritual? Is it future or present? Do your answers to those questions affect the way you do ministry? If so, how and why?

2. Do you long and pray for God's Kingdom to come (Matt. 6:10)? Is this a source of comfort and encouragement to your Christian faith? Why or why not?

3. Would you consider God's Kingdom to be an essential part of a complete gospel presentation? Why or why not?

4. Does Daniel's vision of the future thrill your heart? How does it instill confidence and boldness in God's people?

5. Anyone in Western culture who questions the current view of anthropogenic climate change is branded a "denier" because they don't accept "scientific consensus." Can you think of any other "scientific consensus" that was later found to be incorrect? What is your ultimate source of authority on the ultimate destiny of mankind and the planet?

6. Compare the objects of worship, ethical requirements, and eschatologies of biblical Christianity and Western environmentalism.

7. During the COVID-19 pandemic, we were told to "trust the science." In the US, we even had a particular scientist claim that "attacks on me, quite frankly, are attacks on science," as if disagreeing with him constituted a denial of science itself.[6] How does "trusting the science" fit into a biblical worldview? How does it apply to our eschatology?

8. If our citizenship is in Heaven, and all current political entities are merely secular and temporal, how invested should we be in secular political matters? Should Christians vote, serve a political party, run for office, educate themselves on political candidates, etc.? How much of our time and other resources should be devoted to political concerns?

9. God controls the leaders of nations. "He removes kings and establishes kings" (Dan. 2:21). In your nation, what are the means He uses for that purpose? What is your ethical responsibility as a Christian to participate in those means?

10. We assert in this chapter that God's establishing for Himself a Kingdom is a central theme of Scripture and of history. What other central biblical themes would you identify, and how are they related to God's establishment of His Kingdom?

RECOMMENDED READING:

Heaven by Randy Alcorn

The Greatness of the Kingdom: An Inductive Study of the Kingdom of God by Alva J. McClain

Thy Kingdom Come: Tracing God's Kingdom Program and Covenant Promises Throughout History by J. Dwight Pentecost

He Will Reign Forever: A Biblical Theology of the Kingdom of God by Michael Vlach

---

6. Porterfield, "Fauci on GOP Criticism."

God Doesn't Try to Establish His Kingdom

The Millennial Kingdom: A Basic Text in Premillennial Theology by John Walvoord

Chapter 13

Conclusion

13

We love the sovereignty of God! It's a precious doctrine. The theme of God's supreme sovereignty is ubiquitous in Scripture, permeating the whole of Christian theology. Every element of theology proper will remain a mystery to a student of Scripture if the perfection of God's sovereignty doesn't inform the study of all His works.

God's actions in eternity past, His eternal decrees of predestination and election, are the prerogatives of a sovereign God. He sovereignly created according to His good pleasure. He sovereignly decreed sin in the garden, judged sin in the flood, called Abraham out of Ur of the Chaldeans, sent a famine upon nations to drive His people into Egypt, and destroyed the Egyptians in the exodus. By His sovereignty, He destroyed the nations in Canaan and gave His people the land. By His sovereignty, He judged His people for breaking His covenant, raised up the Assyrians and Babylonians to take His people captive, and then brought His people back to their homeland. According to His sovereign plan, the second Person of the Trinity took upon Himself human flesh and, in the fullness of time, died for His people, was buried, and rose again. He sovereignly ascended to Heaven, where He sits at the Father's right hand. He is sovereignly building His church and will return for His bride. In sovereignty, He will judge the living and the dead, establish His Kingdom, abolish death, destroy this creation with fire, create a New Heaven and a New Earth, and reign as sovereign King forevermore. From eternity past to eternity future, He is the sovereign God. At no point has He abandoned His sovereignty, suspended His sovereignty, or allowed any creature to usurp His sovereignty.

This truth is despised by the world, derided by the untaught believer, doubted by the ignorant, and dismissed by the foolish. Yet it is a source of comfort to the afflicted, courage to the timid, and conviction to the fainthearted. We want you to see the value of embracing and loving God's sovereignty. Healthy churches are churches that apply the doctrine of God's sovereignty to their evangelism, counseling ministry, and worship services. Healthy Christians are those with a robust understanding of this precious truth. Our spiritual health begins with a proper understanding of God. Misunderstanding God and His truth is the mother of a thousand errors and the wellspring of every spiritual poison. Every false doctrine that afflicts the modern church is rooted in a misunderstanding of God's nature. When believers think wrongly of God, their worship is affected. They either offer profane "worship" to God or worship a false god altogether.

This book is a study of specific theologies through the lens of God's sovereignty. In chapters 3–6, we considered God's infallible work in believers. He sovereignly saves, sanctifies, secures, guides, and provides for His people. Our salvation must be understood in terms of God's sovereignty in redemption. Every detail of our lives is in His hands. He ordains our days, leaving nothing to chance. Nothing comes to us unless it first passes through the hands of an all-wise, all-powerful, and benevolent God. Like the psalmist, we rest in this confidence: "Your eyes have seen my unformed substance; and in Your book were all written the days that were ordained for me, when as yet there was not one of them" (Ps. 139:16).

In chapters 7–9, we examined God's infallible work in His church. He's no less involved in the affairs of His corporate people then He is in the affairs of individuals. Every event that befalls His bride is ordained by Him for her glory. Our ultimate good, triumph, and eternal reward is always in view as Christ prepares His bride for her eternal home. He builds His church, rules His church, and prospers His church according to His infinite wisdom and sovereign purposes.

In chapters 10–12, we turned our attention to God's infallible work in creation. God in His sovereignty created everything, controls everything, and will consummate everything. The same sure and steady hand that has ordained all that has come to pass is bringing all things to their appointed end. Not a single detail will be overlooked until that final day when all His elect, redeemed, and sanctified people are with Him in glory.

SOVEREIGNTY APPLIED

We hope this journey has been a tremendous encouragement to you. It's easy to get discouraged when we observe the state of the world and the church. Though we've highlighted some issues that threaten to undermine the health and vitality of the local church, our goal is to magnify the cure—namely, a high and majestic view of God applied to all areas of life and ministry. If you're in a church where these truths are not loved by the leadership, preached from the pulpit, or applied in ministry, you may feel disheartened.

Be encouraged, dear reader, all is not lost! This book isn't intended to inflame your critical spirit, increase your discontentment, or add to the frustrations of your situation. After all, the same God Who has ordained all that comes to pass has ordained your present circumstances. The question you must now ask is, "How must I serve and worship God in light of this truth?" In other words, how will you be part of a biblical, God-honoring solution? How can you encourage others to embrace and apply the precious doctrine of God's sovereignty?

FOR THE SHEEP

Where do you go from here?

The theological weakness that plagues much of modern Evangelicalism isn't going to disappear overnight. Barring a supernatural move of God whereby He raises up an army of doctrinally precise expository preachers and courageous church leaders to confront, encourage, and equip the people of God, we can expect the spiritual landscape to remain largely the same or get worse. What will you do, dear reader? How will you live in these days knowing that God has sovereignly ordained you and your life for this time in history?

Emboldening insights can be gleaned from Paul's instructions to young Timothy in 1 Timothy 4. The passage is loaded with encouragement for a young minister facing difficult times. Paul left Timothy in the church at Ephesus to confront the false teachers who had insinuated themselves into the congregation. Rather than teaching the truth from a pure and loving heart, these men focused on strange doctrines, myths, and endless genealogies (1:3–7). They were misusing the law of God in their teaching (1:8–11), ruining the faith and conscience of many in the congregation (1:18–20). Paul's instructions to Timothy served to reprove the false teachers (1:20) and guide the structure, life, and conduct of the church (3:14–16).

This first pastoral Epistle addresses false teachers (chapter 1), the place of prayer and the role of women within the church (chapter 2), the office and qualification of elders and deacons (chapter 3), the honoring of widows and elders (chapter 5), and the conduct of ministers in the church (chapter 6). In the middle of the Epistle, Paul warned Timothy of the coming apostasy (4:1–5) and instructed him on how to live and conduct himself when some "fall away from the faith, paying attention to deceitful spirits and doctrines of demons" (4:1). Here's his exhortation:

> In pointing out these things to the brethren, you will be a good servant of Christ Jesus, constantly nourished on the words of the faith and of the sound doctrine which you have been following. But have nothing to do with worldly fables fit only for old women. On the other hand, discipline yourself for the purpose of godliness; for bodily discipline is only of little profit, but godliness is profitable for all things, since it holds promise for the present life and also for the life to come. It is a trustworthy statement deserving full acceptance. For it is for this we labor and strive, because we have fixed our hope on the living God, who is the Savior of all men, especially of believers.
>
> Prescribe and teach these things. Let no one look down on your youthfulness, but rather in speech, conduct, love, faith and purity, show yourself an example of those who believe. Until I come, give attention to the public reading of Scripture, to exhortation and teaching. Do not neglect the spiritual gift within you, which was bestowed on you through prophetic utterance with the laying on of hands by the presbytery. Take pains with these things; be absorbed in them, so that your progress will be evident to all. Pay close attention to yourself and to your teaching; persevere in these things, for as you do this you will ensure salvation both for yourself and for those who hear you. (1 Tim. 4:6–16)

From Paul's instructions in this passage, we can glean three encouragements for loving and serving God in difficult times. Since we all, regardless of church environment, live at a time when the truth is

Conclusion

under assault, the church is sick, and the remnant is shrinking, Paul's charge to his son in the faith is germane to us all.

First, be nourished on the words of the faith.

In pointing out these things to the brethren, you will be a good servant of Christ Jesus, constantly nourished on the words of the faith and of the sound doctrine which you have been following. But have nothing to do with worldly fables fit only for old women. . . .

Prescribe and teach these things. . . . Until I come, give attention to the public reading of Scripture, to exhortation and teaching. . . . Pay close attention to yourself and to your teaching; persevere in these things, for as you do this you will ensure salvation both for yourself and for those who hear you. (1 Tim. 4:6–7, 11, 13, 16)

If you're in a barren church environment where the spiritual nourishment of the Word seldom comes from the pulpit, and provided you have no other options, you need to nourish yourself. You don't need occasional nourishment, but to be "constantly nourished on the words of the faith and of the sound doctrine which you have been following" (1 Tim. 4:6). Read Scripture daily and meditate on it throughout the day. Memorize Scripture. Seek out podcasts, radio programs, and teaching series to supplement the teaching you receive on Sundays. Give yourself to the diligent study of the Scriptures! Consider buying a good study Bible[1] or a series of commentaries[2] to help you in your study.

Apply the Word of God to yourself. When you see a sin that needs to be mortified, kill it. When you identify a temptation that needs to be resisted, spend all your spiritual energy resisting it. The purpose of being fed and nourished on the Scriptures is that you may apply them and have the energy and strength to pursue holiness (Heb. 12:14), walking in a manner worthy of the high calling with which you have been called (Eph. 4:1).

Being nourished in the words of the faith doesn't end with reading and studying your Bible. It doesn't end with a diligent application

---

[1] In our view, *The MacArthur Study Bible* from Thomas Nelson is the most biblically sound study Bible available.

[2] We would highly recommend *The MacArthur New Testament Commentary* series from Moody Publishers. It is a very readable and thorough explanation of every passage in the New Testament. Having a series on hand as you study Scripture will help illuminate difficult passages and provide you with numerous cross-references.

of what you read. The truth of God's Word shouldn't stop with you. Share what you're learning with others. You should be a conduit through which the truth of God's Word goes to others. Use His Word to encourage your fellow believers. Disciple, teach, counsel, exhort, strengthen, and, when necessary, correct others with the Scriptures.

Being in a church where the Word of God is neither honored nor preached is no excuse for your own spiritual apathy or indifference. It should motivate you to the diligent study, application, and communication of God's truth. Getting good spiritual food may be more difficult, but, thankfully, even in our day, it isn't impossible.

Second, be disciplined.

Paul commanded Timothy, saying,

> But have nothing to do with worldly fables fit only for old women. On the other hand, discipline yourself for the purpose of godliness; for bodily discipline is only of little profit, but godliness is profitable for all things, since it holds promise for the present life and also for the life to come. It is a trustworthy statement deserving full acceptance. For it is for this we labor and strive, because we have fixed our hope on the living God, who is the Savior of all men, especially of believers. (1 Tim. 4:7–10)

Discipline requires effort, spiritual effort. Notice the comparison of bodily discipline with spiritual discipline. Paul uses the words *labor* and *strive* to describe the endeavor. An athlete will sacrifice desserts, comfort, and leisure in order to prepare for a competition. He puts in time and work at the gym and on the court to prepare himself for the contest. He does this to receive a perishable prize (1 Cor. 9:24–25). How much more should the servant of Christ be willing to sacrifice for an imperishable crown? All the work an athlete gives to preparing for the games profits them little. Their reward doesn't last beyond this life. But God calls us to an effort, work, and discipline that holds promise both for this life and the life to come (1 Tim. 4:8). We "labor and strive, because we have fixed our hope on the living God" (1 Tim. 4:10), knowing that having done the will of God, we will receive what is promised (Heb. 10:36). With that confidence,

> lay aside every encumbrance and the sin which so easily entangles us, and let us run with endurance the race that is set before us, fixing our eyes on Jesus, the author and perfecter of faith, who for the joy set before Him endured the

cross, despising the shame, and has sat down at the right hand of the throne of God.

For consider Him who has endured such hostility by sinners against Himself, so that you will not grow weary and lose heart. (Heb. 12:1–3)

Discipline yourself. Labor. Strive. Run your race with faithfulness! "Pay close attention to yourself and to your teaching; persevere in these things" (1 Tim. 4:16). God has called you to this, and He will strengthen you as you are "nourished on the words of the faith and of the sound doctrine which you have been following" (1 Tim. 4:6).

Third, be an example.

Paul wrote,

Prescribe and teach these things. Let no one look down on your youthfulness, but rather in speech, conduct, love, faith and purity, show yourself an example of those who believe. Until I come, give attention to the public reading of Scripture, to exhortation and teaching. Do not neglect the spiritual gift within you, which was bestowed on you through prophetic utterance with the laying on of hands by the presbytery. Take pains with these things; be absorbed in them, so that your progress will be evident to all. (1 Tim. 4:11–15)

It must be the goal of every believer to set an example in "speech, conduct, love, faith and purity" (v. 12). Other believers are watching you. By your diligent nourishment on the words of the faith and your persistent discipline in spiritual labors, you will demonstrate to those who observe just how seriously you take honoring God in word and deed. You can see the passion necessary to obey Paul's command: "Take pains with these things; be absorbed in them, so that your progress will be evident to all" (v. 15). In the very next verse, Paul encourages Timothy to "persevere in these things" (v. 16).

Nourishment, discipline, and exemplary progress in the faith is the standard we must all pursue. Most reading this book would concur with our assessment that the Western church is weak and sick. We can offer no quick fix. The solution is simple, but it is not easy. That is why Paul used words like *labor, strive, discipline*, and *take pains*.

Our corporate problem has an individual solution. It's easy to be one of a disgruntled crowd. Apathy is effortless. Indifference is cheap. Swimming upstream, going against the flow, and being faithful in unfaithful times is laborious, difficult, and sometimes painful. Living

God Doesn't Try

faithfully in difficult times may require you to say no to some luxuries, entertainments, and conveniences enjoyed by those who live only for this world. You may need to curtail your leisure activities to make room for diligent study. Evangelism, service, and usefulness in the Kingdom may require sacrifice. You can labor toward spiritual maturity and effectiveness in the Kingdom with the confidence that God will use your efforts in some way. He won't *try* to do so. He will.

A GAME PLAN FOR THE REMNANT

One final question remains: how can I effect change in my local church body?

You're either in a good church, a bad church, a sick church, or a recovering church. For those in a good church, keep pressing on. Do everything you can to be an encouragement to your leaders. Pray for them; provide for them; encourage, love, and support them. Your elders may make it look easy. I promise you it isn't. They're fighting battles behind the scenes to keep you safe from spiritual danger that you will never see. They're praying for you. They're laboring for you. They're agonizing over you. Good churches don't exist in a vacuum. They're the fruit of much discipline and labor. Solid churches would be quickly overrun with infighting, division, false doctrine, and compromise if the leadership were to give up the fight.

Remember, your pastors aren't perfect. They're mere men with feet of clay. They have struggles. They fight their own personal battles on all the same fronts as you. Then, with whatever gas they have left in the tank, they show up to help you fight yours. There is no perfect church. Every church has its weaknesses and struggles as it strives to obey everything the Lord of the church has commanded. Don't abandon that ship. Don't be quick to leave a good church. They're few and far between.

For those in a bad church, leave. If you're in a church where an essential doctrine of the faith is being compromised or denied, you're subjecting yourself and your family to spiritual poison. You won't turn it around. Your church isn't your mission field. You aren't going to convince the leadership of their error. Instead, you'll sacrifice your own spiritual health and that of your family, only to realize all too late that the time to leave is long past.

Don't try to split the church as you leave. Don't attempt to take a contingent of people with you. If others seek you out to inquire about your reasons for leaving, it's appropriate to be honest and share your theological concerns without being divisive and vindictive. Don't spew verbal bile all over the congregation as you move on. Leave quietly after making your concerns known to the leadership. Find a church where the Word of God is honored, the glory of God preached, and the people of God fed.

For those in a sick church, serve in hope. Serve the body with the hope of steering the congregation toward a healthy soteriology and ecclesiology. Have conversations with the elders regarding the weaknesses of the church fellowship, not for the sake of airing your criticisms, but with the goal of discerning how you can best encourage, support, and assist the body. The goal is to be a robust source of support, strength, and encouragement. Understanding that change takes time, stay until you are certain that the church body and the leadership have no desire for sound doctrine. Once that's evident, you should begin looking for a better church environment you can join as quickly as possible.

For those in a recovering church, serve patiently. After discussions with the elders, you may find that they see the same issues but lack the bandwidth, spiritual resources, or energy to make the necessary changes. Be patient. Be supportive. Do all you can to assist good leaders serving in weak churches. Keep your eye on the goal while striving with excellence to honor God in everything you do. Show yourself an example in these things.

Find a group of like-minded believers, even those in leadership, and pursue discipleship, edification, and encouragement with one another. Spur one another on in sound doctrine and encourage one another in the disciplines of the faith. In the words of Hebrews,

> Let us hold fast the confession of our hope without wavering, for He who promised is faithful; and let us consider how to stimulate one another to love and good deeds, not forsaking our own assembling together, as is the habit of some, but encouraging one another; and all the more as you see the day drawing near. (Heb. 10:23–25)

Give generously. Pray fervently. Serve passionately. There's nothing more discouraging and disheartening to a pastor than to have a like-minded, solid believer leave their congregation to attend another place because the effort needed to improve their struggling church was too great.

If you're in a church with humble leadership and a hungry congregation, consider yourself blessed. It might not be perfect. There might be blind spots, parts of the service, or traditions that irritate you, but you have the makings of a healthy church. Pursue obedience in all your activities. While being constantly nourished on the words of the faith and disciplining yourself for the purpose of godliness, work, labor, and strive toward spiritual health and vitality. Pray for, counsel, teach, disciple, exercise hospitality toward, give to, serve, sacrifice for, love, and cherish those dear people. Be patient and gracious, trusting the Spirit of God to use the Word of God to sanctify the people of God. Great things are ahead!

FOR THE SHEPHERDS

Our fellow pastors, you know that Paul's counsel in 1 Timothy 4 is addressed to us as much as it's addressed to any other believer. All the same principles apply. All the same encouragements are relevant. To what we have said thus far, we would only add this:

> I solemnly charge you in the presence of God and of Christ Jesus, who is to judge the living and the dead, and by His appearing and His kingdom: preach the word; be ready in season and out of season; reprove, rebuke, exhort, with great patience and instruction. For the time will come when they will not endure sound doctrine; but wanting to have their ears tickled, they will accumulate for themselves teachers in accordance to their own desires, and will turn away their ears from the truth and will turn aside to myths. But you, be sober in all things, endure hardship, do the work of an evangelist, fulfill your ministry. (2 Tim. 4:1–5)

Ministry isn't easy. Let the Word of God do the work. Labor to preach exegetically sound, doctrinally profound, and precise expository sermons. Don't skip over tough subjects. Don't offer up topical tripe. Labor in the Word. Take it slow. Don't rush over rich passages of Scripture simply because you have a church calendar to keep. Feed the sheep, and they will respond. Goats will leave, sheep will thrive. Take the time to teach your people through the doctrinal issues you need to address. Let the Word of God convince them. Pray for the Spirit of God to change them. Give them excellence in everything. Show yourself an example of striving to honor God in all you say and do. Your love for the sovereignty of God, and your desire to honor His Word in the ministry of the church, will be contagious.

And finally, as you live faithfully and obediently in the midst of this difficult, sin-cursed world, find your rest in this foundational, life-altering, God-glorifying truth:

God doesn't try.
Soli Deo gloria!

DISCUSSION QUESTIONS

1. What priority do you place on being nourished spiritually from God's Word? What percentage of your time is spent on reading, hearing, studying, memorizing, and meditating on it? An hour a day constitutes only 4 percent of your time.

2. To what extent would you go to avoid sin? What verbs does the Bible use in relation to our fight against sin (1 Pet. 2:11; Rom. 8:13; 13:12–14; Luke 22:40; 1 Cor. 6:18; Matt. 18:8–9)?

3. James 1:22–25 contrasts a forgetful hearer of the Word with an observant doer of the Word. Where do you find yourself currently along this spectrum? What will you do to become more obedient to God's Word?

4. As a result of reading this book and especially this conclusion, what actions will you take to support your church's development into a more Bible-centered body that celebrates the sovereignty of God?

5. This book ends with one of the great *solas* of the Reformation, *soli Deo gloria*. What does this phrase mean, and how does it apply to the material presented in this book?

God Doesn't Try

Appendix: Discussion Questions

CHAPTER 1: INTRODUCTION: WHY THIS BOOK?

1. What role does your church's doctrinal statement play in directing and evaluating its ministries? When was the last time you carefully and thoughtfully read through it?

2. Have you gone through the stages of discernment described in this chapter? Which group most closely describes you? If you identify with groups 1–3, what efforts are you willing to make to remedy your situation?

3. If you're in group 4, what responsibility do you have to your church body? What can you do to further the influence and gospel impact of your healthy church?

4. Who in your life knows and loves you enough to prayerfully speak God's Word to you for encouragement and correction? Are you providing that kind of encouragement to anyone yourself? What changes do you need to make in your weekly schedule to make such mutual edification more than wishful thinking?

5. How does your view of God affect your worship, either positively or negatively? What does the modern worship methodology communicate about God and His Word?

6. How can we encourage faithful, diligent shepherds in their work?

7. Can you name three modern false teachers and describe their main heresies? Name three biblical doctrines that must be included in an orthodox doctrinal statement.

CHAPTER 2: "DO. OR DO NOT. THERE IS NO TRY."

1. Do you find the teaching of God's sovereignty to be a source of comfort? Why or why not?

God Doesn't Try

2. Do you know anyone who struggles to understand or embrace this truth? How can you help them see God's sovereignty as a glorious reality?

3. Can you name causes of human failure other than lack of knowledge and lack of power? Do those other causes fit under the two categories listed?

4. In what ways do you think your language fails to honor God? How do you misrepresent Him and His works through sloppy language?

5. Is there anything God is unable to do? Why?

6. What does *omniscience* mean? How is omniscience related to God's power?

7. What is the difference between simple, eternal knowledge and incremental knowledge?

CHAPTER 3: GOD DOESN'T TRY TO SAVE HIS PEOPLE

1. Do you have a clear understanding of Who does what among the Members of the Godhead regarding the salvation of sinners? Can one Member of the triune Godhead do a work without the Others being involved?

2. In what ways is a clear understanding of the sovereignty of God in salvation a source of comfort to our souls and boldness in our witness?

3. How can you encourage your pastors/elders to either become or remain faithful to this truth?

4. Do you think the fear of man causes weak gospel preaching? How else does this fear manifest itself in our lives?

5. In what ways does Jesus's clarity on doctrinal truths serve as an example to us? How can we follow that example?

6. How does the doctrine of predestination show the power, love, grace, omnipotence, wisdom, and omniscience of God?

Appendix: Discussion Questions

CHAPTER 4: GOD DOESN'T TRY TO SANCTIFY HIS PEOPLE

1. Have you ever engaged in an extended study of the doctrines of sanctification? In what ways did that study change your view of the subject? In what ways has this chapter changed your view on sanctification? How has it clarified your understanding?

2. How would you utilize your biblical knowledge of the doctrine of sanctification to help a fellow believer who is struggling with sin? To what Bible passages would you turn to help them?

3. Do you struggle to embrace life's difficulties and afflictions as a gift from the hand of a loving heavenly Father? Why or why not? Why does God discipline believers?

4. What are you doing to prepare your loved ones to face the possibility of suffering for the faith? In what ways are you preparing your own heart for this? How does God use persecution to accomplish His designs for the church? What are the negative results of persecution?

5. Discuss how suffering makes us holy. Can suffering have the opposite effect? Why or why not?

6. Describe how sanctification differs from justification.

7. How is sanctification inevitable for the believer?

8. Describe the moral test in one sentence.

9. How do we demonstrate our love for the children of God?

10. What does an unchanged life communicate to the world about the gospel? What does it communicate to other believers?

CHAPTER 5: GOD DOESN'T TRY TO SPEAK TO HIS PEOPLE

1. Does your church experience include exposure to "hearing the voice of God" (HVG) theology? In what ways has this shaped your understanding of the will of God?

2. Is HVG teaching detrimental to Christian growth in holiness? Why or why not?

3. Should you be automatically suspicious of an HVG teacher in other areas of their teaching? Why or why not?

4. Have you believed things about "the voice of God" that dishonor His Word? In what ways do you think your views deny the sufficiency of Scripture?

5. How can we make our language more honoring to God? What does it mean to use biblical language to describe biblical concepts?

6. How does our use or interpretation of Scripture reveal our view of God's Word?

7. Why is the lack of specific guidance for everyday decisions not considered a deficiency in Scripture?

8. What is the significance of John's statement in John 10:6 that Jesus was using a figure of speech? What does it tell us about the Good Shepherd Discourse? Can you summarize the meaning of that passage?

9. Describe the difference between inspiration and illumination.

CHAPTER 6: GOD DOESN'T TRY TO PROVIDE FOR HIS PEOPLE

1. In Philippians 4:11–12, Paul says he has learned the secret of contentment. What are some of the implications of contentment being a knowable secret?

2. Have you learned the secret of contentment? What are some ways you can help others learn it as well?

3. Have you experienced a time when you felt that God failed to provide for something you thought you needed? What lessons did you learn?

4. What kinds of sinful fear afflict you? What things are you tempted to fear? How does the sovereignty and goodness of God address that fear? What characteristic of God are you doubting in the moment of fear?

Appendix: Discussion Questions

5. How much of your sinful worry stems from a concern for what others think of you? Discuss how the fear of man is a snare (Prov. 29:25). In what ways do you fall prey to the fear of man?

6. What does it mean to fear God? What kind of fear should we have of Him? How does fearing man differ from fearing God? Are they different kinds of fear or the same?

7. What is your estimate of yourself, your talents, and your duties? What is God's estimate of those things?

8. Discover and explain four Scriptures that demonstrate that anxiety is a sin and contentment a command.

CHAPTER 7: GOD DOESN'T TRY TO BUILD HIS CHURCH

1. How do the truths explained in this chapter comfort and encourage you? How do they motivate you to service and diligent work for Christ and His purposes? Do you regularly evangelize your community? In what way, and by what means? Have you ever engaged in disciple making? What role does prayer (corporate and private) play in these activities?

2. Have you ever been discouraged by the present state of the church? How does Jesus's promise encourage you?

3. How does a proper understanding of the future, glorious, ultimate state of the church inform how we treat others in this time of incompletion and imperfection?

4. Who is responsible to build the church? How does this inform the way Sunday morning worship is conducted? How does it inform our broader church ministry?

5. Which threats are more dangerous to the church—internal or external? Explain your answer.

CHAPTER 8: GOD DOESN'T TRY TO ORGANIZE HIS CHURCH

1. What unbiblical ideas were corrected by this extended teaching on church leadership? Did you find it difficult to relinquish any of your

previously held beliefs? Which ones and why? Is the structure of church leadership described in this chapter new to you?

2. How does a biblically correct leadership structure prevent sin and problems in the local church?

3. What role does or should a local congregation serve in the qualification, selection, training, and recognition of its own elders?

4. What do the Greek words for *elder* and *pastor* tell us about the work of their ministry?

5. Why are the qualifications given in Scripture essential to the success of the plurality leadership structure?

6. What are the two scripturally defined offices in the post-apostolic church? How do they complement one another?

7. Name the evangelists mentioned in the New Testament. What was their role? How does the role of an evangelist compare to the office of elder? How do they complement one another?

CHAPTER 9: GOD DOESN'T TRY TO PROSPER HIS CHURCH

1. In what ways has prosperity hindered gospel growth in the West? In your own life? In what way is your thinking about persecution, suffering, or affliction affected by the comforts and conveniences of Western culture?

2. Does God's promise to judge the wicked for their treatment of His people comfort you? Do you struggle with rejoicing in that truth? Is it hard for you to rest in it?

3. How does an eternal perspective help us deal with suffering?

4. Is suffering for Christ in this world optional or a given? Use Scripture to prove your answer.

5. Why is the judgment of God on the unrighteous with final adjudication in the lake of fire something for Christians to celebrate?

6. Discuss how the afflictions of this life can be described as momentary and light (2 Cor. 4:17). Would you describe your own sufferings that way? How does your view of your afflictions need to change?

Appendix: Discussion Questions

CHAPTER 10: GOD DOESN'T TRY TO CONTROL CREATION

1. Why is an understanding of God's sovereignty crucial to a stable and productive Christian life?

2. Do you or have you struggled with the implications of God's sovereignty? What aspect of sovereignty is or was most troubling and why?

3. How do you disciple yourself and others to delight in God's sovereignty and experience joy?

4. Have you ever had your view on God's goodness and sovereignty tested by difficulties or tragedy? How did you hold up?

5. How does the doctrine of concurrence help you reconcile God's sovereignty and human responsibility?

6. What do we learn from Joseph's statements regarding the sins of his brothers? How can such a perspective help you forgive others?

7. Balance the sovereignty of God over sin with the clear lack of responsibility for that sin. Can man, through reason alone, reconcile these two things?

CHAPTER 11: GOD DOESN'T TRY TO EXECUTE JUSTICE

1. Have you ever experienced injustice? How did you respond to it? What specific role did the gospel play in aiding and enabling your response?

2. Do you long for the return of Christ so that justice will be done? Do you look forward to escaping this sin-cursed world?

3. Has someone you know and care about been influenced by the social justice movement? In what ways? What help have you offered them? How did they respond? Is there anything more you can or should do?

4. When was the last time you heard an entire sermon on the subject of Hell? How did it strike you? What did you learn?

5. Is it difficult for you to rest in your justification? Why or why not? When are you most tempted to doubt the truth of your righteous standing before God?

6. How does the work of Christ on the cross enable and motivate forgiveness between believers?

7. How can we rest in God's justice? Is it difficult for you to rejoice in God's righteous judgments? Why or why not?

CHAPTER 12: GOD DOESN'T TRY TO ESTABLISH HIS KINGDOM

1. Is God's Kingdom physical or spiritual? Is it future or present? Do your answers to those questions affect the way you do ministry? If so, how and why?

2. Do you long and pray for God's Kingdom to come (Matt. 6:10)? Is this a source of comfort and encouragement to your Christian faith? Why or why not?

3. Would you consider God's Kingdom to be an essential part of a complete gospel presentation? Why or why not?

4. Does Daniel's vision of the future thrill your heart? How does it instill confidence and boldness in God's people?

5. Anyone in Western culture who questions the current view of anthropogenic climate change is branded a "denier" because they don't accept "scientific consensus." Can you think of any other "scientific consensus" that was later found to be incorrect? What is your ultimate source of authority on the ultimate destiny of mankind and the planet?

6. Compare the objects of worship, ethical requirements, and eschatologies of biblical Christianity and Western environmentalism.

7. During the COVID-19 pandemic, we were told to "trust the science." In the US, we even had a particular scientist claim that "attacks on me, quite frankly, are attacks on science," as if disagreeing with

him constituted a denial of science itself.[1] How does "trusting the science" fit into a biblical worldview? How does it apply to our eschatology?

8. If our citizenship is in Heaven, and all current political entities are merely secular and temporal, how invested should we be in secular political matters? Should Christians vote, serve a political party, run for office, educate themselves on political candidates, etc.? How much of our time and other resources should be devoted to political concerns?

9. God controls the leaders of nations. "He removes kings and establishes kings" (Dan. 2:21). In your nation, what are the means He uses for that purpose? What is your ethical responsibility as a Christian to participate in those means?

10. We assert in this chapter that God's establishing for Himself a Kingdom is a central theme of Scripture and of history. What other central biblical themes would you identify, and how are they related to God's establishment of His Kingdom?

CHAPTER 13: CONCLUSION

1. What priority do you place on being nourished spiritually from God's Word? What percentage of your time is spent on reading, hearing, studying, memorizing, and meditating on it? An hour a day constitutes only 4 percent of your time.

2. To what extent would you go to avoid sin? What verbs does the Bible use in relation to our fight against sin (1 Pet. 2:11; Rom. 8:13; 13:12–14; Luke 22:40; 1 Cor. 6:18; Matt. 18:8–9)?

3. James 1:22–25 contrasts a forgetful hearer of the Word with an observant doer of the Word. Where do you find yourself currently along this spectrum? What will you do to become more obedient to God's Word?

---

1. Porterfield, "Fauci on GOP Criticism."

4. As a result of reading this book and especially this conclusion, what actions will you take to support your church's development into a more Bible-centered body that celebrates the sovereignty of God?

5. This book ends with one of the great *solas* of the Reformation, *soli Deo gloria*. What does this phrase mean, and how does it apply to the material presented in this book?

Bibliography

Alcorn, Randy. *Heaven*. Carol Stream, IL: Tyndale Momentum, 2004.

Berkhof, Louis. *Systematic Theology*. N.p.: CreateSpace Independent Publishing Platform, 2014.

Blackaby, Henry T., and Claude V. King. *Experiencing God: How to Live the Full Adventure of Knowing and Doing the Will of God*. Nashville: Broadman & Holman Publishers, 1994.

Bright, John. *The Kingdom of God: The Biblical Concept and Its Meaning for the Church*. Nashville: Abingdon Press, 1953.

Burroughs, Jeremiah. *The Rare Jewel of Christian Contentment*. N.p.: CreateSpace Independent Publishing Platform, 2013.

Calvin, John. *Concerning the Eternal Predestination of God*. Louisville: Westminster John Knox Press, 1997.

Calvin, John. *Institutes of the Christian Religion*. Translated by Henry Beveridge. Peabody, MA: Hendrickson Publishers Marketing, 2008.

Chandler, Matt. "A Supernatural Community and a Personal Word." Sermon delivered at The Village Church, Flower Mound, TX, July 15, 2018. YouTube video, 47:03, https://www.youtube.com/watch?v=n0aB1lolHn0.

Deere, Jack. *Surprised by the Voice of God: How God Speaks Today Through Prophecies, Dreams, and Visions*. Grand Rapids: Zondervan, 1996.

Ehrenreich, Barbara. "God Owes Us an Apology." *Progressive*, March 1, 2005, https://progressive.org/magazine/flip-side-barbara-ehrenreich (https://perma.cc/79DB-MFE6).

Eldredge, John. *Walking with God: Talk to Him. Hear from Him. Really*. Nashville: Thomas Nelson, 2008.

Frame, John M. *Systematic Theology: An Introduction to Christian Belief*. Phillipsburg, NJ: P & R Publishing, 2013.

Grelle, Kaitlin, Neha Shrestha, Megan Ximenes, Jessica Perrotte, Millie Cordaro, Rebecca G. Deason, and Krista Howard. "The Generation Gap Revisited: Generational Differences in Mental Health, Maladaptive Coping Behaviors, and Pandemic-Related Concerns During the Initial COVID-19 Pandemic." *Journal of Adult Development* 30 (December 2023): 381–92. https://doi.org/10.1007/s10804-023-09442-x (https://perma.cc/X36K-RUZN).

Grudem, Wayne. *Systematic Theology: An Introduction to Biblical Doctrine*. Grand Rapids: Zondervan, 1994.

Harari, Yuval Noah. *Sapiens: A Brief History of Humankind*. Translated by the author, with the help of John Purcell and Haim Watzman. New York: Harper Perennial, 2018.

Henry, Matthew. *Matthew Henry's Commentary on the Whole Bible: Complete and Unabridged in One Volume*. Peabody: Hendrickson, 1994. Logos.

Hinn, Benny. *"Rise & Be Healed!"* Orlando: Celebration Publishers, 1991.

Hodge, Charles. *Systematic Theology*. Vol. 1, *Theology*. Peabody, MA: Hendrickson Publishers, 1999.

Howard, Ron, dir. *Apollo 13*. 1995; Universal City, CA: Universal Pictures, 2006. DVD.

Hybels, Bill. *The Power of a Whisper: Hearing God. Having the Guts to Respond*. Grand Rapids: Zondervan, 2010.

Lawson, Steven J. *Show Me Your Glory: Understanding the Majestic Splendor of God*. Sanford, FL: Ligonier Ministries, 2020.

Lucas, George, writer and executive producer. *Star Wars Episode V: The Empire Strikes Back*. 1980; San Francisco: 20th Century Fox, 2011. Blu-ray Disc.

Luther, Martin. *On the Bondage of the Will*. Rockville, MD: A Martin Luther Book, 2012.

MacArthur, John F., Jr. *The MacArthur Study Bible*. New American Standard Bible, updated ed. Nashville: Thomas Nelson, 2006.

MacArthur, John F., Jr. *Matthew 16–23*. The MacArthur New Testament Commentary series. Chicago: Moody Publishers, 1988.

MacArthur, John F., Jr. *None Other: Discovering the God of the Bible*. Orlando: Reformation Trust Publishing, 2017.

MacArthur, John F., Jr., and Richard Mayhue. *Biblical Doctrine: A Systematic Summary of Bible Truth*. Wheaton, IL: Crossway, 2017.

McClain, Alva J. *The Greatness of the Kingdom: An Inductive Study of the Kingdom of God*. Winona Lake, IN: BMH Books, 1974.

Morris, Robert. *Frequency: Tune in. Hear God*. Nashville: W Publishing Group, 2016. Kindle.

Murray, John. *Redemption Accomplished and Applied*. Grand Rapids: William B. Eerdmans, 1955.

Murray, John. *Select Lectures in Systematic Theology*. Vol. 2 of *Collected Writings of John Murray*. Edinburgh: Banner of Truth Trust, 1977.

Osman, Jim. *God Doesn't Whisper*. Kootenai, ID: Kootenai Community Church Publishing, 2020.

Bibliography

Packer, J. I. "Introductory Essay" in *The Death of Death in the Death of Christ*, by John Owen, 1–25. Edinburgh: The Banner of Truth Trust, 1959.

Pink, Arthur W. *The Attributes of God.* N.p.: CreateSpace Independent Publishing Platform, 2012.

Porterfield, Carlie. "Dr. Fauci on GOP Criticism: 'Attacks on Me, Quite Frankly, Are Attacks on Science.'" *Forbes*, June 9, 2021, https://www.forbes.com/sites/carlieporterfield/2021/06/09/fauci-on-gop-criticism-attacks-on-me-quite-frankly-are-attacks-on-science/?sh=308943e45429 (https://perma.cc/H6CC-ASSB).

Ryle, J.C. *John 1:1 through John 10:9.* Vol. 3 of *Ryle's Expository Thoughts on the Gospels.* Anniversary ed. Grand Rapids: Zondervan, 1950.

Sammons, Peter. *Reprobation and God's Sovereignty: Recovering a Biblical Doctrine.* Grand Rapids: Kregel Academic, 2022.

San Juan, E., Jr. "From Race to Class Struggle: Re-Problematizing Critical Race Theory." *Michigan Journal of Race and Law* 11, no. 1 (Fall 2005): 75–98. https://repository.law.umich.edu/mjrl/vol11/iss1/5/ (https://perma.cc/YHA6-8R8T).

Sproul, R. C. "No Maverick Molecule." Ligonier Ministries. *Ultimately with R.C. Sproul.* January 11, 2023. Podcast, 5:59. https://www.ligonier.org/podcasts/ultimately-with-rc-sproul/no-maverick-molecule (https://perma.cc/2P2K-KD2D).

Spurgeon, Charles. "Divine Sovereignty." Sermon delivered at New Park Street Chapel, Southwark, May 4, 1856. Accessed via the Spurgeon Archive. http://www.romans45.org/spurgeon/sermons/0077.htm (https://perma.cc/PZ3Q-53R4).

Stanley, Charles. *How to Listen to God.* Nashville: Thomas Nelson, 1985.

Thomas, R. L. *New American Standard Hebrew-Aramaic and Greek Dictionaries.* Updated ed. Anaheim: Foundation Publications, 1998. Logos.

Tozer, A. W. *The Knowledge of the Holy: The Attributes of God: Their Meaning in the Christian Life.* San Francisco: Harper & Row Publishers, 1961.

Tozer, A. W. *The Pursuit of God.* Mansfield Center, CT: Martino Publishing, 2009.

Watson, Thomas. *A Body of Divinity: Contained in Sermons upon the Westminster Assembly's Catechism.* Rev. ed. Edinburgh: The Banner of Truth Trust, 1965. Reprinted as paperback. 1983.

Wayland, Francis. *A Memoir of the Life and Labors of the Rev. Adoniram Judson, D.D.* Volume 2. Boston: Phillips, Sampson, and Company, 1853, quoted in Burns, E. D. *The Missionary-Theologian: Sent into the*

World, Sanctified by the Word. Fearn, UK: Christian Focus Publications, 2020.

The Westminster Confession of Faith. In *Systematic Theology: An Introduction to Biblical Doctrine*, Wayne Grudem, 1179–96. Grand Rapids: Zondervan, 1994.

White, James R. *Drawn by the Father.* Lindenhurst, NY: Great Christian Books, 2000.

About the Authors

Jim Osman

Jim was born in May of 1972 and has lived in Sandpoint, Idaho, since the age of three. He came to know Christ through the ministry of Cocolalla Lake Bible Camp in the summer of 1987 and graduated high school in 1990. Kootenai Community Church (KCC) has always been his home church where he attended Sunday school, Vacation Bible School, and youth group.

After graduating high school, Jim attended Millar College of the Bible in Pambrun, Saskatchewan. It was there that he met his wife-to-be, Diedre, who was also enrolled as a student. He graduated with a three-year diploma in April of 1993 and married Diedre in August of that same year. They returned to Millar as married students to further his education in September of 1994, and he graduated from the Fourth Year Internship program with a BA in Strategic Ministries in April of 1995. He was inducted into the honor society of the Association of Canadian Bible Colleges and appointed a member of Pi Alpha Mu.

Jim and Diedre returned to Sandpoint, where Jim began working in construction as a roofer until he was asked to take over as the preaching elder at KCC in December of 1996. He counts it his greatest privilege to be ministering in the church that ministered to him for so many years. He is the author of *Truth or Territory: A Biblical Approach to Spiritual Warfare*, *Selling the Stairway to Heaven: Critiquing the Claims of Heaven Tourists*, *The Prosperity of the Wicked: A Study of Psalm 73*, and *God Doesn't Whisper*. You can follow his preaching at the KCC website (kootenaichurch.org) and his writings at jimosman.com.

Jim loves to be outdoors, whether camping, hunting, or working in his garden. He enjoys biking and watching football, especially his favorite team, the San Francisco 49ers, for whom he has cheered since childhood. Jim and Diedre's four grown children and their spouses—Joe and Taryn Adams, Shepley and Melina Osman, Trenton and Ayden Tilton, and Liam and Molly Osman—all live nearby and attend KCC. As of the publication of this book, Jim and Diedre have four grandchildren.

God Doesn't Try

Dave Rich

Dave Rich was born in 1966 in Libby, Montana, and grew up in southern Idaho. He graduated from Burley High School in 1984. The Lord was pleased to withhold from him the blessing of growing up in a Christian home, and he had very little Christian influence in his life prior to going to the University of Idaho in 1984.

Dave was confronted with the gospel by his roommate, Rich Strasser, upon their first meeting at the University of Idaho. Soon after, while reading John's Gospel, he repented of his sins and put his faith in Christ as a college freshman in 1984. He attended Trinity Baptist Church in Moscow, Idaho, where he was baptized in 1984. The Lord was pleased to bless him by bringing his future wife, Diane, into his life shortly after he was saved. He married Diane in 1986, after his sophomore year and her junior year. Dave received his BS in economics from the University of Idaho in 1988.

Dave and Diane moved to Seattle, Washington, in 1988 for Dave to attend graduate school at the University of Washington. While in Seattle, Dave and Diane joined Tabernacle Baptist Church in Shoreline, Washington. It was at "Tab" that Dave was first challenged to teach the Bible by Tom Ruhlman, the teaching elder of the church who would be a tremendous blessing to Dave and Diane. Dave and Diane were active in youth ministry and Sunday school teaching.

After graduate school and receiving his MA in economics, Dave taught at a small liberal arts university in Columbus, Ohio, from 1993 to 1996, where he was blessed with his first two daughters (Megan and Jamie) and introduced to his lifelong love of The Ohio State University Buckeyes. While attending Bethesda Baptist Church in Grove City, Ohio, Dave and Diane started a children's ministry and a youth ministry.

After moving back to Seattle and "Tab" in 1996 to work in private industry, he and Diane were blessed further with a third daughter, Kellie, while continuing to work in youth and children's ministry.

Dave and his family moved to Sandpoint, Idaho, and began attending Kootenai Community Church in 1999. In 2000, Jim asked Dave if he would be willing to be recognized as an elder. After a period of examination from the elders and the church, Dave assumed the office of elder in 2001. He has been active in youth ministry, children's ministry programs like Adventure Club, and teaching youth and adult Sunday school. Many of his sermons and lessons can be found on the website of Kootenai Community Church, including a Sunday school series on biblical eldership, a series of writings on Martin Luther's *On the Bondage of the Will*, and a sermon series on 1 Peter. *God Doesn't Try* is Dave's first book.

Dave has a deep love for the saints of Kootenai Community Church, having been blessed to see the growth of the church and the addition of so many beloved brothers and sisters in Christ over these two decades. While the accountability for a flock is not a light matter, he counts the fellowship at KCC as one of the most profound and humbling of the many benefits that are ours in Christ.

Dave is a huge fan of all the major sports and loves the Atlanta Braves, Las Vegas Raiders, Los Angeles Lakers, Ohio State Buckeyes, Washington Huskies, and Idaho Vandals. He loves to read just about everything and usually has several books going at once: a good fiction story, a good (or bad) theology tome, a biography, and/or a study of a topic in science or history that is especially interesting.

Made in United States
Cleveland, OH
25 September 2025